Footloose in the West of Ireland

Also by Mike Harding

WALKING THE DALES
BOMBER'S MOON
FOOTLOOSE IN THE HIMALAYA
WALKING THE PEAK AND PENNINES

Footloose in the West of Ireland

MIKE HARDING

MICHAEL JOSEPH
LONDON

MICHAEL JOSEPH LTD
Published by the Penguin Group
27 Wrights Lane, London W8 5TZ
Viking Penguin Inc., 375 Hudson Street, New York, New York 10014, USA
Penguin Books Australia Ltd, Ringwood, Victoria, Australia
Penguin Books Canada Ltd, 10 Alcorn Avenue, Toronto, Ontario, Canada M4V 3B2
Penguin Books (NZ) Ltd, 182–190 Wairau Road, Auckland 10, New Zealand

Penguin Books Ltd, Registered Offices: Harmondsworth, Middlesex, England

First published in Great Britain 1996

Copyright © Text, photographs and maps 1996 by Mike Harding

Typeset in 10.5/13pt Monotype Sabon
Colour reproduction by Bright Arts, Hong Kong
Printed and bound in Italy by L. E. G. O. Spa, Vicenza

ISBN 0 7181 3359 5

Contents

Buicas le – (thanks to)

Johnny and Dympna Crowley, Joe and Eileen Cronin, James and Peggy Flahive, Séan Ó Suilleabháin, Feargal and Ainé Mac Amhlaioibh, Steve MacDonogh, Michael Coyne, Bernie Goggins, Joss Lynam, Tony Birtles, John Lahiffe of Bord Failté, Stena Sealink, Irish Ferries, Margaret Curry, and Arthur Guinness and Co., St James' Gate Brewery, Dublin.

A special thanks to Bernard Wrigley, Feargal Mac Amhlaioibh and Tony Sullivan who helped to straighten out the music.

IN MEMORIAM

Eamonn Coyne, Micho Russell, Andrew and Dennis Dineen, Tony Whilde, Davey Gunn and Paddy Campbell.

Acknowledgements

The author and publisher would like to thank the following for their permission to quote from copyright works in this book:

Mike Harding, 'The Cliffs of Moher', reprinted by permission of Peterloo Poets, from *Daddy Egar's Pools*.
Cathal Ó Searcaigh, 'Tearmann' reprinted by permission of Ció-lar-Chonnacta Teo, Connemara, from *An Bealach 'na Bhaile*.
W.B. Yeats's 'Dromahair', 'The Hosting of the Sidhe', 'The Fiddler of Dooney', 'The Song of Wandering Aengus', and 'The Lake Isle of Innisfree', from *The Collected Poems of W.B. Yeats*, reprinted by permission of Macmillan and Co.

Extracts from the following books/poems are also acknowledged with thanks:

BOOKS

J.C. Coleman, *The Mountains of Killarney*, Dundalgan Press, now out of print.
Father James McDyer, *An Autobiography*, Brandon Books.
H.V. Morton, *In Search of Ireland*, Methuen and Co.
Flann O'Brien, *The Third Policeman*, Grafton Books.
Tim Robinson, *Connemara*, Folding Landscapes.
Peig Sayers, *An Old Woman's Reflections*, Oxford Paperbacks.
Lady Wilde, *Book of Irish Legends*.

POEMS

J.J. Callanan, 'Goughane Barra', from *A Writer's Ireland* by William Trevor.
Tir Eolas, 'The footprints of an older race are here', anon., from *The Book of the Burren*.
John Montague, anon. version of 'Bitter the Wind Tonight', from *The Faber Book of Irish Verse*.
Frank O'Connor (transl.), 'Kilcash', anon., from *The Faber Book of Irish Verse*.

SONGS

Séamus Ennis (transl.), 'The Fairies' Lamentation', traditional.
Micho Russell (singing of), 'John Holland', traditional.

Spellings and Things

SPELLINGS

I have tried to keep to the *Suirbhéireach Ordanáis na hÉireann* (Ordnance Survey of Ireland) spellings in this book but, inevitably, in a land where one language has been imposed upon another there will be mistakes and confusions. Let me give you one example. The OS map gives Lough Anscaul but calls the nearby village Anascaul while a recent guide book gives Annascaul. A mound of stones is called a *clochán* in the dictionary though the OS spell it *clocháin*. There are more than thirty-seven different ways of spelling the name of the highest mountain in Ireland. The OS map gives Carrauntoohil, while Sean Ó Súilleabháin gives Carauntuohill and one guide even gives Karen O' Toole, claiming that the mountain is named after a hairdresser in Kilorglin. The name Plover Bay is given as Pol na Feadóige by Tim Robinson although the dictionary gives Feadóg.

I have tried to be consistent and have gone grey in the process. Where I fail, please forgive me. Where possible, I have used the spelling adopted by Tim Robinson. Thanks, Tim.

I have used Irish place names where I felt that they would inform rather than confuse, although there again purists will probably tell me that I have made a right *magairlí* of the job. Again, I can only hold my hands up and tell you that I have requested that upon my tombstone this simple epitaph be chiselled: 'At least he tried'.

CLOTHING AND GOOD ADVICE

I don't really know what to say on this matter. I hate preaching and I've made enough mistakes in my time to know that 'physician heal thyself' has more than a grain of truth in it. But do remember –

1 if it's warm at sea level it could be near to freezing at 3000ft, especially if the winds are strong. If you're going high, even on the best of days, you may need gloves and a hat.

2 in the west of Ireland it can rain at any time so you need good waterproofs.

3 in the west of Ireland the hills are often boggy; stout shoes aren't enough and fabric boots are not much better when there's a lot of water lying about. Good leather waterproof boots are a must. A pair may cost you nearly £100 but they'll last you ten years and what other kind of fun comes as cheap as £10 a year? Don't answer that!

4 If you don't know how to use a map and compass then stay off the high hills until you do. There is only one official Mountain Rescue Team in Ireland and they're in Kerry. They might not want to go all the way to Mayo to haul you off the cliffs of Croaghaun.

5 Enjoy yourself.

MUSIC

I've included music in this book because not to have music in a book about Ireland would be like having fish and chips without salt and vinegar. The tunes are in basic notation and give no idea of the feeling, the lilt of Irish music, but I included them so that those of you who want to, can play them in the safety and comfort of your own homes. There is of course no substitute for hearing the real thing. On record that's no problem, but finding good live music can be more difficult. There are a few pointers to live venues in the book; other than that you will have to do what I do and sniff them out. Sesiún s are moveable feasts and, like the Scarlet Pimpernel, they are here one week, gone the next. (A short discography follows which may be of some use but it is very personal.)

If you do play then remember the unwritten etiquette of the *sesiún*: ask if it's all right to join in. Don't expect trumpets, glockenspiels and drum-kits to be welcome and if you are a *bodhran* player then remember - no more than one to a *sesiún* and check that the floor is level.

DISCOGRAPHY

This is simply a personal list - the kind of things I play to friends at home. There are so many records and tapes of Irish traditional music and song available now that to publish a 'definitive' list would take a book in itself. In fact, if I were to list all my favourite albums here there wouldn't be much room in the book for anything else.

ATLAN *Island Angel*, Green Linnet
ARCADY *After the Ball*, Dara
THE BOTHY BAND *The 1st Album*, Green Linnet
BOYS OF THE LOUGH *Fair Hills of Erin*, Lough
THE CHIEFTAINS *The Chieftains Live!*, Shanachie
MICHAEL COLEMAN *Michael Coleman (1891–1945)*, Gael Linn
COOLEY *Joe Cooley*, Gael Linn
DALY AND CREACH *Jackie Daly and Seamus Creach*, Gael Linn
DE DANAAN *A Jacket of Batteries*, Harmac
DERVISH *Harmony Hill*, Whirling Discs
DES DONNELLY *Remember Des Donnelly*, Celtic Music
TOMMY HAYES *An Rás*, Mulligan
HILL AND LINANE *Noel Hill and Tony Linane*, Tara
DOLORES KEANE AND JOHN FAULKNER *Sail Og Rua*
SEAN KEANE *Jig it in Style*, Claddagh
SEAMUS MCGUIRE *The Wishing Tree*, Green Linnet
JOE MCHUGH AND BARRY CAROL *The Long Finger*, JMB
MAIGHREAD NI DHOMHNAILL *No Dowry*, Gael Linn
MATT MOLOY *Stony Steps*, Green Linnet
CHRISTY MOORE *The Collection*, Warner
MOVING HEARTS *The Storm*, Warner
NOMOS *I Won't Be Afraid Any More*, Grapevine
MICHEAL O'SUILLEABHAIN *Dolphins Way*, Virgin
LEO ROWSOME *Classics of Irish Piping*, Topic
SHARON SHANNON *Sharon Shannon*, Son
VARIOUS *Bringing it all Back Home*, BBC
VARIOUS *Maiden Voyage - Live Music from Peppers Bar*

MAPS

The old 1:126,720 maps of Ireland are lovely to look at, and for cyclists who want to tootle round the back lanes of the country they are superb. For walking in the hills they are next to useless. The new 1:50,000 'Discovery Series' is excellent, although there are still a few teething problems with place-=names being a mile from the place, rivers running uphill and so forth. They are slow coming out and not all the walks in this book are covered by the new series. I understand it will not be too long before the whole of the west is covered. The relevant map number is shown in a small box on each of the walk maps.

There are some excellent maps created by Tim Robinson of Folding Landscapes, Roundstone, Connemara (*see* Chapter 19). They are much more than maps, more a book of the land and if you are at all interested in maps and the subtext of the world they show then Tim's books *Mapping South Connemara* and *The Stones of Aran* will give you joy.

The OS maps don't show walls and hedges, and since hill-walking as a sport is still in its infancy in Ireland there are not too many 'official' footpaths. So far (with the exception of the Sperrin Mountains in County Tyrone) Irish farmers have welcomed walkers on

The author on Mizen Peak

their land and, provided walkers play fair and treat the farmers with respect (close gates, keep the dog under close control, don't start fires, sensible stuff really) then there won't be any problems.

If in doubt about a route up a hill, then ask. If there's nobody about, then pick the least troublesome route and avoid houses and gardens.

CAMERAS AND FERRIES

All but a few of the pictures in this book were shot on Fuji Velvia using an assortment of cameras and lenses. The panorama shots were taken on a Widelux, for the rest I mainly used a Nikon F3 and a variety of lenses from a 20mm wide-angle to an 80-200 zoom. I also carried a Hasselblad with me on most of the trips and used it where time for more measured composition and selection allowed.

The interior shots of musicians were taken using a single Mecablitz flash with a diffusing hood but I have to say that I hate flash and the sooner somebody invents a film as sensitive and accurate as the human retina the better. I used hardly any filtration, though I confess to helping out Ms. Nature on a couple of occasions with a Hoyarex 2X neutral density graduated filter.

Where I could I used a tripod or a monopod so that I could use apertures like f8 and f11 for depth of field. I carried a total of three camera bodies and eight lenses as well as light meter, filters, cable release and film and I don't recommend it. After losing the way off Knockboy and adding an hour's road-walking in falling light to the journey, I would have gladly swapped the back-pack of cameras for a Kodak Box Brownie.

Travel to and from Ireland was mainly by ferry, either Stena Sealink or Irish Ferries. Two people who specialise in Irish travel helped greatly with my arrangements.

Margaret Curry Travel
Wilbraham Road
Chorlton
Manchester

and

Maire Ryan
On Course Travel Ltd
Parklands House
Great Bookham
Surrey KT23 3NB

Bord Failté
150-151 New Bond St
London W1Y 0RQ
were of immense help.

Glossary

bodhran A single-sided skin drum used as a rhythm instrument in traditional Irish music. Arguments rage over the bodhran. In sensitive hands, like those of Johnny (Ringo) McDonagh, it can be a delight. In the hands of an over-enthusiastic and untalented aficionado it can be a sesiún-player's nightmare. At times one can sympathise with the musician who, when asked the best way to play a bodhran, replied, 'With a penknife'. One translation of bodhran from the Irish gives 'a deaf person'. Q. How can you tell when the stage is level? A. The bodhran player dribbles out of both sides of his mouth.

bohareen A narrow lane, from bó - cow; literally a lane the width of one cow.

booley Temporary dwelling erected by cowherds when out on the hills summering cattle.

bulaun Bullán - a stone with a single cup-shaped depression carved into its surface. Thought to be sacrificial.

cailleach A hag or witch.

caoning (pron. 'keening') Ritual wailing at funerals common in the west of Ireland until this century.

ceilidh A night of singing, dancing and storytelling in which everybody is expected to do their 'party piece'.

ceol or cheoil Music or song.

cillín Children's burial ground.

clocháins Stone huts, often bee-hive shaped, of various ages. Some are prehistoric, others were built and lived in in the last century.

cráic Hard to translate, it can involve any one or all of the following to various degrees - conversation, drinking, fun, wildness, music, song, dance.

curragh Skin canoe - see naibhóg.

Fianna The soldiers or Knights of Fionn – from them we get the name of Ireland's main political parties, Fianna Gael and Fianna Fail.

fiacla Teeth.

filí A poet.

focláir Dictionary.

fleadh cheoil A festival of music and song.

Gaeltacht An area where Irish is still the first language of many of the people. The main Gaeltachts are in Donegal, Kerry, Galway and Wicklow.

gardai Anti-cráic - the police.

garsún A boy.

gombeen A 'chancer' – someone who would sell their mother if it benefitted themselves!

green lane An English definition, I'm afraid, but neither cosaun nor bohareen cover it. It means a track fit for walkers, horses or bicycles but not for cars.

jarvey Rapacious rapscallion – AKA driver of horse-drawn carriages now found mainly around Killarney; the original meaning of 'tourist trap'.

naibhóg Skin canoe - Kerry word for curragh.

Ogham One of the earliest alphabets - based on druidic tree of knowledge.

OPW The Office of Public Works about which I have **mixed** feelings. Some of the developments such as that at Clonmacnaoise are tasteful, well designed and exciting. Other ideas they had such as building 'Interpretive Centres' on a lovely coastline at Dunquin and in both the Burren and the Wicklow Mountains I can only describe as Frank Lloyd Wright meets Genghis Khan. I must watch the blood pressure.

pátrún A pilgrimage or a religious procession around a series of stations or holy crosses. Usually held on the feast day of a local saint.

piseog A superstition.

Pookha An Irish fairy similar to the English Puck, Robin Goodfellow.

Potheen Irish moonshine, and I don't mean the kind you spoon under either.

Rath A ring fort often associated with the fairies or little people.

sesiún Open gathering of musicians; everybody is welcome but they do expect you to be able to play to a standard. *Bodhran* players are welcomed casually.

sidhe A fairy. Thus Ban Sidhe - fairy woman, said to be heard wailing before the death of a member of the household.

sile Sheela-na-Gig.

slán Farewell.

sleán A turf-spade.

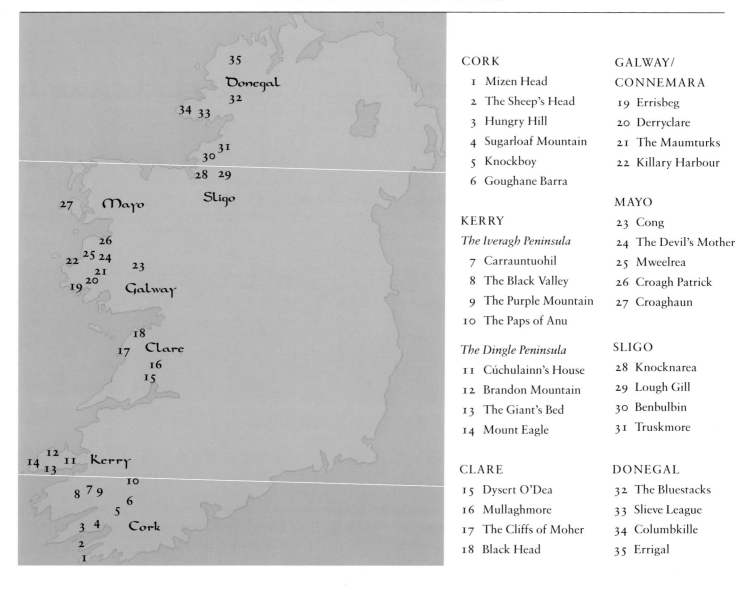

CORK

1 Mizen Head
2 The Sheep's Head
3 Hungry Hill
4 Sugarloaf Mountain
5 Knockboy
6 Goughane Barra

KERRY

The Iveragh Peninsula

7 Carrauntuohil
8 The Black Valley
9 The Purple Mountain
10 The Paps of Anu

The Dingle Peninsula

11 Cúchulainn's House
12 Brandon Mountain
13 The Giant's Bed
14 Mount Eagle

CLARE

15 Dysert O'Dea
16 Mullaghmore
17 The Cliffs of Moher
18 Black Head

GALWAY/ CONNEMARA

19 Errisbeg
20 Derryclare
21 The Maumturks
22 Killary Harbour

MAYO

23 Cong
24 The Devil's Mother
25 Mweelrea
26 Croagh Patrick
27 Croaghaun

SLIGO

28 Knocknarea
29 Lough Gill
30 Benbulbin
31 Truskmore

DONEGAL

32 The Bluestacks
33 Slieve League
34 Columbkille
35 Errigal

A Beginning

I was bound on perhaps the most stupid and thankless of tasks that a man can set himself: I was going to add another book to that mountain of books about Ireland.

H.V. Morton, *In Search of Ireland*

I must have written at least a dozen introductions to this book. Some of them were three pages long and some of them were thirty pages long, but all of them were too long-winded and so purpled with over-ripe prose that they looked like a bucket of aubergines. Often I would write them late into the night, sometimes after the pubs had shut, and they would get wilder and longer and more fanciful, and in the morning I would look at them, tear them up and light the fire with them.

It was like wanting to take a lover home to meet your parents for the first time and rehearsing the words you are going to say over and over before discarding them and then having to start all over again from the beginning. Because, in a way, this book is like a girlfriend. Ten years in the making, thirty years in the courting. And how do I introduce you to her?

I make no secret of the fact that I am in love with Ireland. This romantic notion is partly a result of being brought up in an Irish Catholic household in Manchester by a grandmother who believed in banshees, saints and demons in equal measure and who also believed that it was her job to stop me going to the devil in Protestant England. So she led me to believe that Ireland was a land of saints and scholars where sin was unknown, the

In Ireland it sometimes rains

sun shone all the time and the only things to fear were ghosts, tinkers' curses and certain kinds of mussels that could give you the kind of fever that saw off poor Molly Malone.

I know better now, of course. Thirty years of travelling in Ireland has taught me that there's as much sin there as anywhere else. There's hardship and deprivation too, and the scars of famine and emigration still mark a country that has lost too many of its young people over the years. The country still hurts from the events of 1916 and the Civil War and the 'Troubles' that followed have haunted it since. But this isn't the time or place to speak of such things. And although I won't shirk them when they come up, in the main I'll leave the dark side to other books, other writers. For this book is a celebration.

Hazy nights in old bars with music threading the room like smoke; bitter biting days on high mountains with ragged clouds, bellyful of sleet, racing in off the Atlantic, leaving me holding on to slimy rock with icy fingers as a Fastnet gale tried to peel them free; hot days when I lay on the grass watching small white clouds roll over Dingle Bay and heard the sea muttering on the shore below; nights in a stone-floored kitchen watching dancers weave about the room while the parish priest played a battered old melodeon; afternoons in the Donegal hills drinking tea with people who'd never seen me before in their lives, but who called me in for a drink and a chat; mornings up in the mountains above Bantry, cutting turf with two bachelor brothers, the last of a long line; a glass of potheen by the kitchen stove in a farm on the west Cork coast to warm me up after a wet and windy walk along the sea shore; the faces of little children appearing over the wall as I wandered round an old monastic site, and their open and innocent chatter.

My English teacher at St Bede's College Manchester was a priest called Father Augustus Reynolds. His nickname was 'Foxy' (Reynolds = Reynard = Fox) but a better teacher never walked the face of the earth. Witty and informed and with that great gift of the true teacher that could conjure magic in a dusty Manchester classroom, he could make a class of louts like us sit up and soak up his every word. He is one of the few teachers I've come across that had no discipline problems. In his hands, the plays, prose, poems and essays of E.Lit. O.Level. J.M.B. became a living and exciting thing. He taught me enough to know that, whatever else I did with my life, I would always write. He spoke several languages including Irish and travelled each year to the west of Ireland to cycle round the Gaeltacht playing the fiddle in the houses and pubs, using Irish wherever he could. In my last year at school we read Synge's plays *The Playboy of the Western World* and *Riders to the Sea* together with *The Aran Islands*, the prose piece on the place which had been his main inspiration. Foxy so fired me with his own and Synge's vision of the west of Ireland that I knew I had to go there.

That summer, after raising the money by working as a road digger, I took the night boat from Liverpool to Dublin with Pat, the girl I later married, landing at the North Wall in the grey dawn of an August day to walk through a herd of cows that were on their way to the boat and the abattoirs of England. From Dublin we hitched lifts round the coast to Waterford and then made our way through Kerry and up to Galway and the boat to the Aran Islands. We slept in a tent, under hedges, cooking on an open fire and washing at village pumps. So much of that first journey still lives in my memory. At Bridgetown Co. Waterford an old lady called Stasha Moylan gave us a handful of eggs, a packet of biscuits and a bottle of lemonade which she could probably ill afford, but she gave them because we were travellers and guests in her country. At Salthill Co. Galway a storm tore down the tent and we escaped through the drenching rain to the safety and warmth of the St Valentine's Boarding House, buying a cheap ring from Woolworth's on the way to convince the landlady we were a married couple. The boat from Galway to Inishmore tossed and turned in a force seven and we slid about the deck in the spray trying not to be sick as we looked for the first signs of the island through the gale. Inishmore was a world of stones cobwebbed with more stones, as though they were palimpsests of rock. The Atlantic skies rolled in grey and chill, people huddled round the harbour at Kilronan watching the mailboat dock and we stepped ashore onto a dream.

All that was thirty years ago and I've been back to Ireland over and again through the passing years. Always to the West. When people ask me why, I find it hard to explain. There is a magic in the light there, the mountain light and the sea light. There is something about the pace, too. The east coast is closer to England, closer to what we are told is the 'real world' of insurance and capital and business, the world of humbuggery, fashion and style – the West in the main doesn't care that much about fashion and style.

The language too, I suppose, draws me back. I've been struggling with Irish for years and have mastered only a handful of phrases. It is a difficult language·because it bears no resemblance to French or Spanish or Latin or Greek. It is softer, more musical and yet more angular, it lies beneath the country like the bed-rock and the reasons I am learning it are twofold. First, I want to be able to speak to the people of the country I am walking through in their own language and, secondly, knowing a little of the language helps you understand the land. The simple knowledge that Knock means hill helps you to see what is there on the map underlying the names: Knockboy – *An Cnoc Buí* = the Yellow Hill; Killybegs – *Cill beag* = the little church; Ballysaggart – *Baile an tSaggart* = the town of the priests, as in the ogham circle of that name close by Dingle Town. (In that case it may refer to a seminary or a monastic site.) Mactaggart, by the way, according to a friend of mine who

bears the name, means 'son of the priest', a relic from the days when the Celtic priesthood were allowed to marry.

An understanding of Irish history helps, too. A Mass rock, where priests said Mass in secret during penal times, is not just a lump of stone – it is an uncut ogham, a monolith whose secret text is carved not on its face but on the memories of the people of the townland, a rock whose roots go deep down through the earth back to murdered priests and reach through time, forward to the Falls Road and the Shankill.

As with my other walking books this is not a detailed guide. It doesn't tell you to climb a stile or turn left at the third oak past the pig pens. There are many books that do that and do it well; Paddy Dillon, Joss Lynam, Seán Ó Suilleabháin and Kevin Corcoran have all written accurate and interesting guides to walking in Ireland. This isn't a guide, it is a taste, a gathering of images and impressions.

I've divided the book into sections since the West, in terms of walking, does fall naturally into segments – the Peninsulas of the Cork and Kerry coasts, the mountains of Connemara, the cliffs of Achill Island, the hills of Donegal, the areas are defined by their geography and each has a different soul. The Sheep's Head Peninsula of Cork is nothing like the Burren of Clare; they could be on different planets.

And since walking, to me, isn't just a matter of getting from A to Z but more a way of meeting people and stories along the way, this book is a rambling and meandering stroll through places and music and people. To me, a land isn't just a bare sheet on which we scribble our own story. It is a collection of stories, of threads, of songs and music all weaving together and when I walk, even though I talk a lot, I also try to listen.

The Glanmore Valley below Hungry Hill seen from the Kenmare road

County Cork

They tell lies about each other in Cork and Kerry. It's a little like the Wars of the Roses that are still going on between Lancashire and Yorkshire, a friendly sort of needling between neighbours that never comes to anything much, more like a humorous leg-pulling or slanging match. John B. Keane, the Kerry playwright and novelist, once asked me if I knew why St Patrick had never come to Kerry. I said I did not. 'It's because the Corkmen stole his donkey,' was the answer. The Corkmen (and many other counties in Ireland) are very fond of telling Kerry jokes and though it's all politically incorrect, it has to be said that it is usually quite harmless stuff.

One of my favourite stories is a bit of an about-face because the fool, as so often happens, is shown to be a wise fool. A Kerryman goes for a job on a Cork building site; 'There is an intelligence test,' the foreman tells him. 'We have to know that you can do the job.'

'Fire away,' says the Kerryman.

The question came back, 'What's the difference between girders and joists?'

The Kerryman thought for a moment. 'Girder wrote *Faust* and Joists wrote *Ulysses*.'

Cork is the biggest county in Ireland and, in fact, compared to English counties, only Yorkshire beats it. Cork City is Ireland's second city (although you won't find any Corkman believing that Cork is second in anything) yet, even though it's a

The Irish shop front as a form of folk art

busy commercial town, it still somehow manages to feel warm and human. It has great theatres, restaurants and pubs and the ceol and the craic are as fierce as anywhere in the West. Cork has its own holy well at Lady's Well where, on the site of a medicinal spring that could 'cure lepers and make the blind see again', Murphys now brew a stout to rival that of Arthur Guinness. But if you want to escape the metropolis of Cork and stay a few days in a quieter spot then Bantry is a fine town with good shops and easy access to great walking country, while Glengarriff is small and busy but handy for the Caher Mountains. Macroom for years was just a town I drove through after arriving at Cork on the ferry. Then a few years back I stayed there on my way to Goughane Barra. It is a delight of a place, completely unspoilt with good hotels, great food and friendly people.

The Corkman will tell you of course that the best walking in Ireland is to be had in the Beara or the Sheep's Head Peninsulas, while the Kerryman will tread on the tail of your coat if you dare suggest that the Iveragh and Dingle Peninsulas might not be Paradise fallen to Earth. I'll leave them to fight it out and say that I've had great days in the hills of both counties. The Beara is not as well known or visited as the Iveragh Peninsula, probably because it hasn't got the Lakes of Killarney or the other tourist honey pots, but it is a savagely beautiful place and, as an old friend from Bantry, John Crowley, said to me once when I came off the mountains after a hard day in terrible weather: 'When you get in amongst them there's a lot of mountain up there.'

Like many of the Irish mountains you really do need to know what you're doing in the high hills of County Cork. It's easy to get lost and, because the hills are on long fingers of land thrust out into the Atlantic, the weather can change very quickly. Mist and fog can cover the mountains in a very short time, particularly in spring and autumn, and you need at all times to keep an eye on the weather.

But it's not all high mountain, of course. The Sheep's Head Peninsula has some lovely coastal walking and is quieter and more tranquil than its bigger sister across the bay. Stroll along the back lanes to the bays and inlets with your bag of sandwiches and finish with a pint at the Ahakista Bar and you'll not find a better day out.

I spent a lot of time in Bantry a few years back while working on a BBC television series, staying with the crew just outside Bantry at an excellent bed and breakfast run by Dympna and John (Johnny) Crowley and their large family. They have become good friends over the years, so I won't embarrass them by shouting their praises to the roof tops in this book, beyond saying that you won't find anywhere or anyone better. Johnny is a great guide, with extensive local knowledge; there aren't many people he doesn't know or who don't know him.

One day he took us out to meet Dennis and Andrew Dineen, two brothers who farmed up on rough mountain land in the hills above Bantry. We spent most of the day with them, cutting turf out on the bog and looking at an old Mass rock up on the hill beyond the house. Dennis and Andrew lived simple lives as bachelor farmers, cultivating the land as they had always done. Cutting the turf was hard, painful, hand-blistering work, but Dennis cut with a rhythm and ease that was powerful and yet graceful at the same time, a Nureyev of the *sleán*. When I had a go I made a terrible dog's breakfast of the bog face and got two handfuls of blisters in the process. Patiently and effortlessly, Dennis re-cut the face of the bog, getting it as straight as if a

Bantry Bay Hornpipe

plumb-line had been used, but each time I took the *sleán* I made a donkey's leg of the business again. Afterwards, we had soda bread and butter and hot strong tea in the little cottage and Dennis found a bottle of mountain dew that the fairies had left in a ditch somewhere and we took a drop in case we caught cold, it being such a warm day. Dennis sang a song and then I sang a song and so the day went on. Until the day he died, Dennis said his night prayers in Irish even though this area is not a Gaeltacht.

His mother had taught him his prayers in Irish when he was a child and for eighty years he'd been saying them in the old language.

The brothers are dead and gone now; they died within a few weeks of each other, both in their eighties, and we'll not see their like again. I will never forget them and their gentle shy ways, their hospitality and their courtesy – they were true gentlemen indeed.

1 Mizen Head

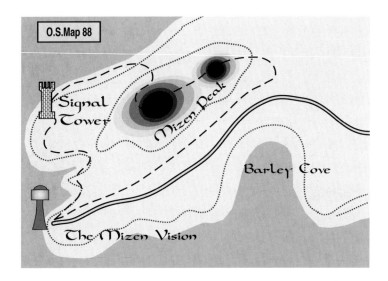

O.S.Map 88

Signal Tower

Mizen Peak

Barley Cove

The Mizen Vision

The southernmost point of mainland Ireland, Mizen Head, looks out towards America; nothing between here and Boston but the waves of the Atlantic. There isn't a great deal here to look at, just a few farms, a scattering of fields and a redundant signal station. But it is a quiet and still place and there's a fine easy climb to Mizen Peak from which, on a clear day you can see the bays and mountains of west Cork. According to Johnny Crowley, if it's clear enough you can see sun shining on the brass overall buttons of the men putting the oil in the Statue of Liberty's lamp, but I've never been there when it's that clear. During the summer holidays there are crowds at Mizen Head, most of them coming to look at the signal station, but when they have all gone you will hear no sounds but the moaning of the wind in the gorse and heather, the screams of gulls and the thunderous mutter of the waves far below drumming on the great sea cliffs.

The fog-warning station was built in 1906 on Cloghane Island, a lump of bare rock just off the Head to work in tandem with the Fastnet lighthouse. In bad visibility, the keepers would set off explosive charges at three-minute intervals to warn ships away from the rocks. The warning was obviously needed because around the Mizen there are more than eighty major wrecks and hundreds of smaller sunken boats. The island was connected to the mainland by an impressive bridge 175 feet long and 150 feet above the waves, one of the earliest uses of reinforced concrete. Later a powerful light was built that could send a beam thirteen miles out to sea. When satellite navigation took over the work of many lighthouses in the 1970s, the redundant station became a tourist attraction with a visitor centre and displays – the 'Mizen Vision' it calls itself, though the words 'Fog Station' and 'Vision' seem like a contradiction in terms.

Mizen Head is like many places in the west of Ireland that are busy tourist spots – if you walk a hundred yards from the car park you will see no one. In a way this isn't surprising because

Pat at cairn on Mizen Peak

the old coastguards' path that leads around the cliffs now has a 'No Entry' sign and a fence across it – though for the life of me, I can't see why, because this path has always been used by walkers and local people as a way along the cliffs and up to the old Napoleonic Tower.

However, I suffer from a strange kind of word blindness when it comes to signs like that and I often see fences as things to be crossed rather than things to keep people out so, one late summer morning, I followed the old footpath under a broken blue sky that held the promise of a better day than the ones that had gone before, when grey Atlantic cloud cover had rolled in and squatted on the land like a gloomy tent.

I left the signal station behind and crossed a short stretch of moorland to an older signal tower, one of the many that were erected all along this coast by the British during the eighteenth and nineteenth centuries, when Boney was a bogeyman and the Wild Geese who had fled Ireland to fight with the French against the English oppressors were more than just a folk memory. I often think, when I see these old towers with their ruined dwellings at their base, how poor footsloggers from the fields and the streets of Britain were sent out here to keep down a people as poor and as exploited as themselves. What would some farm labourer from Yeovil or some weaver from Blackburn, who had taken the King's Shilling, have felt as he sat high up in the tower looking out to sea, the Atlantic gales battering the cliffs, nothing around him but fear and resentment, sea spray and the keening of the gulls? They must have wondered what the hell they were doing there while the politicians back in Westminster sat in their armchairs before the fire. It was ever thus. Now the tower is ruinous and the wind and brambles have taken it over.

The kidney vetch and heather were thick beneath my feet as I left the ruined tower and followed the well-worn path along the cliff edge. Recent falls have meant that the path has veered sensibly inland (the Irish, though they have done many things, have not yet perfected the art of unaided flight), but occasionally there were sudden views down clefts into black voids where white boomerangs of gulls spired on the up currents. It was one of those mornings that got better and better as it went on, rather like a good wine. The few clouds that had been swirling about the south-west seemed to have moved over to the east where the weather certainly looked muckier.

As I walked along the cliffs I could see below me fulmars, kittiwakes and guillemots, though there was no sign of the skuas that are sometimes seen here on their way to and from their summer grounds on the islands of the North Atlantic. I was glad of that. The last time I had seen skuas was on St Kilda in the Hebrides, when I had stood on a much more fearsome cliff than this with the damn things dive-bombing me. They have a fair-sized wingspan and are nastier and more aggressive than any pub drunk. Their favourite trick is to gang up on a gull that has just eaten and harry it until it vomits up its catch. They then eat the loot themselves in mid flight. Very poor table manners.

I stood for a long time looking out to sea, watching for any signs of the dolphins, whales or porpoises that used to be seen here in great numbers, but saw nothing. Either I was unlucky or the war of attrition that Man has been carrying out against the sea is finally being won in his favour. The porpoises and dolphins swallow polythene bags, condoms, ropes and discarded fishing gear, mistaking them for food; the stuff lodges in their gut and kills them. Well done, mankind.

From the cliffs I struck out across rough heath towards *Mizen Peak*, at 765ft above sea level hardly a Matterhorn but a nice climb anyway. I made my way up a mild form of the *benching* that is such a characteristic of the hills of west Cork. This benching is caused by the erosion of folded rocks turning the mountains into giant staircases. It is seen at its most severe in the *Beara Peninsula*. After an easy climb on to the summit I laid my rucksack against the concrete trig point and looked around me. (Did you know by the way that cement, the main constituent of concrete, was invented by an Irishman? Bryan Higgins of Sligo invented the stuff in 1779 and a good few Irishmen since have had cause to curse him while they were, as Dominic Behan once wrote, 'building up and tearing England down'.) To the south I could see *Clear Island* and the beautifully named *Roaringwater Bay*, while standing alone far out to sea was *Fastnet Rock*, that fantastic fang of stone whose name I used to hear as a schoolboy when I listened to the shipping forecasts on the radio. To me it was a word as magical and mystical as Sinbad or Scherezade, only it promised not deserts and flying horses, but grey-green seas, vicious storms and the wrecks of long-lost fleets – from British dreadnoughts to gold-laden Spanish galleons. Dogger, Fisher, German Bight, Forties – Fastnet, the litany still conjures up mind-pictures of great fogs and tiny boats looking out hopefully for that angel light to see them safely home to harbour.

Northwards lay the *Sheep's Head Peninsula* with *Seefin* and *Caher Mountain* clearly to be seen, while beyond were the blue, far-off peaks of the *Beara*, the hump of *Hungry Hill* and the cone of the *Sugarloaf*. I walked from the trig point to a cairn of stones that looked towards *Knocknagree* and *Mount Gabriel*, with the white domes of the tracking station on its summit.

There was a cool wind even though the day was filled with sunshine and that clear Atlantic light, so I dropped down below the peak behind a stone outcrop into a natural sun trap. I must have sat there for an hour or more just looking out towards *Cape Clear* and down into *Barley Cove* where I could just make out the spattering of coloured dots that I realised were families sunbathing and swimming in the cove. It was one of those summer days that you remember from childhood, soft and warm and sleepy and magical. But I had a few miles to go to my bed that night with Johnny and Dympna Crowley so I dropped north from the peak across more heath and heather to follow an old bog road back to the signal tower.

They used to tell a story in Cork of an old farmer coming off the mountain at the close of a hard day on such a bog road, driving a donkey with two creels of turf on its back. As he reaches the main black-top road, he meets an American tourist standing by a hired car videoing the land all about him:

'Is this all yours?' The American asks, sweeping his arm out to encompass the countryside around.

'Indeed it isn't,' answered the old farmer. 'I have only the two good fields of hay up above and a part of the bog and two fields below that wouldn't keep a goat in hair.'

'Back home in Texas I can get in my car and drive for half a day and still not get to the end of my land,' said the American proudly.

The farmer thought for a moment. 'D'you know, I had a car like that meself one time. I had to get rid of it in the end.'

In a car not much better, I drove home to Dympna's scones by lanes that were a riot of fuchsia and montbretia; an easy and unheroic day in the hills but a glorious one.

2 A Walk on the Sheep's Head

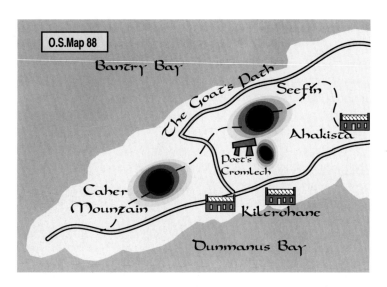

O.S.Map 88

Bantry Bay

The Goat's Path

Seefin

Ahakista

Poet's Cromlech

Caher Mountain

Kilcrohane

Dunmanus Bay

Slung beneath the Beara Peninsula like an outrigger, the Sheep's Head Peninsula is a peaceful and unchanged corner of Ireland. It is one of the best kept secrets in the whole country. Small farms huddle low on the flanks of the hills, sheltering from the inc.oming westerlies, while the mountains are gentle and roll westward, almost calling you up them. Local people are busy putting together a network of footpaths that will thread the length of the peninsula. Called the Sheep's Head Way, it will be a 45 mile long-distance walk starting in Bantry and following

the high land down to Tooreen at the tip of the Sheep's Head. From there the route returns south along lanes and paths close by the coast through the most beautiful landscape in Ireland. There is bed and breakfast accommodation and bunk house barns along the way and the whole walk will take four or five days of easy rambling.

I walked part of the Sheep's Head Way one windy March day with a local farmer, Séamus Daly and his little son, James. (Since Séamus means James, and 'een' is the diminutive, I suppose it should be 'Séamuseen' or 'Jimeen' by rights.) James, a stocky, tough little three-year-old, took special care of me, helping me over walls and down craggy jumps, all the while keeping up a seamless chatter – he must, I assumed, have been breathing through his ears. Séamus loves the area and wants to see it stay exactly as it is. No way-marking, no fencing. Just the way it is. It's uplifting to come across someone like Séamus, a farmer in touch with the land, who welcomes walkers and wants to share in the beauty of the place he calls home.

'You can't eat the view,' an Irish farmer once said, meaning that it didn't put food into men's mouths. Nowadays, it does put food into a lot of people's mouths through tourism but, more importantly, it puts food into their souls. There is something that can't be measured in pounds and shillings in being able to sit on a high mountain and look across Bantry Bay at striding hills and white farms and inlets studded with boats. I'm convinced that

Hungry Hill seen across Sheep's Head Bay

getting out into the open spaces, whether they be wilderness or farmland, mountains or sea coast, makes us better people. It makes us (or it should make us) realise how the stresses, noise and clamour of our everyday lives are really meaningless and that the eternal verities of sun, sea and sky will be there long after the mortgage and the grey hairs have all gone. I have a theory that all politicians should be dragged into the hills at least once a month. It might improve them, and at least it would keep them out of mischief for a while. Somebody I said this to in a bar in Galway once said he agreed with taking them into the wilderness, but didn't see why they needed to be brought back.

Séamus led us over good meadows onto the rougher land of the coastal cliffs where old, deserted copper mines now stand derelict high above the waves. The mines were sunk by Cornish miners who were brought over for the purpose and dumped here on this lonely spot on the edge of Ireland. You can still see the dam they made for washing the ore, while their little row of cottages, each with its fireplace, stands with its windowless wall to the sea. It is said by some that the miners, like those brought over to Allihies at the end of the Beara Peninsula, were bitterly resented and were boycotted by the locals. They are also said to have brought over with them the fuchsia that had just been introduced to England and that it is thanks to them that the hedgerows of the west of Ireland are now so full of these bushes with their red flowers, 'the tears of Christ'. The cottages are very like those you might see close to the tin mines around Botallack in Cornwall, low and squat and thick-walled. Séamus would like to rebuild them as bothies or camping barns along the Sheep's Head Way. I hope he succeeds.

Little James dragged me up the crag in front of the cottages and across the rough, boggy land to a blowhole where spouts of spray flew high into the air as the sea rushed in to an underground cave. The blowhole is not a natural hole; it was a shaft sunk by a local man who used it for drawing sand up. Boats would gather the sand along the coast and bring it into the sea cave and from there it would be hauled up in baskets to the donkeys waiting above. Amongst other things, it was used for spreading on house floors to keep them clean. James loved the noise and the roar of the water as it spouted from the back of this great stone whale, but we got a drenching standing there and even he got fed up in the end so we made our way back to the lane and on to Séamus's farmhouse, where tea and brown bread put some heat back into the old bones. James's elder sisters were home from school, two beautiful little girls with dark hair and blue eyes.

'Your brother's quite a man,' I said.

'He's a monster,' they both said, looking at me wide eyed with wonder. 'He's terrible.' I thought this was sisterly exaggeration. I was wrong.

That night there was set dancing at the local village school and John Crowley and I were playing for the dancers. It's hard to describe Irish Set Dancing. It's much tighter than English or Scottish country dancing, probably because the dancing originally took place in small cottage rooms, where the moves were more restricted. It is amazingly powerful and fluid, with four couples to a 'set' going through a series of complex and wild moves. I enjoy playing for the sets; it is good discipline and the dancers tell you exactly what speed and rhythms they want. That night the dance was going well and everybody was enjoying the *cráic*, when all of a sudden, halfway through a set, the room was flung into total darkness. This was a schoolroom in the heart of rural Ireland so there was nothing so much as a glimmer of a street light outside. The darkness was total, you could have drunk it. Some little girls screamed, then someone struck a match. The lights came on again to show a room full of still and puzzled dancers. The door opened and in was led little James, with an enormous grin splitting his face. As one the room said, 'Oh, no, it's James.' He'd flung the main switch on the fuse panel into the 'off' position just to see what would happen – an Irish Dennis the Menace.

Later that year, Pat and I travelled to the Sheep's Head to walk the ridge from Ahakista over Seefin and Caher Mountain and on to Caher Pier. It's a longish day's walk and means leaving a car at each end, or arranging to be picked up at the western end of the walk, which, through various contacts in Johnny Crowley's Murphyia, we were able to do. We were to be guided over the mountains by a local farmer, James, and his son, John, and picked up by car at the far end. This, by the way, is not the little James you have just met; this is Big James the farmer – but not Very Big James the farmer who is the brother of Dympna who I stay with over in Bantry and who is married to John the farmer. This is another James entirely. I asked James if everybody on the Sheep's Head was called James. 'A few of the women aren't,' was his answer. Fair enough.

James was taking us as far as the Goat's Path where young John would meet me to lead the rest of the way. It obviously helps to have local knowledge when you're walking an area for the first time and in this case we were doubly blessed because James knows these hills like the back, front and middle of his hand and does this walk at least once a year, crossing the moun-

tains to visit his brother John, the uncle of John, his son, and no relation to John, the husband of Dympna. We were also lucky with the day, which was clear and bright with a few clouds far off to the north over the Beara Peninsula. The forecast was for rain later, however.

As we'd driven down from Duras, we'd seen farmers hurrying to get the silage in before the weather broke. All over Ireland, a poor summer had grudgingly handed out a few good days and the farmers were not going to waste them. One farmer we knew had started cutting silage on a Sunday for the first time in his life. Certainly everybody was praying that the weather would hold. It looked set for fair as we headed up the road from James's farm above Ahakista and climbed over a fence onto some rough meadowland. There was a warm breeze and the air was almost motionless as we crossed the boggy land below the Seefin ridge. The way was rough and unmarked, but James was a great guide, as he knows every bog hole and 'soft' piece of ground. The going got better once we'd climbed a little and left the worst of the wet behind. I was dressed in my usual hill gear of walking boots, fibre pile, rucksack and camera pouches, and in the rucksack were film, lenses, a flask, waterproofs and gaiters. James, farmer fashion, was wearing jeans, wellies and a light shirt and his 'lunch' was a tin of hand-rolling tobacco and cigarette papers.

We scrambled up onto the broad ridge between Seefin and Gouladane, and, had I been alone here, I might well have gone wrong. An easy shoulder leading to an unnamed false summit, only 100 feet or so lower than Seefin, snakes off to the south, while the true summit is south-west. In low cloud it would be easy to make a wrong move here and, though you wouldn't be in

Pat and James (note the wellies) on the summit of Seefin: the Slieve Miskish and Caha Mountains seen beyond

any danger, since the hills are almost crag-free, you would have a tedious time finding your way back on to your route.

The benching, so typical of the mountains of West Cork, is just about played out by the time it arrives at the Sheep's Head, although, like the shake of a tail, it can still hold some surprises. As I soon discovered, there were slabs and steps enough to make it a longish slog over a series of false summits until the last pull to the summit of Seefin, 'the Seat of Fionn Mac Cumhail' – for this was his mountain.

The views all around us were wonderful. To the north and far below, was the whole of Bantry Bay and, beyond, the Slieve Miskish and Caha Mountains with Hungry Hill softened and blued by the distance. Below us, somewhere to the south of Derrycluvane, lay the Poet's Cromlech, one of the hundreds of megalithic tombs that are scattered over Cork and Kerry. Close by the Poet's Cromlech is the Poet's Well and whether there was a bardic school here or whether they were named after a famous local poet or *filí* I've yet to find out. We munched on some apples and James smoked one of his roll-ups as we sat in the sun, silently watching the light move across the land and the sea. It was a Sunday and I'd missed Mass yet again, but I've always felt that you can give silent praise just as well (if not better) to whatever god you believe in when on top of a mountain on a day of such glory.

We dropped down off the hill in a series of short scrambles, James, in his wellies, as sure-footed as one of the wild goats you see in the hills here from time to time, and met up with John where our route crossed the *Goat's Path*, once an old way across the mountains and now a black top road. There's a Calvary on the summit of the Goat's Path, put there by a local man who made good in America. A pietá might be a more accurate description of the white marble statue of the Virgin Mary with the murdered Christ in her arms, looking down from the col towards the sea.

At the road, James went home for his Sunday lunch and John took over, leading us up on to a dry rocky ridge which gave pleasant walking for a while, though we soon ran back into benching and bog. As we climbed higher we came across the remains of old turf cuttings high up on the broad shoulder of the mountain, an indication of how desperate and hard life must have once been here. John told us the turf would have been carried off in baskets slung on people's backs, for the ground here is too rocky and steep for even the bravest and toughest ass. There was a disappointing drop of a couple of hundred feet just before the summit of *Caher Mountain*, where a gash has been carved through the hill, but what can't be cured must be endured, so down we went, then scrambled back up the steep grassy slope to the shoulder and the summit.

Behind us was *Seefin*, before us the long drop to the coast and

The pietá at the summit of the Goat's Path

the Atlantic. In the middle distance we could see the newly mown fields on James's farm (James, the brother of Dympna, not James, the father of John) and the man himself on his tractor chugging around in circles like a tiny red snail. John led us down off the hill and through the usual bog and barbed wire to a *bohareen* that led down to the road. There, John's Uncle John was waiting to 'lift us' back to *Ahakista* where we celebrated the end of a great walk with a pint of the very best Liffey water and a bit of *craic*. While we were inside the bar, black clouds rolled over the land, turning the day to premature night. The lights in the bar came on, and the threatened rain fell in buckets. The farmers had the silage in and we were off the hill just in time, getting wet inside instead of out.

[17]

3 Hungry Hill

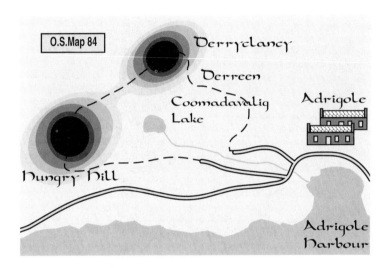

O.S. Map 84

Derryclancy

Derreen

Coomadavalig Lake

Adrigole

Hungry Hill

Adrigole Harbour

The Beara Peninsula was home to the Ó Sullivan Beares, the great battling clan whose ruined castles and strongholds still dot the coastline of west Cork. Beara was the daughter of the King of Castile and married one of the Ó Sullivans, giving him many children and the peninsula her name. The might of the Ó Sullivans is long diminished now and their descendants have been described as the 'water drawers and wood hewers of society', though I don't think my good friend Seán Ó Suilleabháin, the Irish walker and writer of guides to the mountains of the south-west, would applaud that description.

Two mountain ranges lie thrusting westwards, the spine of this peninsula; these are the Slieve Miskish and the Caha Mountains. Caha means 'showery' and, since the water-logged Atlantic westerlies have these hills to climb before they can get further inland, they dump most of their water here. I have sat for hours some summer days waiting for the clouds to clear off Sugarloaf Mountain and Hungry Hill, only to give up and drive down to the Sheep's Head Peninsula which had been in sunshine all along. There are plenty of good days though, and when the sun is on the hills of the Beara and you've a clear sky and plenty of time then the walking is superb.

Hungry Hill is better known to many people by the book of that name written by Daphne Du Maurier (who never in fact went anywhere near the place). The book is a romance based on the true story of the copper-mining Puxley family who came to this neck of the woods from Wales and ended up by becoming extremely wealthy copper masters. By all accounts, they were what my old history teacher would have described as 'blackguards of the direst hue', and when their beautiful stately home was torched by the IRA in 1921 few locals mourned. It was a terrible waste of a lovely old house but the Puxleys had been barbarous employers and landlords, and wrongs meted out to generations of local people brought about the sad destruction. 'We see tomorrow through yesterday' an Irishman once said, and it is true that in Ireland hurts and grievances are never forgotten but go below to smoulder and burn, resurfacing perhaps years later.

People still argue about the name Hungry Hill (*Cnoc Deod* in Irish). One theory is that it is a corruption of 'Angry Hill' from the predominant mood of the mountain, broody and grey. I've often seen it like that on those sour days when the hills have followed the lead of Henry Ford and decided that 'you can have any colour as long as it's grey'. Another theory is that the name is a corruption of 'Envy', the story going that the hills hereabouts were named by a local priest after the seven deadly sins. Having been on intimate terms with the mountain, I would agree with Johnny Crowley that it gets its name because there's not a lot to eat up there for either man or beast. At 2,251ft, Hungry Hill is the highest mountain on the Beara and although there are a good few routes on to it, my favourite walk on to the massif is from the road that leads in to the glen from Adrigole, making a horseshoe of the walk by taking in Derryclancy as well.

One Sunday in the first weeks of summer I left my car at the road end and, climbing a newly erected stile, aimed for the high land of the shoulder. The ground was sodden, but by picking my way carefully round the worst of the boggy areas I made the higher and drier ground and, scrambling through a group of rock outcrops, reached the shoulder. It was a warm but hazy day so visibility was limited but I could see the whole of Bantry Bay, Bear Island and Bear Haven below me. Bear Haven was full of Russian and Spanish fishing boats lying at anchor. I counted more than twenty of them, factory ships in the main. I'd heard stories of how, the previous Christmas, the sailors had bought just about every toy from the shops in Castletown Bearhaven and the shopkeepers had had to rush to Cork to get more so that the sailors could take them home for their children. It might be good for the shopkeepers but I'm not sure what the fishermen of the West feel about their stocks being fished to extinction.

From the outcrop I traversed west and then started to climb over the massive rock 'benches' that are a distinct feature of the hills of the Beara Peninsula. The benches were once rock pleats that were eroded into giant saw teeth. A geological shift moved them to the perfect angle for collecting water and, since the benches are filled with soft peat, the equation 'soft peat plus lots of water equals slutch' holds extremely well in the mountains of west Cork. On Hungry Hill, the rock benches are at their most gruelling. Climbing the benches means finding a place on the rock low enough for you to scramble up, then working your way along the soft ground on top of that until you find a way up the next slab. It's like a giant staircase with risers of near vertical rock and treads of sodden and mushy bog – and makes interesting walking . . .

At about 2,000ft, the gradient grew gentler and I left bog and rocky staircase behind to cross a broad green hump to a large stone cairn. This isn't the true summit of Hungry Hill but the cairn is so well constructed that I can only think it stood as a marker point for ships in the bay, or was perhaps erected as an observation point. Bear Haven is a very safe deepwater mooring, much prized by the British during the First World War when Admiral Beatty brought the Allied fleet in here before the Battle of Jutland. After the Treaty of 1921, the British were allowed to maintain a garrison at Bear Island and a destroyer in Bantry Bay. This arrangement lapsed in 1938 and Bear Haven was handed back to the Irish. Churchill, my grandmother's *bête noir*, was the only one to oppose this. As First Lord of the Admiralty, he wanted to keep Bear Haven as a safe anchorage for British ships.

Pat ascending the saddle of Hungry Hill: typical benching can be seen on the hillside beyond

There was a diplomatic kerfuffle in 1939 after the declaration of war when German U-boats were seen cruising off the coast and Churchill sent an envoy to ask for Bear Haven to be returned to the British. De Valera, the Taoiseach of the day, sent the envoy away empty handed and Churchill, almost frothing at the mouth, asked the Cabinet to authorize seizure of the port under any pretext. The Cabinet refused and Churchill was left to stew. He did go so far as to offer De Valera an end to partition in exchange for use of Bear Haven and the other safe water at Lough Swilly, but the Long Man was having none of it. Interestingly, climbing in the West a few years ago with a good Irish friend who shall be nameless, I heard of a very good and detailed set of maps that had been prepared by the British in case they invaded Ireland during the Second World War to prevent German occupation. The maps were languishing in their thousands in a military warehouse somewhere in England and my friend had managed to get hold of a complete set. Very good they were too.

I took a last look at the peaceful flotilla below me and headed north across green turf to the cairn and trig point at Hungry Hill's true summit. To the west was Knocknagree, to the north Eskatarriff and the Glanmore Valley; beyond, further north still, the mountains of the Iveragh Peninsula were smudged by the heat haze into a series of folds and spires. I sat by the summit cairn and ate my lunch, taking in the view and putting names to the mountains about me from the map. Then I took an easy way down to the saddle between Hungry Hill and Derryclancy by a series of small benches, making sure that I kept well clear of the ferocious cliffs on the east face of Hungry Hill. It's important when following this route to head further north than east for the benches lie in such a way that it is easy to be drawn towards the cliffs.

The mountains of the Iveragh Peninsula seen from the summit of Hungry Hill

From the saddle, it was another slog back up to the summit of Derryclancy, though much easier-going underfoot. The summit of Derryclancy is a series of quartzite outcrops and I ducked in amongst them to shelter from the stiff breeze that was racing across the tops. I had a choice now of either carrying on to Coombane and bagging another peak, or finding a way down by the stream that springs between the two mountains. It was getting late in the afternoon so I chose the shorter path and scrambled down quartzite and over bogs until I hit easier ground to follow a wall that took me over barbed wire and ditches via a peat bog to a gate and a farm track back to the road. I should warn you early on in this book that no descent from Irish hills is complete without a scramble over barbed wire, a drop into a ditch and a step-dance through a slimy peat bog – in no particular order.

Once on the road, I reasoned from the map that if I could walk back into the glen towards the waterfall that hangs down the hillside like a mare's tail, then I could ford the river and get back to my car without a lot of road walking. But an old lady standing at a cottage gate that had a sign painted on it advertising teas and cakes told me it wasn't allowed. 'The people up there don't allow anybody across their land. There's no way through to the river. You'll have to go back by the long way round.' So I thanked her and wandered back to the road and the bridge, the afternoon now turning sunny and bright. Road-walking on a day like this, in any case, is no real hardship. Montbretia and hibiscus studded the hedgerows and the lanes were quiet and lonely and, even though I dawdled and looked and sat and took photographs, I was back at the car in less than an hour.

On the way back to Glengarriff I noticed a pub with tables outside and people sitting in the sun. I have the will power of a brainwashed gnat and, in any case, the car has learnt that it is more than its next MOT is worth to pass a good pub, so it turned in, parked and switched off the engine all on its own and I spent a pleasant hour sitting in the sun with a pint of Guinness in front of me, watching the world go by, telling myself that this was research for the book and therefore work.

That night I stayed at the Eccles Hotel, the grandest in Glen-garriff where George Bernard Shaw is said to have stayed when he wrote *Saint Joan*. The hotel has some of the faded glory of a Victorian watering spot, which is what it indeed was. During those sepia-toned years of Empire, the whole of the Glengarriff area was known as one of the most beautiful spots in Ireland, and travellers from England in search of 'the picturesque' could get a weekend boat-and-rail trip direct from London for thirty shillings.

A few years ago I was here with a BBC crew filming the Glen-garriff Ceilidh Band who were playing at the Eccles Hotel. The sequence began with me arriving by bicycle and walking in through the door just as dusk was spreading over the harbour and the hills behind. At the very moment I dismounted from the bike, an owl hooted and flapped away above me out of shot. When the film was broadcast, a keen 'twitcher' wrote a scornful letter to the BBC saying that they'd done it again and should know better than to let their dunderheads loose in the sound effects library. The owl's call showed it to be an Abyssinian Cross-Eyed Mute Screech Owl (or whatever he said it was – I forget now, it was a long time ago), and went on to point out that this same owl was never found any further north than Barcelona. We were very happy to write back and tell him that if that was indeed the call of the Abyssinian Cross-Eyed Mute Screech Owl then one must have decided to take its holidays in Ireland that year because nothing had been added to the recording at all. We heard no more.

4 Sugarloaf Mountain

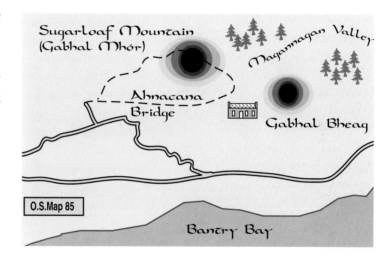

Seen from the Glengarriff to Castletown road, the Sugarloaf Mountain truly suits its name for, like its namesake in the Wicklow Hills, it looks for all the world like the conical blocks of sugar that grocers used to keep on their counters in years long gone. They had died out even when I was a kid and the only time I remember seeing one, apart from in a museum, was in a pub of that name in Manchester where it was kept on the bar as a souvenir.

The Sugarloaf is a great hill for a short walk; it's a tough little climb but the views from the summit are superb. As somebody once said in a bar in Glengarriff, 'Sure you can see to the moon from there, how much further do you want to see?' The hill is quite accessible too since the Beara Way passes under its flank, crossing the saddle between the Sugarloaf and its companion *Gabhal Bheag* at around the 750ft contour, and giving you a clear way up over open ground, following benching to the summit. *Slieve na Goil* is the Irish name for Sugarloaf Mountain – 'the hill of the wild people' – although it is shown on the map as *Gabhal Mhór* while its companion *Gabhal Bheag* also appears as Gowlbeg Mountain. Leaving aside all discussion for the moment of the anglicisation of Irish names, it seems obvious that the Sugarloaf and its companion were respectively the Big Mountain of the Wild People and the Little Mountain of the Wild People.

Paddy Maloney of the Chieftains Irish Music Group tells the story of two fairy queens living on their respective mountains arguing about which was the biggest. I don't remember what the outcome was but the row gave birth to a piece of music called 'Si Bheag Si Mhór'. This was written by Turlough Ó Carolan, the most famous of all the wandering Irish harpers who, though went blind from smallpox in his teens, travelled around the great houses of the west of Ireland with his harp, composing and playing his music and (if he was anything like the musicians I know), drinking and wenching his way around the countryside of Connaught. He celebrated the largesse of his hosts with 'Planxtys',

The Sugarloaf Mountain showing clearly how it got its name

pieces of music dedicated to them, and is said to have written one of his most famous pieces, 'Carolan's Concerto' for a wager one night in a stately home after hearing a piece of Mozart played on the harpsichord. And indeed echoes of Scarlatti and other European courtly composers are plain to hear in his own short piece. After leaving the world hundreds of marvellous tunes, he died with a glass of whiskey held to his lips saying, 'Twould be a shame if old friends could not kiss before they part.'

I walked the Sugarloaf with my old friend Seán Ó Suilleabháin one wild early spring afternoon with a strong wind roaring in from the west and the first of the new lambs in the fields. Seán has been involved in the outdoor movement in Ireland for a long time and is a mountaineer, runner and climber as well as an 'all round good egg'. There isn't much about Kerry that Seán doesn't know. We were on our way to Killorglin from Cork to walk in the Reeks and along the Dingle Way, but 'with the day that was in it' we saw the opportunity for breaking our journey with a short walk on the way and seized it. The wind was cold and it was quite overcast but there was a good light in the sky. Seán wanted to look at a recently designated long-distance walking route, the Beara Way, and since it runs under the Sugarloaf, we decided to climb the mountain from the path and kill two birds with one stone.

We parked the car carefully out of the way at the road end and set out along the old green lane that leads between the Big and Little Mountains of the Wild People, back to Glengarriff. It was walled on one side and well defined, obviously having been in use as a line of communication for hundreds if not thousands of years, perhaps from the days of the Wild People themselves. Tracks like this came to be known as 'butter roads' in the last century when butter from all the townlands of the west travelled along them to Cork; here it was taken on board ship to end up on tables as far away as the mansions of the West Indies. Well drained and culverted, the roads were obviously of vital importance and were well maintained by gangs of stone breakers and engineers.

A few hundred yards along the 'butter road' at Ahnaclana, we crossed a fine arched bridge, broad enough to take a cart and horse – another indication of the importance of this old highway. A farmer and his dog gathering sheep were the only signs of life as we walked on towards the saddle between the two peaks. There was a ruined cottage just off the track and signs of further ruins in the distance. Prior to the Famine, it is likely that there were a good few families living in cabins along this old highway.

Seán Ó Suilleabháin on the flanks of the Sugarloaf: Bantry Bay seen beyond and wild weather coming on

Si Beag Si Mhor

Now they have gone and only the ruined walls of their houses remain, the people who once lived here gone like the wind on the mountain.

We struck up northwards on to rising ground at the point where the old road dropped away before us towards Glengarriff. There was some exciting scrambling on the benches and in slippy gullies before we reached a final great shark's-fin of rock, like a miniature Striding Edge, that brought us close under the summit of the Sugarloaf. The weather had closed in and mist and cloud sailed all round us, breaking from time to time to let great bars of sunlight wash across the land far below. Through the gaps we could make out Bantry Bay and the great curve of Glengarriff harbour shining in the fitful light. The wind was raging in from the west, however, buffeting and pummelling us, far too strong for us to stand there for very long, so we pulled our way the last hundred feet to the summit. And a grand summit it is too, sharp and conical, everything a mountain should be. No broad hump or cluster of shattered rocks, just an honest-

to-goodness peak with a trig point on top. Through tears in the cloud we could see, far below the steep northern flanks of the Sugarloaf, the wild and uninhabited Magannagan Valley and the forestry road that leads into it like a thin scratch on the dark green of the land. Standing up on the summit in the face of that fierce wind was hard work so we didn't stay long. We found our way off to a small saddle and a stream that led us down to the bridge at Ahnaclana and so to the car.

The weather broke yet again into bright sunlight and scurrying clouds as we rolled out of Cork and into Kerry. Once over the border, Seán took off the chain of garlic he had been wearing round his neck in case the Cork vampires got at him. I tried to explain that there were nice people in Cork just as there were in Kerry but he was not for convincing and was only really happy when Macgillycuddy's Reeks filled the windscreen of the car. Then he gave a deep sigh and muttered something in Irish about 'sabháilte faoi dheireadh buíochas le Dia', which I think means 'Safe at last, thanks be to God'.

5 Knockboy and the Priest's Leap

There is an old green lane that leads from Bantry over a remote pass in the mountains to Kenmare and beyond. They call it the Priest's Leap because during penal times, when the practice of the Catholic religion was banned and priests were outlawed, a priest on horseback, who was being pursued by red-coats, jumped his horse from a rock on the pass clear through the air to Bantry Bay, four or so miles and nearly a thousand feet below. If you look carefully, it is said that you can see the hoof marks of his horse on a rock on 'The Lepp', as locals call it, and the marks where the horse landed on another rock in Bantry. Don't ask me whether it's true or not. In Ireland, the truth is not as important as legend, and reality is what you make it.

I first went to the Priest's Leap when I was making a film for BBC Television and, for the purposes of the film, I had to cycle up 'The Lepp'. What viewers later saw was a shot of me trundling up a very steep, unmade road in the lovely west of Ireland with blue skies and green mountains all around me. What they didn't see was the two little boys on bicycles who were watching the action while picking their noses in tandem and who fell off their bicycles laughing when the director made me do it four times to get the picture right.

One April day a few years ago, after a cup of tea and a good helping of Dympna's buns, Pat and I set off for 'The Lepp' and Knockboy (*An Cnoc Buí* – the Yellow Hill). It was midday by the time we set off, late to begin a walk like this, but the weather,

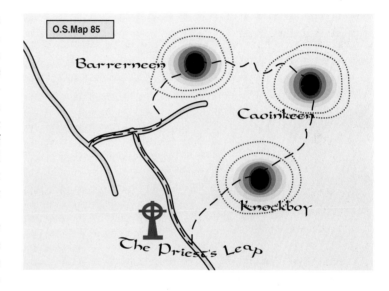

O.S.Map 85

Barrerneen

Caoinkeen

Knockboy

The Priest's Leap

though it had closed in a bit, looked settled. The clouds were down but seemed to be well above the mountains, so we left the car close by 'The Lepp' and struck off for the hill. The ground was a sponge beneath us, sodden from weeks and months of lashing rain, but after half an hour or so of hard walking we were just below the summit of Knockboy. To the north, beneath the ceiling of rolling dark cloud, we could see the Iveragh Peninsula and the Reeks while south lay the Sheep's Head Peninsula

Storm clouds over the Priest's Leap

The Priest's Leap

with Bantry Bay far to the south-west. While the sun constantly shone on the distant sea, all about us was nothing but swirling grey.

The wind promised by the weather forecast got up as we gained the trig point, so there was no point in lingering. We pushed on to Caoinkeen, a minor summit to the north, before dropping to the saddle between Caoinkeen and Knocknamanagh, another small peak. I slipped on my backside in a patch of slime and got a good soaking for my troubles. The wind cutting through the wet trousers caused an arctic experience in certain parts of the corpus that even Heineken couldn't reach. There is, by the way, a rocky combe beneath Caoinkeen which could be a real danger in misty weather and, since the mountains round 'The Lepp' are very prone to fogs and mists, it's important to have a compass and map and to be able to use them.

It was a tough slog climbing Caoinkeen for the winds were fierce, gale-force now, and the light was dropping. We wasted no time crossing the mountain and cutting north-west to Barrerneen, an even tougher slog. It was far too cold to linger on the summit. The cloud had come down until it was just above the peaks and the last of the light was going, so we dropped quickly down to the road by some turf cuttings to what I think was once an old bog road. It was a slippy and rocky descent to the cuttings and I landed on my backside a few times more before we joined a rough farm track close by a ruined building. This was another deserted farm, where at one time there would have been a large family; all gone now to England or America, I suppose.

I made a bad mistake in the poor light on the walk back. Thinking the lane that went to our left was a farm track I carried on until I reached a T-junction and realised I had over-shot our way back by almost a mile. The female side of the relationship was not best pleased. I was looking at the map trying to work out where the road had gone when an elderly lady came along, pushing her old black bicycle up the hill.

'Is this the road to the Priest's Leap?' I asked.

'Sure and it is not. The road is back up there. I'll lead you the way myself. I thought ye were two little boys sat at the side of the road waiting for their daddy. I do be seeing them there some evenings, waiting for him to take them to the sports. Ye have the same colour jackets.'

She pointed us in the right direction and we began the long trudge back up to 'The Lepp'. It was only then that I remembered that old adage of the hill walker. 'Start low, climb high and finish low.' We had left the car on the summit of the pass and it was not a lot of fun trudging through a bitter wind and near darkness with forty pounds of cameras and lenses on my back. Still, as I pointed out, we had walked the horseshoe and blown some of the cobwebs out of the system in the process. It was pointed out to me in return that the same walk on a hot summer's day would be a much nicer way of getting rid of the cobwebs.

6 The Goughane Barra Horseshoe

There is an island in lone Goughane Barra
Whence Allua of songs rushes forth like an arrow
In deep Valley Desmond a thousand wild fountains
Come down to that lake, from their home in the mountains.

J.J. Callanan (1795-1829)

In the heart of lovely Goughane Barra, on a tiny island just off the shore of a great lake, lies the hermitage of St Finbarr. The island is joined to the mainland now by a short modern causeway, and a chapel and reconstructed monk's cell have been built on the original site, but the sense of great peace in a place of humbling beauty is still evident, in spite of the tour buses and the crowds that throng there in summer. Go on a quiet cold weekday in winter or autumn and you'll hardly see a soul; it is then that you will sense the haunting spirit of this fascinating place.

When Finbarr first built his cell on this island in the fastness of Valley Desmond, the land around would have been wild and almost impassable. Dense oak forests with wild boar and wolves would have hemmed him in almost as much as the great cliffs which rise to form a seemingly impassable wall round much of the valley. On grey wet days, the cliffs are dark and threatening – small wonder that they inspired so many Victorian painters and poets. Access to Goughane Barra is easy now, and there is even a hotel looking out over the lake where St Finbarr, were he

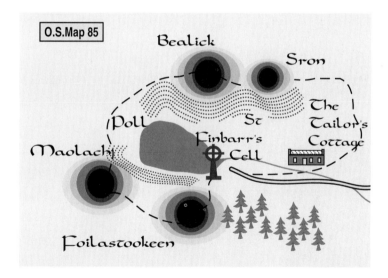

alive today, could go for afternoon tea, using it also perhaps as an excuse to nip in the jacks and wash his duds, laundry facilities in his cell not being perhaps of the five-star variety. St Fin-

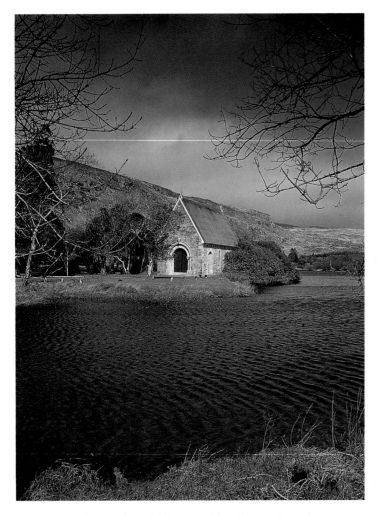

St Finbarr's chapel, the site of his former hermitage

barr, by the way, is the patron saint of Cork and thus, by extension, of Murphy's Stout.

There is a strenuous walk that takes in the whole of the horseshoe above the valley. It is one of the great walks of Ireland, though it does need to be said that on grey miserable days good route-finding is essential. Much of the high land is featureless and boggy, there are no escape routes and there are dangerous cliffs that it would be easy enough to find yourself drawn onto in mist and poor light. Pat and I set off to walk the horseshoe early one summer's morning a few years back. The day promised to be fair with light cloud and a gentle wind and, listening to the radio that morning over the smell of bacon and toast in the B and B, the weatherman had talked of a few light showers and better weather in the afternoon.

Leaving the car at the car park, we wandered round the lake edge and then took an old farm track that leads on to the hill, skirting the edge of an ugly new forestry plantation. I hate Sitka. It is an ugly tree, a foreign invader in this part of Western Europe. It doesn't blend in with the flow of the land, its regimented squares are an intrusion into most landscapes, it's cheap and it's ugly and it's no substitute for the great trees that were here before. It is planted as a cheap cash crop and is symptomatic of the short-sighted, short-term, get-rich-very-quick attitude that has taken a grip everywhere, even here in the land of saints and scholars. And don't give me the old argument about shortage of timber. The government forestry departments of both England and Ireland were set up to replace the great hardwoods that were felled for the First World War, and all they've done is cover the land with Sitka spruce. Thus mused I as I trudged across the bog by the forest towards higher ground.

The clapper bridge leading to the hamlet where the Tailor and Ansty lived

As if that wasn't enough to put me in a bad mood, it started to rain heavily. So much for the weatherman and his 'light showers'. And what's more, it was not just any old rain, it was Irish rain. There is something about Irish rain that makes it different to any other kind of rain in the world. I've been in tropical downpours in the African jungle, in 'the Wet' in Darwin, Australia and in monsoon rains in Nepal and none of them has wet me as much as Irish rain. Irish rain can come sideways and upwards as well as downwards. It can snake up your sleeve and up your trouser leg as well as down the back of your neck. And, since it rarely gets very cold in the summer in Ireland, you put on your waterproofs and carry on walking only to find that they act like a sweat box so that you're as wet on the inside as you are on the outside. This is all great fun, particularly when the midges arrive.

Then you also have to bear in mind that the hills of Goughane Barra are well 'benched' and that this particular year it had rained continuously from January to July and you get some idea of the state of the mountains and the fun we were having. I think I heard the muttered phrase 'grounds for divorce' coming from somewhere below me.

Low cloud added to our problems and as we climbed towards Foilastookeen, (*Fail an Stuaicín* – Cliff of the Little Pinnacle), the first peak of the horseshoe, it dropped to cover the hills completely and wraithed and wrapped around us like something from *The Hound of the Baskervilles*. The map we were using was the only one available at that time, Sheet 24 of the old survey – great for cycling the back lanes of Ireland and very prettily coloured in orange and gold and green and blue, but in reality as much use as a chocolate teapot. Still, I took a quick bearing and we plodded on through the mist until we came to the top

of something. Since there was only one top anywhere in the vicinity I must assume it was Foilastookeen, but because there was nothing but ectoplasm all about us I'll never know.

From the summit we walked south-west through the mist across a giant sponge. The ground was so sodden that the water, even on the hills, was just lying like a skin and, though we didn't sink in to any bogs, it took more than half an hour of splashing about to get us to the summit cairn of Maoloch (Bald Hill), where there was a small peak and a rocky ridge – (for some reason the new Discovery OS Map has the mountain named as Conigar – An Coinigéar). Maoloch was the last nesting site of the golden eagle in Ireland and a wild and wonderful eyrie it must have been. The mist broke briefly as we nibbled a biscuit on the summit and for a moment we could see the lake far below us like a leaden mirror, then the mist closed in again.

I took another bearing and we walked off towards the col. There were sheer cliffs in the mist to our right but, by dropping to gentler ground and keeping a small tarn in view, we got safely down to the head of Poll (hole), the old pilgrims' path from Goughane Barra to the Borlin Valley. Apparently, at one time, this steep stone staircase was in good order, and a lovely book *In a Quiet Land* by John O'Donaghue has a wonderful account of a *pátrún* to St Finbar crossing Poll, but it hasn't been really passable for a long time now.

Poll was the scene of one of the great escapes of the Irish War of Independence when Major Tom Barry, led by a local man who had cobbled together a long rope from odds and ends, brought his IRA flying column over from Cumhalla into Goughane Barra to escape encirclement and capture. His book *Guerrilla Days in Ireland*, is a first-hand account of the Irish armed struggle that led to independence. 'For over an hour,' he writes, 'man after man with the aid of stretched out rifles and that useful rope, swung and slithered down that rough passage to the level ground of Goughane Barra.' Peering down into the slimy stone staircase of Poll on this day it was hard to see how anybody could have climbed that on a black night, much less got to the bottom in one piece.

Barry was retracing the steps of another great Irish leader, O'Sullivan Beare, though the outcome of O'Sullivan's flight was tragic and not triumphal. The O'Sullivans who gave their name to the Beara Peninsula came originally from Tipperary and, like many stories from Irish history, theirs is a tale of treachery and betrayal. Donal O'Sullivan's uncle, Sir Owen, allied himself with the forces of Elizabeth I and helped to drive his own nephew out of Beara and away on a long and murderous march to Ulster. Owen took all of Donal's lands including Whiddy Island and most of the north of Bantry Bay as a reward for his treachery. In 1602 Donal O'Sullivan Beare had been defending his castle at Dunboy against the English for almost a year. By June the castle had fallen and the English began a systematic slaughter of the whole clan. O'Sullivan fled with a thousand of his clan, including many women and children, in a desperate march northwards to the safe havens of Ulster. They left Glengarriff on Christmas Day and made for the fastness of Goughane Barra by that steep and terrible pass. All the way to Ulster they were dogged and harried, and of the thousand who left Glengarriff only thirty-four men and one old woman reached the friendly lands of the O'Rourkes. Donal later fled to Spain where he was made Count of Dunboy by Philip III. Much good it did him though; seventeen years later he was killed in a brawl with his Irish valet.

In Ireland there are stories under every rock and stone, stories breathing from the very earth you walk upon, every footstep opens another page of the secret book – down in the valley, St Finbarr builds his cell in a spot that was probably holy to the druids, Tom Barry and his men cross the path of the thousand O'Sullivans – all of it lies there under the very soles of your boot. Close your eyes and you can hear the clash of rifles and the voices of the men as they scrambled down Poll away from the Tans. Close them again and you can hear the desperate voices of the O'Sullivans scrambling their way to what they thought was safety, all the stories now nothing but dying echoes returning from the cliff walls of Goughane Barra.

The cloud had lifted again and from the col we could see across to Knockboy, where we had walked earlier that year, dark heavy clouds skimming its summit. We climbed again northwards following a line that would bring us by sodden heath and bog to the summit of Bealick. There are many false summits on the great hump that is Bealick so, to find the true summit, look carefully for a cairn on a rock outcrop. One of the stones on it is mine. The day was definitely improving, it hadn't rained heavily for almost half an hour and the cloud now had a few rips in it that showed the blue beyond. Occasional stabs of sunlight laid long washes of light across the mountain, but the wind was too strong to dawdle so we made our way off towards the *Sron* (nose), the last outcrop of rock which marks the only certain and safe way down from the cliffs of Goughane Barra. There are probably some very good scrambles up and down the cliff face and, on a sunny day with time to explore, you might be able to find a fairly safe gully through the cliffs, but today, 'with the day that was in it', we plumped for slow and boring safety. Like all

Irish descents from mountains it had its bog and its bit of barbed wire but eventually we did find the way off and back onto a dusty road that brought us down to the lake.

The sun struck a bargain with the clouds just as we got to the clapper bridge leading to the tiny hamlet where lived one of Irish literature's most famous couples. Not quite a Diarmid and Grainne or a Molly and Leopold but remarkable none the less. 'The Tailor' and his wife Anastasia (Ansty) lived in a little white-washed cottage up the lane; their story, told by Eric Cross in his little book, *Ansty and the Tailor*, is a picture of a way of life and the kind of manners and speech that were disappearing even as Cross was recording them. It is a gem of a book: the Tailor is a wit, a fluent Irish speaker, a great storyteller and hater of the sham. Ansty, like the tailor, is full of life and in the great tradition of Irish women from 'The Midnight Court' onwards, she is earthy and at times ribald. The book is full of the Tailor's stories and sayings and Ansty's often teasing and dismissive commentary gives them all the more salt. Once he tells how, wandering through Belfast, he and some other Kerrymen were caught by a gang of Orangemen and hung by the heels over a bridge 'and with the Lagan flowing beneath us. They told us to say, "To Hell with the Pope!"'

'Yes, but what did you do then?'

'I did a bit of quick thinking. I thought – well, they can always get another Pope, but there's only one me. So, "To Hell with the Pope!" it was.'

It is hard to believe now, but a year after this book was published in 1943, De Valera's government had it banned, declaring it 'in general tendency indecent'. It didn't stop at that; the clergy were even more wild at the book than the mealy-mouthed politicians. Three priests came one afternoon and, forcing the Tailor to his knees at his own hearth, made him burn his own copy of the book. The power of the book in Ireland can be a fearful thing. St Columba went to war for a book and afterwards banished himself in exile from Ireland. The Catholic Church for long years had a list of books on the 'Index' (and still do for all I know) and poor old Ansty and the Tailor were pilloried and abused in their own lovely valley. The end of the tale and the death of the old couple make for sad reading. They are buried together in the graveyard across from St Finbarr's island and, as we passed in the late afternoon sun, with children splashing in the lake and the last of the visitors strolling along the causeway, I thought of the Tailor and of Ansty's words at his wake, 'There'll be great talk Above tonight.'

That night in the Old Triangle on the road to Macroom there was a wonderful *sesiún*, with the flute-maker Hammy Hamilton on timber flute, and the world and his wife on everything else. Close by the pub stands Carrigaphooca (The Rock of the Fairies or Puck's Rock) and the ruins of MacCarthy's Castle. On this rock, King Puck reigned supreme and also from here Daniel O'Rourke flew to the moon on the back of an eagle. But they are stories that will have to wait for another time.

The Kingdom of Kerry

'Kerry is mountain and ocean with a little bit of land in between' according to Des Lavelle, writer, deep-sea diver and fisherman, whose boat *An Beal Bocht* (The Poor Mouth) once took me to the Skelligs through choppy, stomach-churning seas. Like all Kerrymen, Des is not 'backward in coming forward' about his beloved county and states quite baldly that, whatever it is you're looking for in Ireland, Kerry has got more of it than any one of its thirty-one neighbouring counties. I am not going to enter into any argument here but I do have to admit that there is something very different about the Kingdom.

For a start, as any Kerryman worth his pepper will tell you, everybody in Kerry is descended from Ceasair, the daughter of Noah. Ceasair was banned from the Ark by her father for some undisclosed crime and, in a huff, took her own boat and came to Ireland with fifty girls and three men. She landed at Ballinskelligs Bay and set about populating Ireland. Three against fifty is unfair odds and two of the men died in the line of duty while the other went mad.

After Noah's daughter, came, in succession, the Fir Bolgs, the Dé Danann and the Milesians, all of whom seemed to have taken great delight in battering the living daylights out of each other. This may account for the faction fighting that used to take place in Kerry until the end of the last century, when families met on fair days and holy days to knock each other about. So prevalent was this ritual battling that one of the Kennedys, a famous bat-

tling clan from the Dingle Peninsula, became known as 'Who's Afraid' Kennedy.

They still tell a story in the Dingle Peninsula of the Kennedys and the Currans agreeing to give up their faction fighting when the son of one tribe wished to marry the daughter of the other. They shook hands all round and hung up their long fighting sticks and sat down in the pub for a quiet celebratory drink. Within minutes they heard a rattling sound and, looking up at the wall, saw the two sticks 'knocking the divil out of each other'. Interpreting this as a portent, the men took down the sticks and began leathering each other. Joking apart, during a faction fight between the Mulvills and the Cooleens at Ballagh Strand near Ballybunnion, one race day in 1834, almost twenty people were killed.

One of the most westerly parts of Europe, Kerry deviates from Greenwich Mean Time by forty minutes, and therefore from British Summer Time by one hour and forty minutes. It thus follows, according to some Kerrymen, that there are twenty-five hours and forty minutes to every Kerry day in the summer months. This may account for the feeling that life somehow passes slower here and that the pubs, as Des Lavelle says, should shut at Kerry closing time and not according to a line drawn through some congested London suburb.

But Kerry has great claims to antiquity as well as eccentricity. Ptolemy knew of the Kingdom and wrote of the fine, rich iron mined in Kenmare, and Kerry's most famous traveller St Brendan may well have reached America well before Columbus was as much as a twinkle in his father's telescope. Many of the ships of the Spanish Armada were wrecked along the murderous coast and it is said that the colouring and passion of the Kerry people come from the marooned Spanish who were given sanctuary by the local people and who married into the community. It is a county soaked in history and as somebody once said, 'You can hardly turn round in Kerry but that you'd knock your eye out on a ruined church or an ogham stone.'

Kerry is, of course, the tourist honey-pot of Ireland and if you don't like crowds then you'd better stay away from places like Dingle Town and Killarney during the height of summer, and Killorglin in mid August. That quiet little town on the River Laune lets down its hair, teeth and eyes once a year and goes wild at Puck Fair (*Aonach an Phuic*). If you find yourself in Killorglin that week, you may as well throw away the car keys and join in, for Puck is the greatest event in west Kerry. 'Puck', as it is known to all, is a week of horse trading, singing, dancing and music that fills the town with thousands of tinkers, tourists, locals and (I wouldn't be surprised) the odd Martian or two. A wild goat is captured in the surrounding hills and brought into the town where it is crowned King Puck or *Poc* and hoisted aloft onto a platform on a pole high above the heads of the crowd and it there stays for the week of the fair before being released back into the wild. The fair probably originates in prehistoric times with the festival of *Lugh*, the Celtic Sun-God of the Tuatha Dé Danann, and the goat and 'pookha' connections give it a decidedly wild and pagan connotation. Strangely, the clergy have not made any attempt to ban it, as far as I know.

But even in the high season you can still find quiet, backwater spots and, if the towns are crowded, then the hills are wide and empty and, in Kerry, there are some of the finest (and, of course, the highest) hills in all Ireland. The Iveragh Peninsula and the Dingle Peninsula between them have MacGillycuddy's Reeks, Brandon Mountain, Mount Eagle, Masatiompan, Caherconree, Mangerton and dozens more high and hard hills. But if it's easier walking that you are looking for then there's the Kerry Way and the Dingle Way, both of which take you through the Kingdom by old butter lanes, lakeside trails and easy mountain passes.

A trip round the Ring of Kerry, the road that runs from Killarney by Killorglin westward to Cahersiveen and then south and east to Kenmare, is a great way to get a taste of the Iveragh Peninsula, though seeing a place from a car or a bus is no substitute for getting in amongst it on foot or by bicycle.

When it comes to the Dingle Peninsula then I have to admit favouritism and plead forgiveness. There can be few places in Western Europe as magical as the Dingle Peninsula. If a land can absorb something from the lives of those who have lived and struggled there, then that area south-west of Tralee has soaked up the emotions, the fears, the happiness, the worship and the battles of thousands of years.

I have wandered all over the Dingle Peninsula, on foot and by bike, following old ways and paths, looking at the ruined forts, the old churches, the standing stones and the *clocháins* and over the years I have come to love it. It is a place of rare and powerful beauty. It may have something to do with the light, which is liquid and restless and which is never the same from hour to hour. On the hottest summer days the sea can be slack and still, rolling lazily to the shore. On grey, gale-battered winter days, mountain

Dingle Regatta

high waves butt the foreland at Slea Head, sending spume spraying far inland, flecking the drystone walls and fields. The weather can be changeable, too; nothing, it is said, lasts for a whole day on the Dingle Peninsula and incoming westerlies bring in bolts of sun and skirmishes of rain.

There is a bar in Dingle Town called Flahive's. It is one of the great pubs of Ireland. On summer evenings, the lowering sun comes through the windows into the room, lighting the little snug where marriages were arranged and where women would sit for a quiet glass rather than be seen drinking in public. James and Peggy, who run the bar, are known to thousands who have passed this way to 'hold your hour and have another'. The Guinness is beautifully kept and served and, beyond a coat of paint when it needs it, the bar hasn't changed in years. Long may it be so. Go in there 'early doors' of an evening in winter and James will be enthroned in his corner chair, the one-bar electric fire burning on the counter, talking to, like as not, a local fisherman having a pint and a bit of *craic* on the way home.

It was in Flahive's one summer evening that I met a coal-black priest from Nigeria called Father John. He was having a jar and a chat with another priest when I was introduced to them by Peggy. '*Dia dhuit a Seán. Connas ata tú?*' (Hello, John. How are you?) said I, in my best page one, *Teach Yourself Irish*. And he came back at me with the best mouthful of Irish you've ever heard. To while away the evenings in the mission, he had taught the Irish priest Yoruba, and the Kerry priest had taught him Irish. Things like that happen all the time in Ireland.

They say that if you sit at a certain table at a pavement café in the heart of Paris and stay there long enough then you are sure to meet everybody you have ever known in your life. I'm certain that this is true of the Dingle Peninsula too, for I have sat playing in O'Flaherty's great music bar with Fergus the owner, and through the door have come, on numerous occasions, people out of the past – like Peggy Seeger, the singer and songwriter, widow of Ewan McColl, one of the greatest prime movers of the Folk Revival in these islands. Time without number singers, writers

things, entering another world almost. Here, in certain light, particularly in early spring and late autumn, the sea and land are hard to distinguish. Then you can understand the Celtic fascination with boundaries, as places where magic happens.

If you are of a more prosaic turn of mind, however, and regard things like magic and Celtic ways as the ramblings of an old romantic, then I'd better tell you that you can eat as well on the Dingle Peninsula as anywhere else in Europe; the seafood in particular is magnificent, and after you have eaten you can choose any of half a dozen bars to listen to good traditional music. My own favourites are O'Flaherty's and An Droichead Beag in Dingle itself and, out of town, there is Bricks' Pub at the crossroads near Reesk. And, to my mind there is no better way to finish a good day on the mountains than by listening to Micheál Ó Hiarlaithe and Feargal Nic Amhlaiobh playing in the An Droichead Beag – though I may well be biased.

Of all the nights I've spent there I remember one most vividly. I had my banjo with me and was playing along with Micheál and Feargal to the music of a set of reels from west Kerry, when, half way through, a sailor from a Russian fishing ship suddenly started doing a Cossack dance in time to the music. He flung himself round the room, as they do, kicking his legs up, doing the splits in mid-air and dancing on his hands while swinging his legs round under him. I'm sure you know the kind of thing I mean. When he finished there was a moment of deafening silence and then the room burst out in a thunder of applause. The least we could do after that was to play him 'Lara's Theme' from Doctor Zhivago. Ruth is certainly stranger than friction.

James and Peggy in Flahive's Bar on the harbour front, Dingle

and musicians have shouted, 'What are you doing here?' at me across the street and I've asked them the same question.

Along the Dingle Peninsula you will find some of the most ancient and holy places of Western Europe: the beehive huts of the monks who came here to pray and fast on the westerly margin of Europe; the ruined church at Kilmalkedar with its crosses and its stone heads; and the wonderfully preserved oratory at Gallarus which looks for all the world like an upturned stone boat. When you walk to Slea Head, the most westerly point of the peninsula, you are conscious of being at the very edge of

The Blasket Islands seen from Slea Head

7 Carrauntuohil

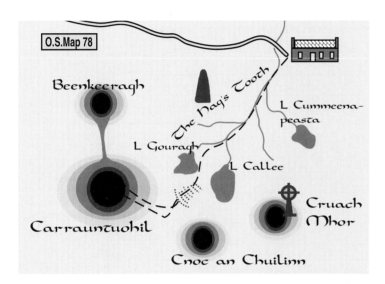

The county that has, in Carrauntuohil (*Corrán Tuathail*), the biggest mountain in Ireland, the crown of MacGillycuddy's Reeks, has some of the biggest hearts in the country too. Like Donegal it is a county of open doors and welcomes. I've made many true friends there over the years and many's the night I've sat and played in crowded rooms in little houses, while the dancing and the singing went on until dawn. Joe and Eileen Cronin's house close under Carrauntuohil is such a house and has been the scene of many a party, with the chairs cleared back and the couples up dancing the sets as the musicians are 'lashing into it' in the corner. It is open house, too, when the Kerry Mountain Rescue are called out, and many's the night Eileen and Joe have been up until dawn making tea and drying clothes for the team.

Their house stands at the end of road, the last house before *Coomcallee* – the Hag's Glen – and, one late May morning, I left my car in the cottage yard and set off to climb the big hill with Seán Ó Suilleabháin. May and June are often the best months for walking in Ireland. The weather is more settled and the statistics show that there's less rainfall during those months than in June and July. Someone once asked an Irishman what the climate was like in Ireland. 'We don't have a climate,' was the reply, 'we have weather.' I think he had got it just about right, because that day was the coldest May day I remember in my entire life; chill and showery, with great splashes of sun, chunky, swift-moving clouds and a blustery wind that threatened to toss us all over the Kerry sky like dumpy kites. The weather was courtesy of the tail end of lows that had been rolling in from the Atlantic for days.

Seán is a marathon runner and hill-walker and at that time was the convenor of the Kerry Mountain Rescue Team. He was instrumental in the development of both the Kerry and the Dingle Ways and is the author of several guides to walking the hills. So I knew I was in safe hands as we trundled along the banks of the swollen Gaddagh River that carries the overflow from the

Old Hag You Have Killed Me

three loughs of the Hag's Glen; Lough Cailee (the Hag's Lake) Lough Cumeenapeaste (The Lake of the Combe of the Serpent or Water Monster) and Lough Gouragh. I think this translates as the Sheep's Lake, as *caora* is Gaelic for 'sheep', but Seán thinks it means Goat's Lake, from *gabhar* or 'goat'. Since Seán is a fluent Irish speaker, and my Irish is still at the 'See Fluff. See the ball. See Fluff chase the ball' stage, then don't take my word for anything. We could probably both be wrong, and doubtless some Irish scholar reading this book will write to tell me that the lake is really named after Finbar Gouragh who played for Kerry in 1923, when they beat Cork seventy-five nothing – 'And do you know', said the Kerryman, 'they were lucky to get nothing!'

On normal May days the river would be easy to cross, but this wasn't a normal May day and we almost began the day with a soaking, trying to cross the flood. It was tricky and involved a good deal of manoeuvring but we did eventually get across. If you do come this way, then take extreme care – this river has, in fact, already caused the death of one walker.

Ahead of us, the Hag's Glen stood dark and dour, shifting bars of light striking the black walls, and grey and dancing clouds rolling over the saddle above the Devil's Ladder. Seán told me that the glen had once been home to a sizeable number of families and that a census taken in the 1850s showed six people living close in under the Devil's Ladder right at the very head of the glen. The Irish word *cailleach* means a witch or hag and may refer to a wise woman who lived in the glen. After the witch hunts that swept Europe in the later Middle Ages, any poor woman who used herbal medicine or who practised the 'old religion' was dubbed a 'witch'. But nobody really seems to know how the glen came by its name, although of course there are theories galore.

Some people believe that the Hag was an old woman with magical powers who fell into the Hag's Lake while chasing her lover and thus became a water witch. There are echoes here of other stories, such as that of the Hag's Leap on the Cliffs of Moher, or the Legend of Anascaul on the Dingle Peninsula.

Carrauntuohil from the Hag's Glen

'Time is a great storyteller' the saying goes, but it may also be true that time is a great confuser, and that naiads, dryads and the water goddesses of the native Celt were turned into crones and witches by the Christians as they gained power. One thing is certain, lakes like those in the Hag's Glen are often the stuff of legend. In the Pennines of England, there are nymphs and mermaids on the Kinder massif and the Staffordshire Roaches, both places where the Celts would have lingered long after the coming of the strangers from the East.

The Lake Serpent of Cumeenapeaste is documented equally well, in that he (or she) comes from a long line of lake monsters that stretches back to the Loch Ness Monster and beyond. In the Fenian cycle of Irish sagas we read how Fionn Mac Cumhail slaughtered a lake monster that had swallowed several of his followers. The battle was fierce and long and resembles that of Beowulf with Grendel (another lake monster). Like Beowulf, Fionn eventually kills the monster, so staining the lough with its blood that ever after it was known as Lough Berg (the Red Lake). The seventh century life of St Mochua tells of a *peasta* devouring a swimmer in the Shannon, while St Colman is supposed to have saved a girl from a similar fate in Lough Ree.

But lake monsters are not just the stuff of ancient myth and legend, there have been numerous sightings in Ireland in recent years. In 1960, three Dublin priests fishing on Lough Ree saw a dinosaur-like creature some sixteen feet long, swimming close by the shore. Now, unless they had been at the potheen, three priests with nothing to gain are hardly likely to invent a lake monster. So the mystery remains.

We passed between Lough Gouragh and the Hag's Lough with no sign of lake monsters; in fact, no sign of anybody, for the glen was deserted. The rest of Ireland's walkers must have known something we didn't. We pushed on, heading for the Devil's Ladder, the rocky scramble that would take us on to the col between Carrauntuohil and the Reeks' ridge. Behind us to our right, hanging high over the glen, was the Hag's Tooth, a massive nunatak, standing like a stone fang above the valley. I've always felt nunatak to be an unfortunate word, particularly in such a Catholic country as Ireland. I can't help seeing, in my mind's eye, a picture of a mugger relieving one of the Little Sisters of the Poor of her collecting box.

Leaving such thoughts unuttered, I plodded along behind

Carrauntuohil in the mist – Ireland's highest mountain and at times its most dangerous

Seán to the jumble of scree and boulders clustered about the foot of the Ladder. The Devil's Ladder is a narrow gully, a fairly steep rocky scramble, quite safe as long as it is not too wet; in ice or snow, however, it becomes a different proposition. In fact, if there is ice or snow, unless you have an ice axe and crampons and know how to use them, I recommend that you steer clear of the Reeks altogether and come back another day. People have fallen to their deaths in this area and the Kerry Mountain Rescue Team is the busiest in Ireland, so commonsense and good map reading is essential. Only weeks before our day on the hill, a Dutchman had fallen to his death because of poor map reading when low cloud had gripped the Reeks.

Once out of the Ladder and on the saddle, the way to the top of Ireland's highest mountain is easy to see, for the iron cross that marks the summit is clearly visible, even though you still have more than fifteen hundred feet to climb. And a long climb it seemed, too, because a cold but clear summer's day suddenly turned grey and wild and, by the time we'd got to the summit, a fully-fledged blizzard was on us and we were in a total white-out. We huddled in what shelter we could find by the summit cairn and poured two cups of coffee out of the flask. Within seconds, our bare hands were numb with cold and we were fishing gloves and mittens out of our packs. It was my daughter's birthday, 29 May, and around us snow and ice swirled. The views from the summit, which normally take in half of Ireland, took in our feet and one solitary, laughing sheep that seemed to be saying, 'I have to be up here, it's my job, eating grass and growing wool and that – what's your excuse?'

Then, as quickly as it had arrived, the storm abated, and we could see the land below us, drenched but sparkling in a bright watery light. Broken clouds were flying eastwards above us and the weather looked anything but trustworthy. We had originally intended to follow the arête to Beenkeragh (*Binn Chaorach* – the Peak of the Sheep or Goat or Kerry Football Player) and then drop down back to the glen by crossing rough ground under Knockbrinnea, but, as Seán said, there was now a fair spattering of hail and snow on the arête and the winds were strong enough to make a crossing quite dangerous. He also pointed out that it wouldn't look good if the Kerry Mountain Rescue Team had to be called out to rescue its own convenor and the President of the Ramblers' Association, as I was then.

One thing I would always caution against on descent – trying to slide down on your backside. On dry grass, when you're wearing ordinary clothes, that may just about be manageable, on wet and icy slopes when you're wearing slippery waterproofs you'll turn yourself into a human sledge. If in doubt, always face into the hill, make sure you know where your next foot and hand-holds are coming from, and take it slowly.

So we retraced our steps back to the saddle and, taking great care, descended by the Devil's Ladder. And a slippy and shaky descent it was, too, with rocks that had earlier been dry, now slicked with verglas, and every hand and toe-hold freezing and slimy. We both breathed a lot easier when we made it to the level ground between the lakes again. As Confucius the Mountaineer used to say: 'Knowing when to get off a hill is as important as knowing how to get up it.'

We got even wetter and colder on the walk out when another batch of storms hit us but then, as it does in the West, the whole thing blew over and it was sunny and fine and pleasant once more. We set off back in sunshine while, behind us, the walls of the Hag's Glen were still black and dour. Then just as quickly the window closed again and black rain pelted at us from big-bellied clouds and the wind had a bite like a tinker's dog. Once back at the Cronins, it took a good few cups of Eileen's tea to warm up the marrow of our bones again.

My last memory of 29 May that year is of the impromptu *ceilidh* that took place that night in the cottage, with the parish priest singing that beautiful Kerry song by Sigerson Clifford, 'The Boys of Barr na Sráide', and Seán himself giving us that old rebel rouser, 'The West's Awake'. A local lad played melodeon, others played tin whistle and guitar and I plonked along on the mandolin. Eileen scuttled about as usual, filling cups of tea before they were half empty, and Joe moved around with a wide smile on his face handing out cake and sandwiches. The chairs were pushed back against the wall, and friends and neighbours danced the sets and sang, while outside, just to show us who was boss, the clouds cleared and a burning silver moon rode an untroubled sky over the Hag's Glen.

8 A Walk in the Black Valley

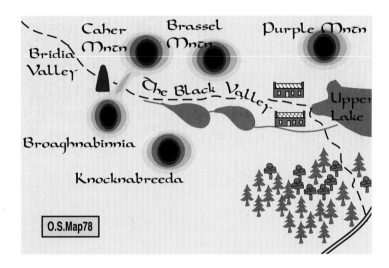

Caher Mntn
Brassel Mntn
Purple Mntn
Bridia Valley
The Black Valley
Upper Lake
Broaghnabinnia
Knocknabreeda

O.S.Map78

The Kerry Way is a long-distance footpath that rings the Iveragh Peninsula, beginning and ending at Killarney and along its way taking in MacGillycuddy's Reeks, the Black Valley (*Cumeenduff*) and a good stretch of the Dingle Bay coastline, as well, of course, as the world-famous Lakes of Killarney. I've never had the time to walk the whole of the way (ten days would make a pleasant walk of it, I guess) but over the years I have done a good bit of it. I had never been in the Black Valley, however, that lonely but lovely glen that runs from the head of the Upper Lake between the hill of Knocknabreeda and the southern flanks

of the Reeks until recently when I had a phone call from Seán Ó Suilleabháin asking me if I would like a day out with him and a few friends. He was planning to walk from Killarney through the Black Valley and over to the Bridia Valley. It took me all of one and a half nano seconds to consider his offer, so a few days later I met him and a band of fellow walkers and we set off for the hills.

It was one of those lovely spring days that comes out of nowhere in the middle of weeks of grey and cold and gloom, one of those days when you could almost swear that you feel the earth awakening. The sky had been grey and unpromising as we rolled up the road towards Derrycunnihy church, but as soon as we set out along the path into the woods, the sun ripped the clouds wide open, tore them up into bits and scattered them all over the sky, and it stayed like that for the rest of the day. A sheet of blue, polished by high, white clouds, too cool for midges, but warm enough, in the valley at least, to walk along in shorts and bare arms.

We'd arranged to be picked up by Tom, a friend of Seán's, and his minibus at the point where the road turns into an impassable track at the head of the Bridia Valley at about four o'clock so we had a whole day ahead of us and could take our time. The way from the church follows easy paths through lovely old oak forests. This kind of relict woodland must have been common all over Ireland at one time, but the ravages of landlords saw an end to most of the old forests, and the bits of bog oak that are found in the peat bogs of the West and the number of place names that begin with Derry (*Doire* – an oak wood) are the only reminders of the great forests. I was reminded, as we walked that morning, of that lovely old poem 'Kilcash' that tells of the taking of the trees and links the felling of the trees with the destruction of the last of the Irish aristocracy, the Flight of the Earls after the Battle of Kinsale.

> What shall we do for timber?
> The last of the woods are down.
> Kilcash and the house of its glory
> And the bell of that house are gone,
> The spot where the lady waited
> Who shamed all women for grace
> When earls came sailing to meet her
> And Mass was said in the place.
>
> My grief and my affliction
> Your gates are taken away,
> Your avenue needs attention,
> Goats in the garden stray.
> The courtyard's filled with water
> And the great earls where are they?
> The earls, the lady, the people
> Beaten into the clay.

The way through the woods led past the ruins of a cottage built to lodge Queen Victoria when she came to visit Killarney. It lies under Looscaunagh Hill, where the woodland opened out to

The Upper Lake, Killarney

give us a view back over the Upper Lake to Arbutus Island and Torc Mountain. There is a Victorian parlour ballad entitled 'My Love is an Arbutus', and for years I wondered what an arbutus was. I got it mixed up in my mind with an albatross and imagined it some kind of bird. It is, according to the dictionary, a kind of bush, in particular the strawberry tree. So now you know; his love is a strawberry tree – that has to be one of the strangest fetishes I've ever heard of. The lakeside here is a place of special interest to botanists because, as well as arbutus, there are several species of Lusitanian plants which are unique to the area. But it was early in the year and the winter had been particularly wet and long, so there was little to see beyond clusters of early primroses.

The Kerry Way follows the edge of the Upper Lake for a while before crossing a small stream and emerging from woodland into the grounds of Lord Brandon's Cottage where, in season, you can get tea and scones and other refreshments. Lord Brandon, being the pukka chap that he was, built himself a round tower in the grounds of his cottage, not so that he could meditate there, or copy the Book of Kells, safe from the Norse raiders, but so that he and his gamekeepers could keep an eye out for poachers.

We wanted to reach the end of the Gap of Dunloe for our lunch, so we left Lord Brandon's Cottage and look-out tower behind and pushed on through the bright sunshine, striking west over open country to meet a metalled road. A few minutes' walking along the black top brought us to the Youth Hostel at the head of the Gap, and there we had several fine pots of tea as we sat on benches in the warm sun. It came to me, as I sat there under Purple Mountain, that this was my first walk in Ireland this year; and, the year before, the last walk I had done in the country had been over Purple Mountain, when again the day had been unseasonably fine, a summer's day at the end of October. I told Seán it was Manchester weather I'd brought with me and he told me to bring another bucketful next time I crossed the pond.

As we sat in the sun, I mentioned the Serpent's Lake, *Lough Cumeenapeaste*, that lies high above the Hag's Glen on the other side of the Reeks. One of the group said that there is a lake in the Gap called the Serpent's Lake, though it doesn't appear as such on the maps. Whatever these 'serpents' are, giant eels or some kind of extinct life form that lives on in folklore I don't know, but there certainly are a lot of lakes associated with them.

We left the Youth Hostel and headed along the road for a lit-tle while before cutting off to follow an old green lane, that would lead us into the heart of the Black Valley. The way led on through another belt of woodland where the going was a little muddy underfoot, though this was only to be expected after the rains of the previous winter, and after a short if muddy and acrobatic trek through the silent pine woods, we broke out of cover into the valley proper. Below, to our left, the land ran down to two lakes and, standing at their head was a solitary farm; it must be a wild and lonely spot in winter. The Black Valley now has few people living in it but, like many of the glens of Ireland, it was quite heavily populated at one time. H.V. Morton was told that the people of this valley were very strange: 'He told me of queer, hidden places which no man really knows, and of a shy, hostile race, different from ordinary Kerry folk, who live by poaching and mix only with their own kind.'

As we walked on, the valley closed in about us and, striking up onto higher ground, we turned north-westwards between Brassel Mountain and Broaghnabinnia, making for the head-waters of the Cumeenduff River. Seán pointed up at the flanks of Brassel Mountain. 'People say that's where the last Dane in Ireland buried his gold. He must have been a Viking, I suppose, and legend has it that when other invaders were approaching the Black Valley he dug a hole up there and buried it. A lot of people have been out looking for the gold but nobody has ever found it.' Looking at the great expanse of wild and open country up there you could be digging for ever. I wondered if the old Dane was like the bank robber who wrote to his wife from prison telling her that the loot from his last bank job was buried in the garden. The police intercepted the letter, and went right round and dug the garden over and, finding nothing, dug it over again.

What Will We Do For Timber?

There was nothing there of course but the garden was ready for him to plant his potatoes when he got out. I can just imagine that old Viking hiding out in the rocks while half Kerry dug up his mountain for him.

The day grew hotter as we walked on, and the path rose before us, leading us under Broaghnabinnia by an empty cottage. An old man living here used to walk his ponies nine miles to Killarney every day during the season for the tourists to hire and then walk them back again in the evening. People thought nothing of walking many miles at a stretch then and there was any number and kind of travellers and packmen walking through these valleys, selling their wares door to door. Seán said that there used to be a ballad-seller who travelled around these lonely glens and hills selling old ballad sheets door to door and singing the tunes to the people if they didn't know them. That was how many of the old songs must have spread about the country at one time.

Ahead of us the path climbed towards the col between the Black Valley and the Bridia Valley, and by the path lay another empty cottage, apparently the last one in all Ireland to be linked to the electricity supply. Two elderly sisters lived there at the time and when the electricity came at last, the television crews came, too, to make a film of the last house getting linked to the ESB grid. Now the cottage is empty and all about the walls of the valley rise clear and silent of anything but the bleating of the sheep and the call of the ravens, and I doubt that anybody will ever need 'the electric' here again.

It was a gentle trek to the col, the valley falling away behind us. On the skyline lay a standing stone marking the way we were to go. For years I puzzled over the purpose of these great stones, but I have read recently that the stones were seen by Patrick and other early Christians as the gods of the pagans. Although they may not have been carved into elaborate shapes, the stones could have been imbued by the people with all the attributes of the gods they were supposed to represent. Alone on the col, this stone stands at a magical Celtic boundary where one valley gives

Walkers on the Kerry Way below Broaghnabinnia

way to another. On the col, too, there are cup and ring carvings, mystical symbols of the Celts, and growing on one of the great boulders was some St Patrick's Cabbage, a kind of saxifrage. Seán reckons that this is one place that he never fails to find it.

From the col it was a steep and interesting descent into the Bridia Valley where Seán's mother had been born and where wild and wonderful people (too wild and wonderful to describe without the help of a good lawyer) still live. It was late afternoon as we passed through the farms at the head of the valley, making for the road and our lift. Thankfully, Tom's minibus developed the same kind of engine problem my car has, just as we were passing the Climbers' Inn, and we were forced to stop and have a few on our way. And why not?

Descending into the Bridia Valley at the end of the day

9 Purple Mountain and Tomies Mountain

O.S.Map 78

Kate Kearney's

The Reeks

Tomies Mntn

Lough Leane

Shehy Mntn

Cruach Mhor

Glas Lough

Purple Mntn

The jarveys (the drivers of the little horse traps) of Killarney were described in Victorian days as a rapacious bunch of rapscallions and, at the risk of having my legs broken the next time I approach the Gap of Dunloe, may I say that things haven't changed all that much. I once had a short afternoon to fill and wanted to walk Purple Mountain from the head of the Gap to Kate Kearney's Cottage. Rather than spend an hour or more walking to the end of the Gap, I asked a jarvey how much he would charge to take me there.

'Thirty pounds,' was the reply. When I pointed out that it was hardly four miles and, furthermore, that it was only the horse's skin that kept its bones from flying apart and maiming us, while the gig he was sat on was only held together by strong rust and holy water and the woodworm holding hands, he replied that not only had I been present at my parents' wedding, but that, as far as he was concerned, I could walk back to where I came from and the sooner the better. As a parting benison, he further reminded me that my teeth were better off where they were, in my head, rather than scattered about the roads of Kerry. Then, as I started off walking, he whipped his horse and took his cart over the way to pick up a group of four Burberry-clad Americans and to relieve them, no doubt, of several thousand dollars and the deeds to their ranches back in the USA.

Later that year, I parked the car close by Kate Kearney's Cottage and the craft shop that is run by the father of Con Moriarty, mountain climber, mountain guide and general *bon vivant*, who is rapidly becoming a legend in his own lunchtime, and set off for the Gap. It was one of those early autumn days that promises to be nothing less than wonderful. A low mist was slowly dissolving the morning sun, and now the hills were coming through clear and sharp in the early light. A couple of jarveys looked in my direction as I passed and muttered something about 'ride' and 'jaunting car', but I pretended to be Icelandic and unable to understand them. It was early in the morning any-

MacGillycuddy's Polka

way, so their solicitations were halfhearted, more a practice for the crowds to come.

The walk through the Gap is lovely on a day like this. The last cottony strands of mist were clinging to the crags that looked down on the narrow track and the sun as it moved higher burnt them off. The day grew warmer as I walked, so that, by the time I got to Auger Lake, the trout were jumping at a late hatch of flies. The lakes of the Killarney region are, of course, its major claim to fame, and even though the area is a tourist honeypot, they are still truly beautiful. I remember John B. Keane, the Kerry writer, best known perhaps as author of *The Field*, telling me once that it was Killarney that inspired Tennyson to write the following:

> The splendour falls on castle walls
> And snowy summits old in story
> The long light shakes across the lakes
> And the wild cataract leaps in glory.

I once had to learn that poem, 'The Princess', set to music by our music teacher, 'Frostie', and when I think of those lines, I am always transported back to a dusty classroom in Manchester and the sound of the music-room piano jangling round the high walls of that Victorian pile. The poem goes on:

> Blow, bugle, blow, set the wild echoes flying,
> Blow, bugle: answer, echoes, dying, dying, dying.

John B. claims that these lines were inspired by the old man who used to stand by the Turnpike, the two massive boulders near the head of the Gap. An old guide book written by J.C. Coleman in the 1940s found him (or his son) there still: 'Here lurks the man with the bugle to wheedle a "consideration" from your pocket and an echo from the mountain.'

The bugler's cottage is still standing, though the bugler himself is now nothing but an echo, too.

At the head of the Gap there is a small, deserted farm called

The deserted Gap Cottage at the Gap of Dunloe

Gap Cottage. It is in a beautiful spot and on a day like this it seemed strange that nobody lived there, but then I had to ask myself, what would it be like in winter? Probably a wild and desperate and lonely place. A little further on from the cottage is Madman's Seat, and it was from there that I started the slow, long climb to the summit of Purple Mountain. Looking back down the valley it was obvious why the mountain got its name. Whether it's the heather or the way the light strikes the outcrops of rocks, I don't know, but from where I stood, the whole mountain was a deep shade of purple. It was amazingly warm for October and, as I climbed, the sweat began to roll off in torrents, some of it undoubtedly the previous night's Guinness seeking to escape.

The small lake of Glas Lough, under a high rock outcrop, was worth a stop both for a look and a drink. It was quiet and still and, in the sun trap formed by the rocks and the tiny cirque, you would almost have thought it a summer's day. As I climbed further, the Reeks across the valley began to show themselves; the jagged head of Carrauntuohil off to the west and, closer at hand, *Cruach Mhór*. From the flanks of Purple Mountain you can make out quite clearly a tiny grotto on the rocky summit of *Cruach Mhór*. It was built by an old man from Ballyledder in an extraordinary act of devotion. He hauled everything he needed for the job – sand, cement and even the water – all the way to the 3,062ft summit in plastic bags, and when the grotto was finished, he bicycled to Tralee, where he bought a statue of the Virgin Mary, cycling all the way back with it balanced on the handlebars. Sadly, some vicious clowns took the statue from its grotto and threw it down the mountain a few years back and, as far as I know, it has not yet been replaced.

Seán Ó Suilleabháin once told me a droll story about the

Walkers descending the ridge to Tomies Mountain

The Paps in the evening light - displaying clearly how they got their name

day, with people hay-making in the valley below, I left the 'blue tar road' and headed up the old green lane. It was a fair day with broken sunlight and a strong breeze blowing, a good day for walking. Where the road reaches its height, I climbed over a barbed wire fence to make my way up between two stands of forestry onto the hillside. The ground between the stands was boggy and slippery, but once out onto open country it was better drained and the going was good. It was a tough slog but rewarding, with heather and tussocks at first then smoothing out to green grazing as I climbed higher. I passed by what looked like a cluster of hut circles or *booleys* just beneath the last pull, but a glance at the map showed nothing. And that is hardly surprising, since to carry out a full archaeological survey of Kerry would be the work of several lifetimes.

On the summit of the eastern Pap is a massive stone mound twenty feet high with a cairn surmounting it by another ten feet. The books have it down as a burial chamber and I agree, but if it has not been constructed to resemble a nipple then I'll eat my balaclava. It was windy on top, so I got down in the shelter of the cairn and had a drink from the flask, remembering as I did so the episode in *Gulliver's Travels* where the hero finds himself sat astride a giant lady's nipple in the court of Brobdingnag. I wonder if Swift, who was of course Irish, had been inspired by the Paps. Then the whole thing began to get too complex and the thought that I was sitting, drinking stewed tea, leaning on a giant nipple began to disturb me, and when I heard Jesuitical voices spouting about hellfire in my brain I decided to move on.

The descent to the col between the two Paps is easy but frustrating. I never like losing high ground that I'm going to have to regain but 'what can't be cured must be endured' as the old song says, so I rambled off down to the cleavage. On the col is a small peaty pool. Scummy and uninteresting now and home only to a few water-boatmen and a family of beetles, it was by this pool that Finn (the great Fionn Mac Cumhail) fell asleep one Hallowe'en night and woke to see a magical fire burning in each of the breasts. He heard fairy voices and saw a man come out of one of the Paps, carrying a trencher with a cooked pig, a cooked calf and wild garlic upon it. Finn threw his spear, but the man vanished and all Finn heard was wailing and chanting coming

The summit cairn of the East Pap

out from the underworld. The man was a fairy, the Lord of the Underworld Feast.

There was no pork crackling cooked in wild garlic for me, so I climbed the western Pap by the jagged rock spikes of the *fiacla* (teeth) and so came to the second cairn or nipple. This contains within its fallen jumble another burial chamber, the door of which is just distinguishable. We think of fairies as flossy little gossamer things, courtesy of the Victorians and Mabel Lucie Atwell. To the Celts the dead became spirits – *sidhe* – that could pass in and out of this mortal world at will. The Banshee (*Ban sidhe*) is just such a spirit, a fairy woman who appears and wails at the coming of death into a household. My grandmother heard it on several occasions. Cynics say it is often the call of a seal on the shore or a bird like a curlew on the mountain but you wouldn't have got that one past my gran. Dead kings buried under hilltop mounds would thus become very powerful fairies and obviously gave the early church some trouble, for there is a prayer of St Columba's asking God to 'dispel the host around the cairns that reigneth.'

It was bright and sunny as I sat and ate my cheese and apple, but the wind was so biting from the Kerry plain that, even though I had both fibre-pile and waterproofs, I had to huddle in the shelter of the cairn. I don't want to teach egg-sucking to anybody, but never underestimate mountain weather. It can be hot enough to cook a rasher of bacon on a donkey's back down below, but once you get over a thousand feet, you enter another world and the wind makes a tremendous difference. That sunny summer's day on the Paps was bitterly cold.

I made my way off the hill following a broad shoulder to an outcrop marked on the map as Roger's Rock, by which time I was out of the wind and warm enough to be back down to shirt-sleeves again. From the rock I headed down to the stream that runs from the cleavage and followed it south until I came to the usual obstacle course that meets me on every descent from an Irish hill, and I had to scramble over rusty and high barbed wire, through squelching bogs and over deep scum-filled ditches to reach the road.

As I made my way to the car, I passed a family making hay in the field, the old way, by hand. They had been turning the hay that morning when I had left, and now they were raking and stacking it into jockeys, shoulder-high cocks that would then be piled into thatched stacks. They worked together, the women in sun hats, the men in shirt-sleeves or stripped to the waist, laughing and talking as they laboured. I know there is nothing remotely romantic about farming and that it is a hard and often heartbreaking job, but watching that family working in the afternoon sun made me think that there must be a lot of people stuck on assembly lines in factories who would have gladly changed lives with them, for that golden afternoon at least.

11 Cúchulainn's House and Back by the South Pole

The lake of Anascaul lies in a steep-sided glen north of Anascaul village. It is a place with a powerful atmosphere. On grey, dour days it can have an air of menace and gloom, yet on bright days in late spring and early summer it seems a place where magic still rides on the breeze that creases the dark peaty waters of the lough. The lake has a story, of course. A beautiful woman called Scál lived alone by the lake at the foot of the glen. A savage giant, hearing of Scál and her great beauty came to claim her for his own. Scál appealed to that great hero and womaniser, Cúchulainn, for help and the two adversaries squared up on opposite sides of the lake, Cúchulainn on Dromvally (*Drom an Bhaile*) and the giant on Knockmulanane (*Cnoc Mhaoilionáin*). For seven days they hurled insults at each other and, because this was in the times of the *filí* or poets, the insults were doubly barbed by being in verse. For days the battle of words rattled the cliffs of the glen. Then the words turned to stone and Cúchulainn and the giant began hurling boulders at each other – you can still see them scattered all over the summits of both mountains. Cúchulainn was at a definite disadvantage because he was on Dromvally, the lower of the two mountains, and whether it was that or a following wind nobody knows, but a boulder hit Cúchulainn in the chest, he gave out a great groan and Scál, believing that her champion was dead, threw herself into the lake and was drowned. The identical story can be found in Chew Valley near Oldham in

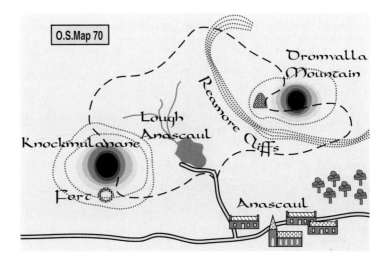

Lancashire and a similar one is told of Pen Hill in Wensleydale.

Seán Ó Suilleabháin recommends a circular walk taking in the horseshoe above Lough Anascaul, and I followed his steps one June day, scrambling up the high ground near the Carrigblagher Cliffs to the summit of Knockmulanane. It was a fair old scramble but the views as I gained height were wonderful. It was a cloudy day with a stiff breeze coming in off the sea, the hills beyond Anascaul village were clear to see and, further still, the glimmer of Dingle Bay. Climbing higher, I looked down and saw,

Standing stones lead the way to the collapsed burial chamber of Tíg Cúchulainn

on a small spur of the mountain below me, the remains of a pre-historic hut, perfectly formed and yet unmarked on the map. It was definitely not a *booley* – the kind of shelter that cow herders would build when living out with their cattle on the summer pastures – it was more like a small watchman's hut where, perhaps, warriors would have been stationed to keep look out for the tribe on the hill behind. The whole Dingle Peninsula is so spattered with early remains that it is probable that a great number like this hut circle still lie unrecorded.

A last pull brought me to the summit of Knockmulanane, a rocky ridge with the teeth of stone outcropping. It was too cold to do anything more than duck down in a hollow out of the wind and have a quick cup from the flask before cutting over a featureless boggy moor, making for the saddle at the head of the glen. An old green lane makes its way out of Anascaul, crossing the col and heading north for Ballyduff under Stradbally Mountain, and close by the green lane are the ruins of a cluster of houses. It was here on the high ground above the houses that the last wolf in the Dingle Peninsula was killed and a large flat slab of rock there is called the Wolf's Step. A group of walkers far below me crossed the pass heading northwards as I dropped down towards the saddle and, as I drank from the stream above the ruins, they were gone away down the track – dayglo dots.

It was a long slow haul from the pass, climbing above the northern cliffs of the glen. According to one local, there are gashes in the fiercest of the cliffs, *Faill Dubh* (Black Cliff), that are twenty feet long and more than two hundred feet deep. In mist, this cliff could be a dangerous place to be. Sudden slashes in the rock showed the lough far below me and the flanks of Knockmulanane across the valley. I followed the edge for a while

Lough Anascual seen from below Cúchulainn's House

before cutting up and across more bogland to the summit of Dromvally and the great collapsed burial chamber of. *Tig Cúchulainn* (Cúchulainn's House). I'm not sure if he regained his strength here after his great battle with the giant or whether his bones lie here in their final resting place, but a fifteen-foot-high stone cairn with a hollow at its centre that is almost certainly a collapsed burial chamber stands on the end of the summit ridge looking out over the valley. A short cursus of standing stones, some more than six feet high, leads to the grave of Cúchulainn and the locals have a name for them: *Fianna Cúchulainn* – the Warriors of Cúchulainn.

The light was breaking now, with shafts of sun patterning the far flanks of Knockmulanane, but the breeze was still cold enough to make me look for shelter. I was sitting in the lee of *Tig Cúchulainn* when I heard a rustling in the grass and, looking down, saw a small frog staring at me. I wasn't sure if St Patrick had banished the frogs from Ireland as well as snakes and for a second I wondered if this was a magical frog. I had been surrounded by myth and fable all morning and there was a strange and wonderful light in the air so that, for a brief moment, the thought trickled through my grey matter that this little creature might be a princess that had been turned into a frog by a wicked pookha – but I decided against kissing it unless it spoke first, and in Irish.

The descent back down to Lough Anascaul was a steep and slippy featureless slope of grass and heather that ended in the usual barbed wire, a ditch and a detour round a bog and stream. The light was changing yet again as I headed back to the car park by the lake and a last wash of brightness caught a white foxglove, casting the cliffs behind in dark shadow.

I stopped for a pint at the South Pole pub in Anascaul. Tom Crean, who accompanied Scott and Shackleton to the Antarctic, owned the pub earlier this century. Shackleton, in particular, thought him a fine, strong, quiet, reliable man, a typical Kerry-man, you might say. He shared the terrible struggle of Shackleton's last journey, sailing in an open boat to South Georgia to fetch help for their ice-locked crew on the Antarctic ice-shelf and endured exposure, frostbite and starvation. Ironically he died not in the white icy wastelands but at home in Kerry on his way to hospital, suffering from a burst appendix. Relatives of his still live in the village, and though the pub closed for a while a few years back, it is open and flourishing again.

Up the street from the South Pole is Dan Foley's, another of the great pubs of the West. The man himself – storyteller, actor, ventriloquist and magician – used to do special shows for the schoolchildren of the area, carrying his props in a box on the back of his 50cc motorbike. I ended up there one Sunday lunchtime after a walk on the Dingle Way, and a wet and cold walk it had been too. There was a big turf fire warming the room. I took off my dripping cagoule.

'Can I move my chair nearer the fire?' I asked.

'You can do anything at all, only that it's legal', he replied and made me a great pot of tea and a plate of fine sandwiches and gave me a drop of the Black Bush to drive out the cold. I was soon, as they say in Bratislava, 'in no pain at all'.

12 Brandon Mountain

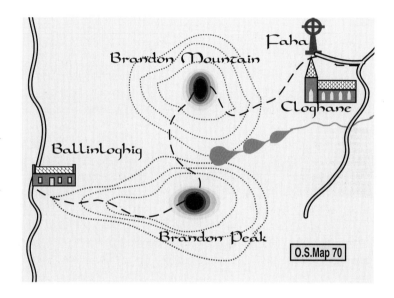

Like Croagh Patrick, Brandon Mountain (*Cnoc Bréainn*) is one of Ireland's holy mountains. St Brendan, who gave the mountain his name, fasted and prayed here, another hermit on yet another mountain-top oratory. The more I have journeyed about this island, the more I have come to understand why it was called 'the land of saints and scholars'. Islands like the Skelligs and mountains like Errigal, Croagh Patrick and Brandon seem to have been places where the men and women of the early Church could go to wrestle with whatever demons were within them and without, and so purify their souls.

Brendan was born around AD 486 in the coastal village of Fenit close to Tralee and a great shining light is said to have shone all over the area at his birth. When he was baptised three magical rams leapt from the well at Tobar na Molt near Ardfert – the rams were used to pay the priest's fee! My poor Irish translates Tobar na Molt, which is a place of pilgrimage to this day, as The Well of the Umpires – cricket in Ireland! I'm wrong, surely. St Brendan was taught by St Ita, a nun who so believed in the mortification of the flesh that, according to one book I read, night and day, weekdays and holy days, she carried in her undergarments an enormous stag beetle 'to nip and tickle her about' (and don't ask what an 'about' is because I've no idea).

Brendan became one of the Twelve Apostles of Ireland and after years of training and travels, came to his holy mountain to fast and pray. He founded an abbey at Ardfert, the ruins of which

are still standing, and men came from all over Europe to learn and pray and labour in the scriptorium. From the creek named after him, at the foot of his mountain, Brendan and a handful of his monks set sail for Hy Brasil, the Isles of Paradise, around AD 525. Their vessel was a skin-covered boat, a larger version of the skin canoes or *naibhogs* they still race down in Dingle Bay every regatta. On his journey across the Atlantic, Brendan and his monks made landfall on a small island. Feeling cold and hungry

Walker on the ridge between Brandon Mountain and Brandon Peak

they lit a big fire to warm themselves and cook a few fish they had caught along the way. As the fire blazed merrily away, the island suddenly jumped up and swam off, for they had landed, not upon solid land, but on the back of a whale called Jasconius.

Brandon's writings would indicate that he travelled round the coast of Greenland and then sailed westward to make landfall in Newfoundland or Labrador, thus 'discovering' America well before Columbus. The explorer Tim Severin made a skin boat similar to Brendan's and sailed across the Atlantic to America proving that such a journey was possible and that the stories the Elizabethan explorers heard from the native Americans of white men having been there before may well be true. He tells the whole story in his book, *The Brendan Voyage*. After discovering America and founding religious houses all over Europe (the Brandenburg Gate in Berlin leads to the area named after him), Brendan died in AD 578 and is buried in Clonfert, in County Galway.

So revered is St Brendan in his native Kerry, that on 28 June 1868, twenty thousand people made their way to the summit of Brandon Mountain to hear Mass celebrated by the Bishop of Kerry. The crowd climbing to the top was so thick that, when the bishop realised he'd left his missal at the bottom, he sent word back down through the crowd and the book was passed up from hand to hand, reaching him before he gained the summit.

Brandon Mountain rises high above Dingle Town, the highest hill on the Dingle Peninsula. From the sea it looks like a great hump, from the Connor Pass to its south-east, a series of peaks separated by combes and ridges. Much of the time, Brandon is under its own individual cap of cloud and even on the clearest of summer days there can be a strange hood of mist on the summit,

Ben on the ridge of Brandon Mountain

almost as though the mountain has its own weather system. Because of this, and because of the sheer cliffs that fall from its northern ridges, it isn't a hill that should be taken lightly, particularly since escape routes are hard to find and sometimes the only safe way off is back the way you came. If that means descending south towards the paternoster lakes, you could have a very uncomfortable climb down.

All of that said, Brandon is a wonderful mountain and if the weather is kind you can have one of the finest days out that you'll ever have on a hill. My favourite walk on Brandon is from Faha by the paternoster lakes carrying on to Brandon Peak and then following the long shoulder down to the road to Ballyferriter. This means either leaving a car at each end or arranging lifts or a taxi.

Faha lies at the end of the road that leads into the mountain from an inlet of Brandon Bay to Cloghane. A few years back, I set out to climb the mountain, calling in at Cloghane on my way to look at the old ruined Protestant church where there was a wonderful Celtic head. Originally the Celts collected the real thing: when victorious in battle, they cut off their enemies' heads and mounted them on the walls of their houses as symbols of their power. The head was the seat of the soul in Celtic mythology, thus, possessing your enemy's head meant that you also possessed his soul and therefore his power. A stone doorway discovered in France had niches on jambs and lintels in which human skulls had been placed. As you entered through the door (to the Celts all boundaries – shore/sea; day/night; spring/summer; inside/outside – were very important) you therefore crossed a magical divide.

Later, real heads gave way to wooden and stone heads, the symbol being as powerful, perhaps, as the genuine article, and these heads, like their fleshy counterpart, were often placed over doorways as magical symbols. Think of the number of cathedral and church doors that have stone heads set into them. Why stone heads? Why not flowers or fruit or geometric symbols? The answer must surely be the enduring power of the mystical symbol.

The head at Cloghane was very special, nobody knew how it found its way into the church – whether it had been part of an old Celtic church that had stood on the site or whether it had been brought from somewhere else – but tradition had it that this was the head of *Crom Dubh* or Black Crom, the powerful god of the Celtic underworld with whom Patrick had wrestled, finally driving him from the holy mountain. Perhaps Brendan, too, had driven *Crom Dubh* from his place on Brandon Mountain. Steve MacDonogh, the poet and publisher who has written an excellent guide to the Dingle Peninsula, suggests that this stone head was the very head used in the pre-Christian Lughnasa festival that took place on the summit of Brandon Mountain when Lugh the Sun God and Crom the God of darkness battled symbolically, and Crom's head was buried to show the death of winter. Somewhere along the way it found its way onto the wall of the chapel.

On this day, on my way to the mountain, I parked the car nearby and walked up the lane to the ruined church. I had a little terrier with me at the time, belonging to my daughter, one of those dogs that thinks he's human and follows you everywhere. At the door of the church he stopped and his fur rose up. He refused to come in to the church even though I whistled and called him again and again. He stood there shaking and whining, showing his teeth in a sickly grin, obviously frightened of something. I went over to the stone head and stood beneath it. I'm not superstitious by nature and tend to treat aliens, UFOs, abductions and ectoplasm with a wheelbarrow full of salt, but that day, as I looked up at the stone head, I felt as though somebody had just stuck a cattle prodder on the top of my head and given me a shot. A powerful physical shock of some kind almost knocked me over. It was as though I had just earthed some strong electrical current. Quite shaken, I looked over to the dog who was still standing at the door of the roofless ruin, and he looked back at me as though to say, 'I told you so. That thing's not to be messed with, Dad. Us dogs know a thing or two – we might run for sticks but we ain't stupid.'

I heard recently that the head had been prised from the wall by thieves and had been shipped abroad, to be sold, no doubt, to some collector. I hope he knows that a curse goes with these heads. Whether you believe it or not, I know of at least one case where a head was given freely to a family, who very quickly asked for it to be taken away after a chain of tragedies and disasters had ruined their lives. I hope the thieves and the collectors get their comeuppance too.

Where the lane ends at Faha there is a grotto to the virgin and, from there, the pilgrims' path to Brandon, clearly marked by stakes and easy to follow, leads into a great combe and onto the mountain by a rocky, but easy, path. I followed it that day, a soft summer light warming the morning, and the summit clear and cloudless ahead. To my left as I climbed, I could see the paternoster lakes ('paternoster' because they lie strung out like the beads on a rosary) and ahead the black cliffs of the *Grain Ceol* (Ugly Music), so-called because of the noise made by rock falls from the walls of the combe. It was a wonderful day, hot and

still, although a heat haze muted and softened the distant views. I followed the well-trodden path into the heart of the combe, the face rising up ahead of me. What looked like a scramble turned out to be an easy, if steep zig-zag up the face of the combe and onto the ridge. Behind me I could see the east ridge opening out as I climbed. It is perhaps, a more adventurous way on to the mountain, with a fair bit of scrambling involved, but it is one of the greatest ridge walks in the country.

A cross marks the summit of the mountain and close by is St Brendan's holy well and the tumbled stones of what remains of his oratory. I sat there for a rest and a drink and to take in the view. The holy well stands only a couple of dozen feet below the summit yet it is said never to dry up. I have to say that on the day I was there it was muddy and overgrown and you would have had a job to get much water out of it.

From Brandon Mountain to Brandon Peak (*Barr an Ghéaráin*), the second summit of the massif, is a wonderful walk. The track takes you along the edge of cliffs, which drop sheer away to your left. In poor weather or high winds, this way could be deleterious to health and should be avoided. From the peak, I followed a long but easy stroll along the shoulder that would take me down to the road at Ballinloghig from where I was hoping to hitch a lift back home. I could see the valley below to my right, the distinct trail of the Pilgrim's Route making its way to the mountain, worn bare by the feet of countless worshippers. That is a way off Brandon often taken by walkers who only want to climb the one peak, but I had stuck to the high route so I followed the shoulder all the way, dropping down at the end over barbed wire and ditches but no bog, coming down at length to a track that led me to the road. An old lady was standing at her cottage door as I passed. It had been a fine day, we both agreed.

'Would you like a glass of milk?' she asked, showing the kind of hospitality that is still to be found in the West. I was just about to say that that would be very nice when a grubby Transit van pulled up and a handsome face framed in a halo of red gold hair loomed out of the window and shouted at me: 'Mike Harding, get in and we'll go and have a jar.'

It was the legendary Con Moriarty, who had recently come back from the Irish expedition to Ama Dablam in the Nepal Himalaya. I said goodbye to the old lady and climbed in. There were climbing ropes, boots, rucksacks, maps, helmets and all manner of trade and tackle in a jumble inside the van. It looked like a hurricane had hit a climbing shop.

'It's a bit of a pigsty, but I'm going to tidy it up tomorrow,'

Con said. It was still like that when I climbed in three years later. A new van, but the same jumble.

We had a pint at John Long's bar and a very good pint it was too, in what must be one of the least spoilt pubs in Ireland – stone flagged floors, little benches, an old wooden counter and old Giraoid, the owner, behind the bar. Later that night at the An Droichead Beag in Dingle town, we listened to Cillian O' Brien, the piper, and Brede his wife, a fine flute player, making some of the sweetest music you'll ever hear. What an end to a glorious day.

I'm often seen in Ireland walking round with a permanent grin on my face. People think I'm mad, and jump out of the way crossing themselves and dragging their children with them. I'm not mad; it's just that for all its faults, and it has many, Dingle town is still, to me, one of the best places on God's earth.

13 The Giant's Bed and Ventry Strand

Above the lovely sweep of Ventry Strand, just below the summit of *An Cathair Aird* (The High Fort), there is a collapsed burial chamber known to locals as The Giant's Bed, a megalithic tomb with a massive cap-stone that was the bed for all time of a chief or high king of the tribe that ranged these hills. The cyst is also known as *Leaba an fhir Mhuimhnig* – the Munsterman's Bed – though nobody I have asked seems to know why. This whole area of hills above Ventry is so rich in history that an easy ramble of a handful of miles can take hours if you are of the mind that seeks out odd corners and old stories.

Ventry village, for example, was founded as a home for converts from Catholicism to Protestantism. Missions based around soup kitchens were set up by wealthy Protestant landlords, well-meaning but arrogant nonetheless, who used the soup to coerce and convert the hungry Irish when they were starving in their thousands during the years of the Potato Famine. Until a few years ago you could still hear the phrase 'he took the Protestant soup' and the word 'souper' was a term of contempt. One branch of my family were O'Neills, the other, Pynes. The O'Neills were Catholic as far back as I can find, while the Pynes were originally Protestant planters. I can only assume that the Pyne's took the Catholic soup.

One late spring afternoon I left the pub in Soup Town and followed the road west for a few yards before turning off to follow a tiny *bohareen*. The lane was rough and muddy, the hedges

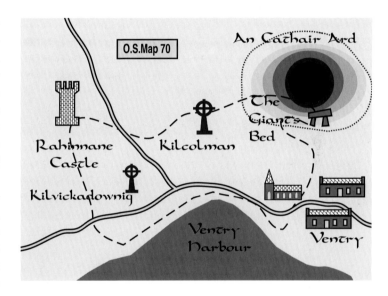

thickly clotted with fuchsia, and it led me up to the road that skirts the hill's flank. From the road I climbed a barbed wire fence near an old quarry and scrambled through heather and brambles onto open country and the shoulder of the hill. There, just below the summit, lay the Giant's Bed. Much of it is collapsed now but you can still climb into the main chamber and imagine you are a dead chieftain. Watch out for the sheep dung though. In most of the old Celtic countries, Ireland, Scotland,

Wales and in the Pennines of England, the cairns of dead Iron Age chieftains stand on the shoulders of many of the hills, looking down on the valley. They are rarely on the summit, almost always on the edge where they can look down on the land below. Again, I wondered whether this was the Celtic sense of boundaries and edges coming into play, the dead chieftain lying on the edge of the mountain neither in the sky nor on the earth but somewhere between. From the tomb I could see the whole of the Iveragh Peninsula and the Reeks, Carrauntuohil clear to be seen, while closer at hand, Brandon Peak stood stark against the broken cloud and Brandon Mountain itself was lost in its usual cap of mist. Below, the whole of Dingle Bay shone in the sun, clear enough for the dolphin boats to be seen.

From the Munsterman in his perpetual sleep, I dropped down to the Dingle Way and followed it over the pass. *Mám an Óraigh* means (I think) the Pass of the Oratory, since *óráidocht* means 'oratory', and that is the only word I can find in the dictionary that comes anywhere close. I am ready, however, to be shot down in flames. The Dingle Way comes down under *An Caithair Aird* and follows a quiet lane that leads by Kilcolman (*Cill an gColmán* – the Church of Colman) where there was an early Christian settlement, though the remains are now quite hard to see. A roughly circular enclosure holds the ruins of several huts and some gravestones. On one of them is a finely inscribed cross and an inscription in ogham which reads 'Colman the Pilgrim'. The cross, like many a cross and standing stone in this area, stands unmarked and unprotected in a field below the road. There is hardly an acre of ground in this part of Kerry that is without a cross, oratory, standing stone or *bulaun*. The definitive archaeological survey of *Corca Dhuibhine*, as the Dingle Peninsula is known in Irish, lists thousands of crosses, standing stones and ruined chapels. It is no wonder the area still has a feeling of great spirituality.

From Kilcolman, the Dingle Way follows a lovely *bohareen* down to Ventry but I was in no hurry to get back so I took the old lane to the crossroads and the ruined high walls of Rahinnane Castle, one of the strongholds of the Knights of Kerry. Steve MacDonogh tells how Rahinnane, like similar small single-unit castles of its type, was built with the help of a £10 grant from the English government. Like many other castles there is a legend about its construction and its mortar is said to have been mixed with the blood of the local people. The castle was 'slighted' by the forces of Noll Cromwell. Rahinnane was built on the site of an old *rath* or fairy fort, and there are said to be a maze of souterrains running from the castle in all directions. Some of the legends associated with such fairy forts may be due to these very souterrains. Stories tell of men falling asleep on the hillside below a fairy fort and suddenly finding the ground open before their eyes and little people coming out. Country people in Ireland often associated the old ring forts with the Little People, and whether these were the race who were here before the Celts, or whether they were imaginings, I don't know. I do know, however, that a man called Dan Ryan from Tulla in Clare, whose honesty I wouldn't dispute, told me that one summer's night he went into one of the old raths to fetch out a cow and then wandered about half the night, lost and bewitched, unable to find his way out of the field.

Fairy music, too, came from these hills and 'The Gold Ring' is one such tune. The story goes that a fiddler, famous throughout the land, fell asleep one night when he was on the way home

The Lark on the Strand

from a dance, a drop having been taken. As he lay there, he was suddenly awakened by the sound of a fiddle coming from inside the hill. He listened intently and the music went on and on, a wonderful tune, but such a complex tune, one he had never heard before. Presently, a tiny fiddler came out of a hole in the side of the fairy hill, followed by a troop of Little People. They spied the stranger from the Big People lying on the bank, but instead of fleeing as they normally did, they stood and watched him, for the human fiddler had taken out his fiddle and was playing the first part of the tune.

'What will you take to teach me the rest?' he asked.

Now the Little People love gold and the human fiddler had a great gold ring on his hand. 'Give us the ring from your finger and we'll teach you the tune.'

And if you want to hear 'The Gold Ring' played by a master, search out the music of Matt Molloy from Westport, County Mayo, a flute player with The Chieftains.

The priests around these parts were no fans of the music, however (perhaps they saw it all as the work of the fairies or the devil) and they did all they could to stamp it out. They particu-larly hated the crossroad dances when people would gather on a fine evening, before the days of parish halls and ballrooms, and would dance in the open air to the music of pipes and fiddles. It was a social occasion and was one of the only ways young people in the country areas could get to meet each other. They were, by all accounts occasions of great joy and fun which meant of course that the clergy saw them as wicked and sinful. Breandean Breathnach in his book, *Dancing in Ireland*, tells of Father John Casey, parish priest of Ballyferriter in the nineteenth century, who was the scourge of all pipers, fiddlers and card players. Once, when he came upon a piper playing at a crossroad dance, he rushed over to the unfortunate musician and 'kicked, cuffed and beat him unmercifully, broke his pipes and completely dis-persed the whole assembly'.

I stood at the heart of the *rath* in the sunshine, and something burning golden in the sun on the edge of the ring caught my eye. It was a dead fox, freshly dead, the bloom still on its coat and the brackish scent still coming from the dead body. Whether it was shot or poisoned I couldn't tell, but I buried it under a mound of stones and left it in the fairy ring.

The Giant's Bed on the summit of An Cathair Aird: in the distance are the mountains of the Iveragh Peninsula

Back on the road, I followed the old lane that leads to the southern tip of Ventry Strand and rambled along the tideline through a glorious afternoon back to Ventry. The soft low murmer of the surf on the long strand was counterpoint to the song of a skylark that had climbed from the rough grass beyond the dunes to become a singing speck against the clear blue sky. The silver strand of Ventry is one of the great places of Ireland. Ventry is said by some to be derived from *Cean Trá* (the Strand of the Headland) but it is more probable that it is the English version of *Fionn Trá* (Fionn's Strand), for it was on this beach that Fionn Mac Cumhail (Finn McCool) fought a hundred kings, including the King of France, the King of Spain and the King of the World. After a battle that lasted a year and a day, his Fianna (the Knights of Fionn) defeated all before them, leaving the beach and the fields round about strewn with thousands of dead. Then the remnants of Fionn's army marched in victory through the Gates of Glory. The tomb of the King of the World lies in a field near Kilvickadownig below the eastern slopes of Mount Eagle. It's hard to find, lying close by a hedge, in a field behind the old schoolhouse, but it has a lovely Greek cross within a simple but graceful circle.

The story of the Battle of Ventry may be based on something much more mundane. The pre-Celtic people who settled first in this area and who worshipped the god Bolg, were called the Fir Bolg, the Men of Bolg. Another name for the King of the Fir Bolg was the King of the World, so the battle may have been nothing more than a skirmish between the old tribe and the invaders, and the Kings of Spain and France may have been nowhere in it at all. Still, you should never let the truth get in the way of a good story. And on that glorious strand under a warm late spring sun you could believe anything.

Back at Ventry I followed the road to the Pottery of Maurice Sheehy, a writer of excellent walking guides to the Dingle Peninsula, where they make lovely pots and tiles, and the best Porter cake and tea you'll taste in a long mile.

The cross of Kilcolman

14 Mount Eagle

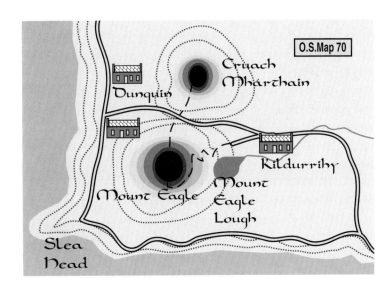

The absence of clearly-marked footpaths in the Irish mountains can be a little off-putting to walkers who are used to the well-trodden routes of English or Welsh hills, or the way-marked routes of Western Europe, but it can give an added spice to the experience too, giving you the feeling that you're walking somewhere that hasn't yet been pounded down into a motorway. That said, if all you have to hand are the old, nicely-coloured, but useless 1:126,720 maps, you can have a frustrating job just finding your way off the road and on to open country.

A few years back I found myself in that position, looking up at Mount Eagle (*Sliabh an Iolair*), in one of the lanes close under the mountain, wondering just how I was going to find my way out of the high-hedged *bohareen* I was standing in and up on to the mountain's flanks, when a farmer and his sheepdog came along. After we'd talked for a while about the weather and sheepdogs and where I was from and how I liked Ireland, and after I'd confused him with my poor Irish, I asked him if he could show me a route I could follow to the summit. He pointed out a way through a couple of field gates and over rough, rushy ground amongst thorns and brambles onto higher land. 'It's hard going for a bit but then you'll be on open ground and with those strong boots you have on your feet you'll have no trouble at all.'

I thanked him and set off, reflecting on the many times farmers in Ireland had commented on my boots. 'They're a fine strong pair of boots' was a phrase I'd heard over and again through the years. Irish farmers run around the mountains all day in a pair of green wellies and think nothing of it, but I'm sure they'd be better off in a pair of good boots. Rubber might keep out the bog water better than leather, but it fries your feet too. After a day on the hill in wellingtons, your toes look like a pound of badly-cooked pork sausages.

It was a perfect day for walking, a blue sky above, with the slightest hint of small, fluffy cloud and the air clear and still. I climbed steep banks, scrambling through thorn bushes and deep heather, gaining height slowly until I cleared the shrub and made my way through coarse grass to a shoulder that led to the summit. Below to the east was Mount Eagle Lough with its ugly transmitter aerial, and beyond that again, the lovely half-moon of Ventry Harbour. In the far distance stood Brandon Mountain, her summit capped with a wisp of cloud. To the north-west lay Dunquin and the Blasket Islands, those lonely and lovely rock-bound havens that face the roaring Atlantic.

This group of islands, *An Blascaod Mór* (the Great Blasket), *Inis Na Bró* (Island of the Quernstone), *Inis Mhic Aoibhleáin* (possibly the Island of Meic Oíbleáin – King of Kerry), and *Inis Tuaisceart* (the North Island) were, like St Kilda in the Outer Hebrides, the last island outposts of a way of life that can hardly have changed much since medieval times. There was no shop, no tavern, no policeman, no priest and no doctor. The islanders lived by fishing and from their fields of potatoes, cabbage, turnips, parsnips, corn and wheat. Sheep were sheared for their wool and a few cows kept for their milk. Life was unbelievably harsh. In times of storm, the islanders could be cut off for weeks, unable to get food or aid from the mainland that lay so tantalisingly close across the sound.

In 1838, Inis Tuaisceart was stormbound for six weeks and, towards the end, a poor couple who were living in a prehistoric *clocháin* on the island began to starve to death. Before help could come, the husband died and after a short while his body began to putrefy there in the stone chamber. His wife was too weak to bury him so she dismembered the body and cast the pieces out of the hut. She later went insane.

The Blaskets are now uninhabited. The last of the islanders left for the mainland in November 1953 when life had become too hard for even the hardiest. Yet, harsh though life on the Great Blasket was, the islanders bore it with a great strength and humour and managed not just to survive but to do so with a dignity and a creativity that is an indication of how 'the peasantry' of Western Europe, poor though they were, had a rich folklore, music and language that only died with the invasion of mass culture. Before they left their homes, a handful of the islanders produced a library of their writings which told in clear and powerful Irish the story of their lives. It is sobering to think that these tiny islands produced such a wealth of writing; that from the pens of a few native Irish speakers came some of the greatest works of European literature. Scholars from England like Robin Flowers and George Thompson encouraged and translated the works of the islanders, such as Muiris O Súilleabháin's *Twenty Years a Growing*.

The writers of the Blasket tradition, Tomás Ó Criomhthain, Muiris Ó Súilleabháin, Peig Sayers and her son, the poet Mícheál Ó Gaoithín, all wrote in Irish, for the Gaelic-speaking world and, most importantly, for the islanders themselves. They wrote because 'art will out' and the desire to create is as powerful amongst the cabins of the storm-battered West coast as it is in the salons of any of our cities. The stories they told are simple and passionate and filled with a translucent and rare beauty.

'I was born on St Thomas' day in the year 1856,' Tomás Ó Criomhthain's *The Islandman* begins. 'I can recall being at my mother's breast, for I was four years old before I was weaned. I am "the scrapings of the pot", the last of the litter. That's why I was left so long at the breasts. I was a spoilt child, too. Four sisters I had, and every one of them putting her own titbit into

Dunquin lying below Mount Eagle and Cruach Mhárthain facing the wide Atlantic

my mouth. They treated me like a young bird in the nest. Maura Donel, Kate Donel, Eileen Donel, and Nora Donel – those were their names. My brother was Pats Donel, and I am Tómas Donel. They were all well grown when I was a baby, so that it was little wonder that I was spoilt among them all. Nobody expected me at all when I came their way.'

Peig Sayer's book, *An Old Woman's Reflections*, begins: 'My sorrow, isn't it many a twist life does! Isn't youth fine! – but alas! she cannot be held always! She slips away as the water slips from the sand of the shore. A person falls into age unbeknown to himself. I think there are no two jewels more valuable than Youth and Health. There's me now, sat in a heap on a green sward beside the house, reflecting and musing on the days of my youth. Och! wasn't it I was agile and light then! Small thought I had that I'd ever be a worn old one like this!'

Where else will you find, from a 'peasant pen' such simple but powerful and poetic writing. Hemingway spent years trying to achieve such a simple, direct style; to the islanders it came naturally because their everyday speech was direct, poetic and musical, their writing simply an extension of that. Synge had discovered the same rare gift when he lived amongst the Aran islanders and his writings on the Aran islands, together with the collected writings from the Blaskets, give us a vivid picture of a way of life that had hardly changed since the Middle Ages.

The musical tradition on the Blaskets was as rich as its literary outpourings although it was sadly uncollected until fairly recently. One of the most fascinating tunes to come from the Blaskets is a slow air from IInis Mhic Aoibhleáin called 'Caoneadh na bPeucaí' – the Fairies' Lamentation. It was said by the islanders that one night people sitting in a house heard a

Sunset over the Dead Man, also called the Sleeping Bishop

fairy woman *caoining* in the night outside. Fortunately, one of the listeners within had a great ear for music and memorised the tune and the words which were later translated into English by Séamus Ennis, the great Irish piper.

I am a woman of the fairies who has travelled over the waves
I was carried off by night far over the sea
I'm in their kingdom under control of the fairy women
And I will not be back in this world until after the cock crows
Then I will go to the fairy fort
I do not wish to go but go I must
And this world and all in it I must leave behind

❖

Port na bPucai

I turned away from the Blaskets, the air of the lament lilting in my mind and walked north from the summit of Mount Eagle following the shoulder, and dropping down to the pass far below. Here a snail's track of the road wound up to the saddle, this being the old route from Dingle to Dunquin. A perfect summer's day and a cool breeze to keep the flies away. I crossed a cluster of bogs and climbed the fence to the road. The path to the summit of Cruach Mhárthain (the Mountain of St Martin?) is well worn because, so I have been told, this is a holy mountain and people still make pilgrimage here. It was an easy climb to the summit, but the sun was hammering down and when I finally made it to the cairn I was more than glad of the flask of tea and the sandwiches I'd stuffed in my sack. I dropped down a little, west of the summit and sat in a suntrap watching the waves roll up the beach at Dunquin. If you can think of a better way of spending a sunny summer's afternoon than sitting on a mountaintop looking out at the Blaskets and the hazy coast below, with a cup of tea in one hand and a lump of cheese and soda bread in the other, then I'd like to hear of it. You can keep your Côte d'Azure and your Mustique; give me the west of Ireland any day.

As the light turned towards evening, wall shadows grew long and the sea took on the hue of bronze, I left the summit and dropped down to the road again to follow it back to the *bohareen* and my starting point. I was in the lee of the hill and the breeze had dropped and the afternoon was golden. So beautiful was it, and so full of my good luck with the weather was I that, just by way of Celtic mystical balance Mr and Mrs Midge and their two billion children came out for afternoon tea and took it out on my skin.

County Clare

The footprints of an older race are here
And memories of an old heroic time;
And shadows of an old mysterious faith
So that the place seems haunted
And strange sounds float upon the wind.

Anon

Though Sligo and Donegal would argue me blue in the face about this one, I have to say that Clare is quite possibly the most musical county in Ireland. There are more great musicians to the square mile there than anywhere in the world. Tony Linane, Sharon Shannon, Tommy Peoples, the Russell Family, Mary Custy, Tola Custy, Bobby Gardner, Noel Hill, Miclín Conlon, Mary McNamara – the list is endless and every year sees another crop of young musicians who are not just good but are amazingly so. P.J. Curtis, who has produced some of the best recordings of Irish music, lives at Killinaboy in the Burren and his book, *Notes From the Heart* has become one of the standard works on Irish traditional music. At Ennis each year the *Fleadh Cheiol Nua* attracts thousands of visitors while, in July, the Willy Clancy Festival chokes the streets of Milltown Malbay with banjo players, flautists, pipers and fiddlers, and every *bodhran* player worthy of the name is battering a lump of goat with a stick.

The late Micho Russell, from Doolin on the coast north of the Cliffs of Moher, was always there whenever the *craic* was mighty. Micho was a wonderful man, a fine musician in the old style and an inspiration to many younger musicians. He was a gentle, shy man, with eyes full of life, and a smile and a story always ready to burst out. He was filled, too, with a quiet wisdom, the earthy commonsense you often find in people who have lived simply and quietly. Micho once said, concerning people who rush about trying to do a million and one things: 'If you try to do too much it will come to nothing in the finish – all only a bottle of smoke.'

It is a little known fact that Muhammad Ali, three times World Heavyweight Champion, had Irish roots; his grandfather was an O'Grady from Clare, and although nobody has yet written a song about Ali's shamrock past, I remember Micho singing a song about another famous son of Clare, John Holland, who built the world's first submarine. He was a Clare schoolteacher who emigrated to America, where his researches were financed by the Fenian Brotherhood. They hoped that his craft might serve to sink British ships. In Ireland the song-writing tradition

Black clouds rolling above the limestone pavement - a typical Burren scene

is alive and kicking and they write songs on every subject under the sun – the coming of electricity to rural Ireland, a goat's desire to be turned into a *bodhran*. All is meat and flesh and more to the songwriter. Why *not* the submarine?

Come all you young Irishmen who walk upon the land
There's feats indeed and fairy creeds that you may understand
There's one of them that comes to mind the like was never seen,
He was John Phillip Holland who invented the submarine.

Now the US Navy, they thought he was crazy, his plans they threw aside,
But Holland paid no heed to them in his boat beneath the tide.
Far down below where only fish go, the yoke was plain to be seen
It was John Phillip Holland inside his first submarine.

Micho travelled the world playing his music, the seemingly simple, yet extremely subtle and complex music of west Clare that he and his brothers, Gussy and Packie, had recorded on an album, 'The Russell Family of Doolin, County Clare'. I remember that record being made, and remember also how, soon after that, Doolin changed from a sleepy fishing village to a busy tourist centre. Some bemoan the popularity of the place, but the *cráic* and the music are still there and, at McGann's or Connors, you'll hear some of the best in the West. There is so much music in Clare that it seems to pour from the very stones themselves.

As well as its music, Clare has a tremendous natural beauty and history: the great sea cliffs of Moher run south from Doolin to the Hag's Head, while north-west of Corrofin lies a land of lakes and quiet country lanes. But the gem of Clare is the great

Michael Coyne in sesiún at Cruise's Bar in Ennis

karst land of the Burren that spreads from Corrofin north to Ballyvaghan and west to the sea. People have written millions of words on the Burren and I'm sure nothing I can say will add anything new. It is a place of vast, bare limestone and rare plants, of ruined churches and old round forts, of caves and crags. 'Not enough wood to hang a man, not enough water to drown a man and not enough earth to bury a man,' one of Cromwell's officers observed of the moonscape of the Burren as he was going about his business of genocide. Well, that may be true, but there were saints and hermits here before Cromwell had ever been heard of. There are flowers here that are seen nowhere else, growing in vast profusion and often strangely neighboured, so that alpine and Mediterranean plants grow side by side quite happily.

The Burren

Spring is the time to be here for the flowers, when the early orchids appear and the stars of blue gentian poke up amongst the limestone slabs. Then the Burren truly is a very magical and mystical place.

I read somewhere that a Dubliner once asked in a shop in Ballyvaghan where exactly the Burren was. 'You're exactly in it,' was the reply that came over the counter, free of charge.

'Well, what *is* the Burren?' the exasperated man asked back.

It's hard to say what it is, because it isn't just stone, or flowers or ruined chapels and forts, it's a living community, too. It is said that bone-setters were more common here than in other parts of Ireland because of all the broken bones people got from falling down the cracks in the great limestone pavements. Cows can winter out here longer than anywhere else in Ireland because the stone holds the warmth it has absorbed through the summer, releasing it in the winter like a giant storage heater. But I remember the Burren most of all for the silence; for the quiet of a summer's day on Black Head and the total stillness of a mild autumn day on Mullaghmore. There may be more than a sprat of truth in the answer the Dub was given that day when he asked what the Burren *is*.

'It's a state of mind', he was told. So now you know.

15 A Walk Around Dysert O'Dea

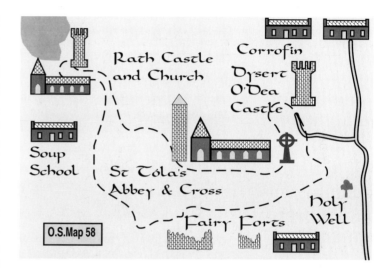

Corrofin stands in the heart of some of the most beautiful country in all Ireland, a land of lakes and woodlands, limestone crags and rich green meadows on the edge of the Burren. The village was one of the first places I visited in Ireland and I still have a very soft spot for it. Any place with a pub called Kenny's Drinking Emporium has surely got to be worth a look. Over the years I have walked and cycled over many miles of the surrounding hills and lanes, and one cold March day, when a westerly wind was making biking both hard and miserable, I found myself at the Clare Heritage Centre in the old Church of Ireland church in the village.

The curator was Dr. Ignatius (Nacey) Cleary, who had been schoolmaster at Corrofin. While researching the Famine and emigration of his own area, he built up a mass of documentation which now forms the basis of the most important body of source material for exiles of Irish descent seeking out their roots in Ireland. Nacey was a kind and thoughtful man, still remembered with great affection by his pupils, and every time I went back to Clare I would go and visit him in his little church. It was Nacey who showed me a grave with, carved upon it, the lines

> 'Here as ever sleeping sound
> Lies our Audrey in the ground
> If she wake as wake she may
> There'll be fun on Judgement Day.'

Sadly, Nacey died a few years back, but so thorough was his work that a new centre, close to the old church, now houses the parish registers of every parish in Ireland. When I was last there, the information from these registers was being put on computer, so Irish emigrants abroad can now trace their family histories with even more speed. Ironically, researching my own family's past, I discovered recently that a female antecedent on my grandmother's side was sent to Australia, only to be deported back from there to Ireland for killing a man who had attempted

The castle of Dysert O'Dea, one of the best preserved in Ireland

to rape her. But that was the Quinlan side of the family, they were rough people from Tipperary and we don't talk about them much.

According to Nacey's records, there was a tremendous amount of emigration from this part of Clare both during the Famine and after, and not all the emigration was voluntary. Deportations from this part of Clare to Australia were terrible. One old lady was transported for stealing a handkerchief, and a boy of fourteen for stealing four eggs. I can just imagine the judge passing sentence on 'these feckless Irish' and sitting down to his dinner that night, confident that justice had been done.

The castle of Dysert O'Dea lies close to Corrofin. It is one of the best preserved castles in Ireland, rescued by the money of an O'Dea in America, and by the imagination and hard work of the locals. At the castle, you can see the murder hole, a gap in the floor of the first storey, through which they would pour nasty boiling stuff and other things, like the contents of the privy, onto the heads of any attackers that had managed to breach the first defences – which, nowadays, would of course be well beyond the terms of the Geneva Convention. At the castle you can buy a map of the Dysert O'Dea Archaeological Trail, a self-guided walk put together by the local community and designed by children at the nearby school. The walk wanders around quiet lanes, linking ruined churches with holy wells, high crosses and lonely lakes. If the cloud is down and the high hills seem better left for another day, or if you just fancy a gentle ramble rather than a climb through bog and heather, then the area round Dysert is a wonderful place for a low-level stroll, particularly if you have children who are interested in high crosses and holy wells. (Well, somebody must have.)

St Tola's Cross - note the missing arm

The Corrofin Jig

On a grey, cloudy summer day, I wandered into the castle and bought a map from the lady who sold the tickets. There was traditional music playing on a cassette player behind her.

'Who's that playing now?' I asked.

'That's the Kilfenora Ceilidh Band. My daughter's friend is in it. They were in the All-Ireland competition last night and I'm waiting for a phone call to see how they got on.'

Kilfenora, a bonny village on the southern edge of the Burren, has a ruined cathedral, one of the great high crosses of Ireland, the Doorty Cross, and the Burren Display Centre which stocks books and maps of the Burren and has a very good tea room that serves locally made scones and soda bread. Because of some politico-religious wrangling centuries ago, the Pope is Bishop of Kilfenora and the *ceilidh* band, in which the Pope occasionally plays spoons, is one of Ireland's best-known *ceilidh* bands, having won the All-Ireland many times.

I wished the band luck and set out from the castle, following the lane and the field path to St Tóla's Cross. The cross dates from the twelfth century and, like the Doorty Cross, is one of the great high crosses of Ireland. It was toppled by Cromwell's men as he was driving the Irish 'to Hell or Connaught', but was re-erected by Michael O'Dea in 1683 and restored by the Synge family in the late nineteenth century. On the shaft of the cross is the carving of an archbishop – perhaps St Tóla himself. The cross was also known as *Croch Bheanála* – the Cross of the Blessing – because at one time there was a removable stone arm, raised in blessing. Now there is only a hole in the archbishop's chest. But this wasn't the only detachable part of the cross. The head of Christ could also be taken down from the cross, and kissing it was said to be a cure for toothache. The head is now cemented firmly in place, perhaps at the request of the local dentists who were losing trade.

I wandered down the field from the cross and spent some time looking for a holy well which is shown on the map. The well was rediscovered a few years ago when bushes and whins were cleared away, but it seems to have dried up and disappeared again under vegetation. I got myself well scratched in the search – vicious Irish brambles surround the site.

The church of St Tóla stands on the site of a much earlier foundation, a monastery founded by the saint himself in the eighth century. Although it is now in ruins, this tiny church has one of the finest Romanesque doorways in Ireland. Nineteen carved stone heads form the arch, twelve human and seven animal. The keystone, though, has always puzzled me because it seems to have been carved by a different hand. It is a human head, much smaller and more primitive than the other carvings, and appears to have been packed out with a thin stone on one side, as though it were placed after all the others. I suppose it might be an important Celtic head from the earlier, eighth-century foundation, perhaps the head of St Tóla himself?

By the church is a ruined round tower, one of many that are found all over Ireland. They were places of retreat into which the monks could go in times of trouble, taking with them the valuable books and ornaments of the church. They may have been some defence against Vikings and the marauding armies of tribal chiefs, but they would not have withstood the cannon balls of later armies.

From the churchyard stile, I followed the road to Rath and, as often happens in the West, the grey beginnings of the day had now given way to broken cloud and sun, with more blue sky showing by the minute. I walked with my jacket in my backpack, a bottle of water in my hand and, on either side, purple loosestrife grew rampant in the hedgerows. There was not a car or a person in sight. The ruined church at Rath lies up a lane beyond a farm, and in amongst its brambles and nettles, high on the inner wall, is a lovely sheela-na-gig, very Romanesque and ornate, possibly at one time a door lintel that was mortared into the wall for safety. The sheela-na-gig or *síle na gcioch* (Julia of the Breasts in some translations) is a fertility symbol, the origins of which are lost in time. She runs in an unbroken line from the Venus of Willendorf, that plump, stone idol with the rounded breasts and swollen vulva, to the Romanesque little doll at Kilpeck in Herefordshire and the spiral dame of Rath. She is found all over Europe with her legs held apart, representing the fountain head of life, the most magical and mysterious and holy of all symbols.

Perhaps the greater number of *síles* in Ireland can be explained by the fact that Ireland celebrated the cult of the goddess later and more fervently than anywhere else in Europe and so the *síle*, as one aspect of the goddess, was revered much later here too. It was no accident that the country which took most ardently to the Marian Year (1953 – the year set aside by Rome for the special veneration of the Virgin Mary) was Ireland and, in that year, grottoes and statues were constructed all over the country, and are places of special worship to this day. From St Brigid to the grottoes by the holy wells is merely a breath in time.

Sheela-na-gigs are also found all over Ireland, the best study of them being *The Witch on the Wall* by Jørgen Andersen, which lists scores of sites in Ireland. Andersen concludes, on the evidence of the intertwining loops and coils, that the carver of the high cross at Dysert and the *síle* at Rath was the same. There is said to be another *síle* in the ruins of the church but, though I spent a long, pleasant, sunny hour looking for it, I couldn't find it. However, I did find a wonderful saint's head instead. I remember hearing that when the sheela-na-gigs were being moved around the National Museum in Dublin at the turn of the cen-

The romanesque arch at St Tola's church

The ruined castle below by the lough at Rath stands alone, so picturesque that you would almost think it had been planted there by the Bord Failté. It was blown to pieces, of course, courtesy of Oliver's Army. I cursed him and made my way down the hill and along a *bohareen* to the castle and the rushy lake. Below the castle walls are stone-lined cooking pits. In the days when this and similar castles were important as military and social centres, there must often have been many bellies to fill. The pits answered this purpose. They were filled with water and then meat, wild deer or boar, perhaps, was placed in them. Large stones were heated in fires nearby and dropped into the pits. As the stones cooled, they were replaced by more hot rocks and this went on until the water boiled and the meat was cooked. Archaeologists from an Irish university have tried the method and managed to cook a substantial amount of meat in a few hours.

I climbed back up the hill, loath to leave that quiet place of stones and water, and wandered back along the road, looking for what the guide describes as an old medieval road that once connected the monasteries and castles of west Clare. It is a rough (and on that day muddy) green lane that leads up to two old *raths* or ring forts in a commanding position on a hill. The way to the forts took me through a chicken-pecked farmyard and, as I was looking at the massive walls of the forts, an old farmer came through the yard for a chat.

He knew a good friend of mine, Noel Hill, the concertina player from this area. 'Sure and he used to come on his bicycle to Frank Custy's down below, learning the music. You'll know Frank's children then, Mary and Frances and Tóla.' I said that I did, for the Custys are one of the legendary musical families of

tury, they were covered with nappies, in case the lady typists should be scandalised at the image. The invoice for a dozen nappies is said to be still there in the accounts, a story which, if not true, should be.

Clare, all great players who have appeared on many a stage and made many a recording.

'Do you know the area well?' he asked.

'Not as well as I would like.'

'Well, that over there is Synge's Rock', and he went on to tell me the story as though it had happened that very morning. 'Synge was a local landlord and he wasn't liked because he was trying to convert people with the Protestant Soup. He had a school over near Carhue House there, and he was offering the children soup and education if they would become Protestants. Well, some of the local people didn't like it and decided to do away with him. One day he was out in his pony and trap when they ambushed him down near that rock. His driver was killed but the bullet they fired at Synge hit the Bible he had in his pocket just in front of his heart and saved his life. Sure and if 'oo don't believe every word of it, there's his Bible still down below in the Heritage Centre in Corrofin to this very day.'

I asked him if he'd ever seen any fairies round the forts since *raths* like these are known as 'fairy forts' and local people often tell stories of strange happenings on midsummer nights, but he just smiled and said no, he didn't believe in fairies.

From the forts I followed the lane down the hill to the Holy Well of the Assemblies (*Tobar Oireachta*). The water was sweet and pure and cool, the best water in the whole Dysert area, so people say, and as is often the case with holy wells, a whitethorn (as the hawthorn is known in Ireland) hangs over the water. There is a *piseog*, or superstition, about the whitethorn which says it is a magical tree and bad luck follows for whomever is foolish enough to cut one down. Farmers have been known to alter the course of a wall rather than destroy a tree and it is thought unlucky to bring whitethorn blossom into the house, though why this should be I do not know, except that the thorn is certainly a virulent tree, and a scratch from a whitethorn will fester very quickly.

I sat by the well a while, enjoying the afternoon light, then walked over to the church at the lane end where there is a *cillín*, an ancient burial ground for unbaptised children. Wandering around the Dingle Peninsula a few years back, I came across another *cillín* at Ballintaggart near to Dunsheen, close by the site of the Dingle Races. There are some fine ogham stones there, and the place is said to contain the remains of many babies who died before they could be baptised. 'Ah,' said a local I met at the site, 'that was by way of being a cod. There would be a priest in the area right enough who would baptise the babies, but the English would have had a priest-hunter after him to hang him if it was admitted, so they would pretend that the baby hadn't been baptised at all and bury it here.'

Nothing illustrates the way the Irish have had to deal with the English over the years better than that 'double blind'.

Back at the castle of Dysert O'Dea, I treated myself to a pot of tea and a bun, and heard from the lady who was running the café that the Kilfenora Ceilidh Band had won the All-Ireland yet again. There would be a hot time in the Pope's Parish that night.

16 Mullaghmore

The Irish are so very odd. They refuse to be English.
Winston Churchill, Letters

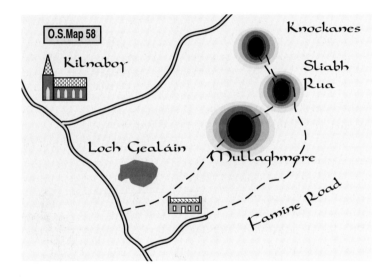

The ruined church at Killinaboy, three miles north of Corrofin, has a sheela-na-gig on the wall above the main door, plainer sister to the síle in the church at Rath. Some say that she represents the Earth Mother, with her splayed legs and her vulva held wide open, and that entering the church beneath her is a symbolic re-entrance to the womb. There could be some truth in that, for many of the great burial chambers were said to have been laid out in the shape of a woman and thus, by entering the chamber, the dead re-entered the Earth Mother from whom we all came. Others say that the sheela-na-gig is simply a good-luck sign to ward off the evil eye. Whatever the truth, there she stands, a pagan 'hag on the wall', and, passing beneath her gaze on the road, you enter another mystical area, the outdoor church of the Burren. Co. Clare may not have any great high mountains, but it has cliffs and prehistory and flowers enough for anyone, and at the heart of the Burren (some have said that it is *the* heart) lies Mullaghmore, a great hump of stone, the layering of the rock clearly visible from the north. The name is the English version of *Mullach Mhór* (Great Summit) and all about Mullaghmore is an area of peace and tranquillity, of narrow lanes and drystone walls and thorn hedges.

If you look at the map you'll see that Clare, like much of the west of Ireland, is covered with a tightly-woven web of roads and lanes. Cycling around Corrofin a few years back, it struck me that there were more roads here than anywhere else I had been. I read later that many of them had been built during the Potato Famine as 'relief' roads. They were not particularly necessary, but it was felt that to give the Irish bread without work would make them feckless. So it was thought far better to employ them on road-building projects that went nowhere than give them money for nothing. This was in spite of the fact that money from the land was flowing out of the country, while the people who had once owned that land were starving to death. Forcing them to work on the road schemes meant that, whatever time they should have spent tending the poor bit of land they had, was spent breaking stones for the few pence afforded by relief.

The Famine, or the 'Great Hunger' as it is sometimes called, is embedded in the Irish psyche like a rock in a blackthorn root; it has left a deep scar in the soul of the Irish that may never fade. The failure of the potato crop, the only one the people could grow for themselves, over three successive years meant that there was literally nothing for them to eat. It has often been likened to the Holocaust and, in a way, it is a just comparison, in that the English Government had it in their power to alleviate the sufferings of the peasantry but failed to do so. While the Irish were dying in their hundreds of thousands, English ships were carrying Irish corn overseas and there were cattle fattening in Irish fields for landlords that were often absentees. Food was plentiful in the nearby markets, while the people of Skibbereen were dying like rats in their hundreds.

My great-grandmother was born not long after the Famine and remembered the tales of the old people from her childhood, stories of women crawling through ditches looking for snails and grubs, and men dead at the side of the road, their mouths rimed with the green foam of grass that they had been trying to eat. The only time I ever remember her flying into a terrible rage was once when I wouldn't eat some food she had prepared for me, and the look on her face that day was frightening.

Records are notoriously unreliable but, at a conservative estimate, more than two million people died of starvation and disease and as many more emigrated, leaving on the infamous 'coffin ships', not knowing whether they'd reach America alive or dead. Those who did reach America were often so weak and exhausted that they died in the very act of crawling up the beach from the ships. At the mouth of the St Lawrence River there stands a monument to the thousands who reached the promised land, only to die on its shores. The population of Ireland halved in a handful of years, and the plight of those that remained was terrible. The story is told brilliantly and dispassionately in Cecil Woodham-Smith's book, *The Great Hunger*. It is a sorry tale of tight-lipped and stone-faced English bureaucracy and the total inability of the Government to cope either with the scale of the disaster or its underlying cause of landlordism.

There is a famine road running under the southern slopes of Mullaghmore, and one glorious Sunday afternoon in late October I made my way down a quiet lane past a neat whitewashed farm and along an overhung *bohareen* that would take me out into open country and on to the famine road. As I wandered along between the high hedges of the lane I met an elderly man gathering firewood.

'Where are you from?' he asked.

'England,' I answered.

'I have a daughter in Gloucester, a nurse,' he said. 'I've been over there to see her. 'Tis awful noisy in England.'

I agreed that it was indeed, compared to Clare, and that he must enjoy the peace and quiet of his own little spot. He laughed and said that nothing on earth would make him move from there.

The sheela-na-gig at Killinaboy

I followed the green tunnel for a short while until it opened out on scrubland and limestone and, picking my way along the remains of the road, I saw the terraced flanks of Mullaghmore ahead of me, shining like bright polished bone in the sun. The famine road crosses an expanse of limestone pavement before losing itself in shrub but its course is still plain to see, marked by the piles of cleared stones that edge it. As I drew near the base of the hill, a pair of horses came racing out of the distance: it was beautiful to see them so free and wild in the bright sun. They galloped towards me, stopping only a couple of yards away, snorting and stamping the ground and tossing their heads. The limestone pavement ended at a low thorn-covered wall that led me under the hill where I began climbing through bushes and

briars and over limestone shelves that were similar to the benches of west Cork, though these were dry and warm and filled with flowers.

A wet Irish summer had given way to a glorious Indian summer and it was ridiculously hot for late October. I was climbing in T-shirt and shorts, where a few months earlier, in July, I'd been dressed for winter storms. Terraces of limestone that gave good scrambling led me up the bare bones of the mountain, and here harebells and ox-eye daisies were still in flower, alongside clusters of herb Robert that peeped from the slots and crannies of the rock. I climbed the last of the terraces onto the shoulder of the hill and onto the smaller summit of *Sliabh Rua* (the Red Hill). The air was shimmering and there was a definite sense of magic about the place; I felt that I was somewhere very spiritual and very important. It was something to do with the view, I suppose; a great moonscape of stone, the colour of old bone, rolled away beneath me, to melt into the soft warm light of an autumn afternoon. In the distance, not a house, not a sign of man to be seen, just stone and shrubs and beech thickets and a spattering of loughs and reedbeds. I was reminded of Micho Russell's saying: 'What fills the eye fills the heart.' I clambered back onto Mullaghmore and sat in the autumn sun. There were birds calling far below in the stands of beech that are clustered round the foot of the mountain, and away in the distance I could see two men working sheep with their dogs.

Not a breath stirred and as I sat on the sweet turf on the hilltop it seemed crazy to think that anybody would be soulless enough to want to turn this area into a theme park. Yet that was very much what the Office of Public Works wanted to do here, build a massive coach and car park and Interpretive Centre

Mullaghmore, the beating stone heart of the Burren

directly under Mullaghmore, the very soul of the Burren. There was terrific opposition and a local group of people formed the Burren Action Group, mortgaging their homes and devoting hours to fighting the faceless bureaucrats in Dublin who thought it a grand idea to destroy an area of stillness and majesty. There were concerts and fundraising walks, and people from all over the world wrote in support. After a similar scheme had been dropped in the Wicklow Mountains, the Mullaghmore scheme was abandoned – for the time at least – and, although the Burren has been reprieved, the future is in no way certain. I would argue that there are some places that are of such importance in terms of world landscape sites that they should be left entirely alone and the Burren is one of them. If people have to have an Interpretive Centre, then let them build it in Corrofin or Kilfenora, in an established village, not in the very beating heart of the land. Let people come here but let them walk, let them find their own way and not be led around by the nose by some bored tour-coach driver.

There will come the day when I won't be able to get up the mountains I once scrambled over, and when that day comes then I hope I'll be generous enough to leave them for those that can. I don't want you building cable cars up hills, or roads into the mountains just so that I can make a quick trip in and go back with my 'seen it done it and this is the T-shirt' T-shirt on. A little boy once said, 'An architect is a man who doesn't like fields.'

In the same way, there are people who have so little soul that they can look at somewhere like Mullaghmore and see it simply as a source of revenue. It's the gombeen mentality all over again.

I sat in the sunlight, musing on the way people fail to see that by developing a place they actually destroy the reason for people going there in the first instance, but I found that the thoughts were depressing me so I made my way off the hill. It was harder finding the way down the terraces and meant a bit of fro-ing and to-ing and scrambling and threading my way through thick beech coppices, but I arrived at the road and made my way back to the car just as the light was dropping. Beyond the still waters of *Lough Gealáin*, the mountain lay quiet in the last of the day. I called at the home of P.J.Curtis, the record producer and broadcaster, on my way back to my B&B and we sat and nattered over a cup of tea in the house his family have lived in for centuries. Across the way lie the forge his father worked when he was the blacksmith of Killinaboy and the old village school, now empty, that must have echoed to the chatter of long-stilled voices. That night, Michael Coyne, the piper, took me to a pub at a country crossroads; here old farmers, in Sunday-best suits and caps, danced the sets with shiny-faced women, and nobody seemed to know what a clock was. When we came out into the cool, still darkness, a low moon hung over the Burren, and I swear that, though the music from the pub was still ringing in my ears, there was another music too. The stone was singing.

17 The Cliffs of Moher

Waves that left America roll up the base
Of these hung tapestries of stone,
Voices from the coffin ships mutter
And thunder at their base
Beating the drums of under-sea jungles.
The Author, *The Cliffs of Moher*

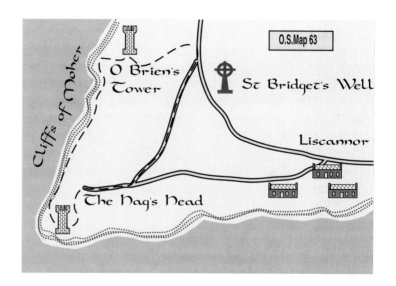

A few years back, I stayed at the Aberdeen Arms in Lahinch and, walking around the Burren and the Cliffs of Moher having myself a good time, I tried to convince everybody that it was really work. Michael Vaughan kept the hotel in those days, a wry man with a great sense of humour and a bottomless barrel of stories. He was once approached by an American tourist who was quite puzzled by the laid-back approach to things in the west of Ireland.

'Do you have any word in Irish like *mañana*? asked the Yank.

'We do, but it doesn't have quite the same sense of urgency,' Michael replied.

The Cliffs of Moher have been a tourist attraction since the early nineteenth century when Cornelius O'Brien, son of Turlough O' Brien, the MP for Clare, built himself a tower on the cliff edge with a stone table and chairs that were fixed to the rock by chains and bolts. (I can only assume that this was to prevent Fenians from hurling them over the cliff edge.) This was the same Corney O'Brien who used ropes to lower his goats on to

Goat Island for pasturage, giving the island its name; he also had a monument erected to himself in the nearby village of Derreen,

Looking north along the cliffs to O'Brien's Tower

four years before he died, praising his compassion and warmth and hard work in the interest of his tenants. The inscription on the monument doesn't point out that the money to build it was raised by forcible subscription levied from the same tenants. The stone chairs and tables are gone now, but O'Brien's tower still stands at the highest point in the cliffs, seven hundred feet above the rollers. Close by to the north is the place named *Aillenasharragh*, (the Cliff of the Foals). Legend tells us that after St Patrick had converted Ireland to Christianity and had driven out the last remains of Druidism, the Túatha Dé Danaan, using their magic powers, turned themselves into horses. They galloped off to some far away caves and there they remained for centuries. One morning, seven foals born to the horses came out of the cave and were so startled by the bright sunlight after their life in the underworld that they panicked and galloped over the cliffs into the sea.

The name, Moher comes from *Mothar Ui Ruis* (O'Ruan's Ruined Fort) and commemorates the ruined promontory fort that used to stand at the Hag's Head, further south. The fort was built sometime between 500 BC and AD 500, but it was demolished in 1808 when there were fears of a Napoleonic invasion, the stones being used to build the signal tower that stands there now. (The James Joyce Martello Tower, just outside Dublin, dates from the same period.) I've walked the cliffs many times, in fair weather and foul, and they are truly impressive. One winter's day, the winds were so fierce that it would have been crazy to have gone within a dozen yards of the cliff edge without being tied onto something. I clung onto the low wall near the car park and peeked out over the stone lip. Below, even the fulmars were staying home, grounded by the gale. I watched

Offerings on the walls of the well house at St Bridget's Well

as a young man swung a leg over the wall and walked to the edge. He was only six feet from the overhang when a gust of wind picked him up and threw him straight back over the wall. He was lucky that particular gust had come from the west, since the winds were swirling about that day. He was in his car and gone before I'd peeled my fingers from the slab. On summer days, particularly during the high tourist season, there can be just too many people on the cliffs to make it a pleasure, although if you walk more than a donkey's spit from the car park, you'll often find yourself leaving the crowds behind, even in high summer. But in general, spring and autumn are the best times to visit Moher. In late spring, the flowers are coming into their best and, if you're lucky, the ever-present wind off the Atlantic might have

The Cliffs of Moher

dulled to a gentle breeze and you'll have time to ramble and look around.

One day in late summer I arrived at the Cliffs in the mid afternoon as people were beginning to pack up their picnic things and head for home. I loaded up the rucksack and set off south along the cliff path from the car park, leaving the crowds behind. The footpath is edged for much of its length by walls of Liscannor flags, with the distinct coils of fossilised worms giving them a *repousée* effect. The cliffs are constantly eroding, the hard flagstone of the middle layers give way to soft shales on the cliff top which are undercut by rain and the lashing gales of winter, so that sections of path and flag wall are washed away into the sea each year. I kept well back from the edge as I walked, and a warm breeze blew in off the sea, tossing the fulmars about on the updraught.

I lay on my belly to try to get some shots of the seabirds nestling on the Cliff of the Gulls, but it was hard work. The things wouldn't keep still and in the dark shadows of the cliff face it was hard to get a light reading on them. Thousands of sea birds colonise these cliffs in the summer – razorbills, black-backed gulls, kittiwakes, herring gulls, puffins and shags as well as the ubiquitous fulmar. Like the Burren, the Cliffs have a unique eco-system, with arctic-alpine plants growing side by side with more temperate plants, and ocean-going seabirds hunting alongside peregrine falcons and choughs.

On the cliff top the light was beautiful and the sun was warm enough for me to lie out lazily in a bed of scurvy grass and sea pinks. Scurvy grass isn't, in fact, a grass but it does have a connection with scurvy. In centuries past, it was taken on board ship by sailors who ate it to combat the scurvy they suffered from through lack of Vitamin C. Growing close by the flagged wall was kidney vetch, yarrow and the pale pink lousewort; in the space of a few yards on the Cliffs of Moher you can find dozens of species of flowers and plants from early purple orchids to angelica. The late Tony Whilde, a local botanist, claimed that the cliffs have never fully been mapped and surveyed botanically and that there may be other species yet to be discovered, although you'd have to be brave enough to hang off a long rope since many of them lie well out of normal sight on the sheer cliff face.

I ambled on, taking it nice and slow. As an Irishman long ago once said, 'What's your hurry? When God made time He made plenty of it.' No one would want to rush an afternoon like this. Down below, waves were crashing over Donal's Rock, a partially submerged rock that could rip the bottom out of any boat unlucky enough to come against it, and also over *Branaunbeg* (The Little Stack), an isolated sea stack close by the cliff. At Malmore there is a disused quarry with abandoned flagstones stacked on pallets still waiting for the lorry that will never come now to collect them. Liscannor flags were transported as far away as England where they were used as paving stones and for the floor of the Royal Mint. The cliff-top quarries are all unused now though Liscannor flags are still quarried further inland, five hundred men were employed here in the last century.

As the sun moved westward I came to the Hag's Head, *Cean Caileach*. The Head is supposed to look like an old woman, and from some angles it does, although another legend has it that the Hag or Witch, Mal, was chasing Cúchulainn across Loop Head when he leaped on to a rock twenty-five feet offshore. The Hag attempted the leap, fell into the sea and drowned, and her body was washed up later at the Hag's Head giving it its present name.

Loop Head itself was originally known as *Léim Cú gCulainn* (Cúchulainn's Leap) and was changed to Loop Head by the Danes.

From the Hag's Head I followed an old quarry road to Kilcormel and then wandered along lovely back lanes to my starting point. You could, if you wanted, make a longer day of it by walking north from the Hag's Head to the main coast road, visiting O'Brien's Monument and St Bridget's Well en route. St Brigid, the Christianised version of the Celtic goddess, Brid, has wells named after her all over Ireland, while in England we commemorate her in the many Bridestones to be found scattered across the northern uplands. The well was originally visited mostly at the time of Lughnasa, the Celtic harvest festival, but now people come here all year round. The well is in an open garden with a glass-encased Madonna and Child. A stone door leads you into the well house (built by Corney O'Brien, the man himself, in gratitude for some miraculous cure he attributed to the holy well), at the end of which is a stone trough where the holy water runs. Along the walls are sacred pictures, statues, walking sticks, rags and photographs, all left behind by worshippers. When I went there first I was dubious about drinking the water, and even more dubious when I saw that beyond the well there is a long-established graveyard. The phrase, 'This water's got somebody in it' thus takes on a whole new meaning.

18 Black Head

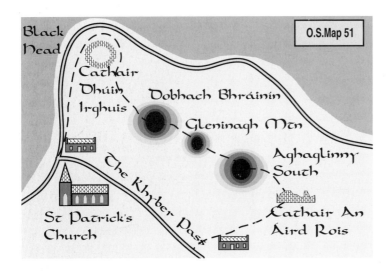

Walking in the Ballyvaghan area one summer, I arrived at Rusheen Lodge, the little B&B that was to be my home for the night, just as the last fire of a sunset, which had brought people out onto their doorsteps all along the coast, was dying in the clouds of the west. In front of the lodge was a lovely garden and, sitting washing its face on the doorstep in the last shaft of sunshine, was a big cat. I asked John McGann, the owner of the B&B, how old it was. 'Thirty,' he said. I reckoned that made it the oldest cat in Ireland and yet the moggy looked as fit and well

as a cat a third his age. 'What is the secret of its long life?' I asked John. 'It's probably something to do with its not dying,' was the answer I should really have known was coming all along. Later that night, planning the walk I was to make the next day, I noticed from the map that the narrow strip of land between the road and the coast west of Ballyvaghan is designated as a Gaeltacht – an Irish-speaking area. 'You won't find many Irish speakers round here now,' John told me. 'My father and uncles were all Irish speakers. But my generation packed their suitcases and went to England to work and left their language behind.' After thirty years in the building trade 'over the water', John had come back to Ballyvaghan to run the bed and breakfast and look after Ireland's oldest cat.

Next morning at breakfast I showed John a picture of a stone head I had come across while researching the Burren. A crude but powerful image, it stared out of the picture with a savage beauty. 'I'd like to get a shot of this head if I can but the book doesn't give any indication of where it's to be found,' I told him.

'Go down to the paper shop,' he said. 'Your man there, John O' Loclainn, knows everything there is to know about the area.'

O' Loclainn's was dark and comfortable and, typical of so many shop/bars in Ireland, had a paper shop at one end of the counter and a bar at the other. John himself was counting newspapers and pulling pints at the same time, because, although it was only ten o'clock in the morning, there was a customer with

O'Lochalinn's newsagents/bar in Ballyvaghan

a pint of Guinness in front of him. This was Seán, an elderly man wearing a tweed cap, with a face that looked as though it had seen a great deal of weather in its time; he was the last native Irish speaker in Ballyvaghan. I came out with my '*Cupla focal Gaelge*' (a few words of Gaelic) which I was quite pleased with, though I'm sure it must have sounded pretty poor to Seán. Once I had got past the weather and my name, I had to admit that I had only a little Irish.

John O' Loclainn told me that the head I was looking for was the one I had heard about on the radio news just the previous day. It had been stolen from one of the chapels of the Burren by some form of pond life on legs, and the rumour was that, like the head of *Crom Dubh* at Faha and a sheela-na-gig that had similarly been looted in Tipperary, it had already been shipped out to an antique dealer in Germany or Holland. A curse on the lot of them. I thanked John, said '*Slán go fóil*' (Goodbye for now), to Seán and set off for a day's walking on Black Head.

The northernmost tip of the Burren, Black Head (*Ceann Boirne*) juts out into the Atlantic north-west of Ballyvaghan. Tim Robinson has published a superb map of the Burren with all the sites of antiquity and mythology so well marked that you are conscious when using the map that you are walking not just through a landscape but a mindscape or soulscape too. Old green lanes, ruined chapels and holy wells thread and cluster on the landscape, calling you out to walk amongst them. One such green lane leads north from Fanore, following the curve of Black Head well above the modern motor road. From the green lane it is possible to strike up to the old fort of *Cathair Dhuin Irghuis* and from there the limestone stretches for miles. I could follow whatever path I chose. It looked set for a fair day, so I bought some bread and cheese and drinks and drove to Fanore. I left the car at St Patrick's Church, pulled on the rucksack and set off along the road towards the green lane. An old farmer, leaning on his cottage gate, waved as I passed.

'Do you think the weather will stay fair for the day?' I asked. 'I'm off up onto the mountain and could do with a bit of good weather for the walk.'

'Ah, sure, hasn't the weather been terrible through the last weeks; sure there must be something the matter with it. Everything's changed. We used to have snow in winter and we hardly get any now and the summers are nothing but rain and wind.' It was a complaint I'd heard not just all over Ireland that year, but from the farmers of the Yorkshire Dales, the Sherpas of Nepal and the porters of Baltistan. All of them had looked at the sky and said, 'There's something up with the weather,' and I'm not sure whether this is just a typical farmer's moan or a more serious indication of global warming.

The old green road left the tarmac at the end of a lane and followed the contour of the hill north. Crumbling walls lined the way of what was almost certainly a prehistoric road, now long disused but full of the most beautiful wild flowers – harebells, bloody cranesbill, mountain avens, Irish eyebright in vast mats, thyme, ox-eye daisies, scabious, herb Robert, convolvulus and many more, the names of which were beyond me. It took a long time to walk the road because of all the photographs I took, and the sheep watched, greatly amused I'm sure, as I crawled around on my belly with my camera.

The lane curves round the headland above a lighthouse to meet up with the main coast road. I left it where it turns to the east and, crossing open country and limestone pavements,

The Limestone Rock

scrambled up an outcrop onto a giant's staircase of limestone cliffs and slopes that brought me eventually to the promontory fort of *Cathair Dhuin Irghuis*. From the outside, much of the wall seems to be in fair order still. Inside, though, all is ruin. It must have commanded a good military position in its day, for from this stone shoulder you can see half of County Clare and a good deal of County Galway. Even on this hazy summer day, I could see the Cliffs of Moher to the south, and Spiddle, the Twelve Bens and the Maumturk Mountains far away across Galway Bay. There were cairns standing on the shoulders of the hill and it struck me that one explanation for these cairns, which appear all over the western hill country of Ireland and Britain, is that they were possibly boundary markers and look-out positions, from which the men on guard could watch for hostile incomers. From the fort (646ft) to *Dobrach Bhráinín*, the first of the summits of Gleninagh Mountain, was another climb by a series of 'steps', some of them good scrambles. On the summit of *Dobrach Bráinín* stands a huge artificial stone mound, and though there is nothing on the map or in the guide books to say so, I'd bet a gallon of Guinness it is a chieftain's grave.

A light cloud had rolled in from the west by now, though breaks in the cover sent flashes of light scudding across the land. The second peak of Gleninagh Mountain, Aghaglinny South, is capped by a huge, dark, peaty mound and to get there meant dropping by more limestone steps to the rocky saddle. There was a massive collapsed cave to my right, and wild goats were rutting on its rim as I dropped down past it. I was glad that my children weren't little again and there with me, asking me those wonderfully awkward questions of childhood.

'What's happening, Daddy?'

'Well, the little goat is sick and the big one is pushing it to hospital'.

It was warm enough to sit for a while on Aghaglinny reading the map and eating lunch. But the clouds were closing in and becoming more threatening, and a cool breeze was sweeping the tops, so I hit off across the plateau, going south on a compass bearing. I crossed rough ground with a network of grikes that were concealed by grass and shrub, dangerous enough if you were to slip down one and snap your ankle. It is no wonder that the land hereabouts was famous for its bone-setters; they must

Harebells at the side of the green lane

have been in fair demand. Eventually, as the light was failing, I came to another old green road that brought me to *Cathair an Aird Rois* – a corruption of *Caher an Aird Durrish*, the Fort of the High Door. The map refers to a ruined chapel and the remains of a shebeen. The shebeen or drinking house was a place of refuge and a place where *potheen* was sold. It reminded me greatly of places I have seen in Zanskar and Ladakh in the Himalaya, where there are high 'shebeens' with rubble walls and earth floors and the smoke finds its way out through the roof as best it can. I have sat in such places with ponymen and traders who were making their way across the mountains, their clothes smelling of mutton fat and smoke, our own bodies unwashed and grimy. Standing in the ruins of the Fort of the High Door, it struck me that, although the mountains here are nothing like the Himalaya, in many ways life in Ireland would have been fairly similar a hundred or more years ago.

The old road meets the 'blue tar' down by the Caher River, and follows what the map calls the 'Khyber Pass' back down to St Patrick's church. It was a pleasant walk by high hedges and small cottages. The threatened rain finally arrived, first filling the air with that strange electric smell as it slaked the dust, then lashing down in grey sheets that washed in off the sea like curtains. I made the car just as the worst of the storm hit me.

That night I stayed in Doolin, where the music in Gussy Connor's was great as usual. At the end of the night someone played 'The Limestone Rock', and sadly I remembered that it was one of Micho Russell's favourite tunes. He had been killed earlier in the year in a car crash. We will never see his like again.

Looking from Black Head to Connemara, the Maumturks and the Twelve Bens

County Galway – Connemara

Neither a map nor a text can do justice to the web of cross-references that Time, the old spider, has spun across the spaces of Connemara.

Tim Robinson, *Mapping South Connemara*

It would be a poor man who could not love Connemara. On a dark winter day, when the wet and the wild and the wind have taken over, there is a savagery and a sadness about the place. But on summer days, when there are only a few small, white, high clouds coming in from the west, then there seems more sky here than anywhere on earth. In an instant, there is something majestic and joyous in the fragmented coast and the great 2,000ft quartzite humps of the Twelve Bens and the Maumturks rising straight up from the coastal plain.

When 'Foxy' Reynolds, my old English master, took us through J.M Synge's writings he conjured up a vision of the west of Ireland that I am sure he hadn't intended. Romantic fool that I was, I thought the West was still peopled with old ladies in shawls smoking pipes, and old men with donkey-drawn carts full of turf while there was a *shebeen* at every crossroads full of fiddlers, dancers and singers. Connemara was my goal when I first came to Ireland more than thirty years ago and of course it was nothing at all like my imaginings. Notwithstanding, I fell in love with it then and the love hasn't diminished with the passing of time. Coming back again and again over the years, I've learned to understand how somebody like Padraic Pearse (himself half-Eng-lish) could come to love a country so much that he was prepared to die for it, to be taken and stood up against a wall in Kilmain-ham Jail and riddled with lead for 'a terrible beauty'.

Pearse had a cottage in Connemara where he would go to write. As a poet he wrote in both Irish and English, and his lovely poem *Mise Éire* he translated himself:

> *Mise Éire:*
> *Sine mé ná an Chailleach Bhéara.*
> *Mór mo ghleoir:*
> *Mee a rug Cú Chulainn cróga.*
> *Meor mo náir:*
> *Mo chlann féin a dhíol a máthair.*
> *Mise Éire:*
> *Uaignei mé ná an Chailleach Bhéara.*

> I am Ireland:
> I am older than the Old Woman of Beare.
> Great my glory:
> I that bore Cúchulainn the valiant.
> Great my shame:
> My own children that sold their mother.
> I am Ireland:
> I am lonlier than the Old Woman of Beare.

Connemara Cradle Song

The name Connemara comes from *Conmaicnemara* (the tribe of Cormac by the sea) and the land of Cormac's kingdom covers all that country that runs south of Killary Harbour to the outskirts of Galway City and westwards from the shores of Lough Corrib to the ocean. It is a land of high mountains and great boglands, of filigree coasts and low-lying sea plains studded with hundreds of lakes. Because of the poor nature of the land, life has always been a battle here and yet the people are warm and hospitable and have held onto their language more tenaciously than anywhere else in Ireland and Connemara has the largest of all the Gaeltachts.

The towns of Clifden and Roundstone are good places to base yourself for a walking holiday. You can find good bed and breakfast accommodation, excellent restaurants and fine traditional music in both places, and if you want to buy a *bodhran* and learn to play it properly (without a pen-knife) then Malachi Kearne's workshop in Roundstone is the very place.

The paintings of Paul Henry, Charles Lamb and Jack B. Yeats convey better than any words or photographs of mine the light and colours of Connemara, the breadth of sky, the rich, wet light and the way the land and the sea and the air seem to flow together. And walking through a landscape is better than any photograph or painting, better than any dry words on a dry page.

There is great walking in Connemara whether you like scrambling in the high mountains or rambling along beaches by rock-pool and strand and even in high summer you will be able to find quiet spots where you will be alone with the wind and the sun and the cry of the curlew.

19 Errisbeg and Tin Whistle Bay

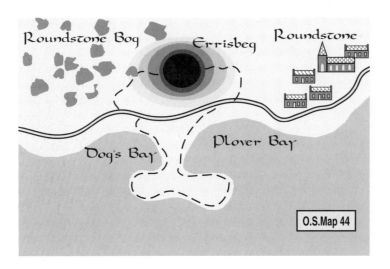

Roundstone Bog   Errisbeg   Roundstone

Dog's Bay   Plover Bay

O.S. Map 44

South of the Twelve Bens, the land reaches towards the sea; miles of low and level peat bog laced with lakes where, on certain soft days, the sky and the land meet and melt into each other without demarcation. The great peatlands of Roundstone Bog are amongst the last great raised boglands in Europe, a place of intense beauty and rare eco-systems. At the southern edge of the bog lies a gnawed coastline of sandy beaches and rocky bays – the only village is Roundstone with its tiny harbour, the only hill, the hump of Errisbeg. The name is an anglicisation of *Iorras Beag*: the dictionary gives *iorras* as headland

or peninsula and Errisbeg thus becomes the 'little headland', which seems a rather low key name for a fine hill.

The old maps have a dot just below the summit and alongside it the letters 'Mont'. Could this refer to a monument and could there at one time have been an oratory there, as on Errigal? The patron saint of Connemara fishermen, St Mac Dara, had an island SSE of Errisbeg across Bertraghboy Bay which still holds his finely built chapel. Might he also have had an oratory on the mountain? It would make more sense than calling the mountain after the headland. Just a thought.

Roundstone is a bonny cluster of houses with a fine hotel and a good music bar and though you are a long way from any big hills here, there are miles of lonely and lovely coastline to wander and, if the weather is glum, then there are far worst ways of spending your life than walking along a wild and windy beach.

Under Errisbeg lie the two bays of Dog's Bay (*Poll na Madrai*) and Plover Bay (*Pol na Feadóige*) Interestingly the word *feadóig* also means tin whistle or fife so the bay could in fact be named after a Spanish sailor from the Armada who was washed ashore clinging on to a tin whistle, but that would be *Poll Na Spáineach le Feadóige*. However, I digress. There is a lovely short walk that follows the coastline around the tombolo taking in both bays. I was directed this way first by Tim Robinson – *fear na mappa* (the Man of the Maps) – who has his studio in Roundstone. Tim is a Yorkshireman who left Cambridge with a degree in mathe-

Errisbeg under a cap of cloud seen across Tinwhistle Bay, sea thrift the only colour to brighten a threatening day

matics and, after various jobs and wanderings which included working as a teacher and artist in Istanbul and Vienna and exhibiting his own paintings in London, ended up on the Aran Islands off the coast of Connemara in 1972. There he fell in love both with the landscape and the people, began to learn Irish – just as J.M Synge did all those years ago – and is now fluent.

One day feeling that he wanted to explore the island a little more than he had already, Tim asked for a map at the post office. When the postmistress told him there was none and Tim expressed his surprise, the postmistress suggested that he make one. And he did. His training as a mathematician and an artist was ideal for the job and having Irish added another dimension because he discovered that most of the place names that had been put on the only maps extant, by the British Ordnance Survey, were all bastardisations or mishearings or confusions. Round-stone, for example, doesn't mean a circular stone but the Rock of the Seals – *Cloch na Rón*. He also discovered the stories under the land, like the *Steip Na Peiler*, the stepping stones used by the *gardai* 'peelers' to try to catch the *potheen* makers in the parish of Cane. After miles of walking and countless conversations, the first map of the Aran Islands appeared. Since then, he has mapped the Burren and the whole of Connemara in a similar way, and has written several books – *Setting Foot on the Shores of Connemara, Mapping South Connemara* and *The Stones of Aran*. His maps are truly wonderful. Gerard Manley Hopkins coined the word 'inscape' to describe that inner mystical land-scape that is much more than mere names and contours. Tim's maps get closer to that feeling of inscape than any I have seen.

One wild spring day when it looked as though the sky really had fallen on Chicken Licken's head and had not bounced back up again, I ruled out any idea of climbing Errisbeg for the views since I would have seen the same things at 987 feet that I would have seen at sea level, mirk and more mirk. Instead, I threw a few things in the rucksack and set off for Tin Whistle Bay in a stiff wind under a slate-grey sky. It was one of those dour Connemara days that never lets up, with leaden Atlantic clouds rolling in off a sullen sea just 100 feet or so above the waves so that you feel as though you are walking under a very low ceiling. There was a small, miserable watery sun that fought its way pitifully through a crack in the clouds as I walked along the beach, the pinpricks of gold fingering their way through the great welt of cloud. Close by the shore the water was a beautiful turquoise, and the wind flung spume high over the rocks.

I followed the line of the coast south, Errisbeg coming and going under a sullen cap of cloud and the sandy beach melting into the failing light behind me. Fishermen in tiny boats were hand-hauling nets just offshore and they waved as I passed by. The grasslands above the wave-worn rocks were spattered with vetch and thyme, sea thistles, thrift and flag iris. Common spot-ted orchids, small and more densely coloured than any I have ever seen, peeped from amongst the scrubby grass. Many of the flowers were the kind you'd expect to find in bogland and I won-dered as I walked whether this would be what botanists call a holophytic bog? This kind of habitat is only found where raised bog meets the sea coast and the combination of salt sea spray and peat produces a singular mixture of bog and sea coast flora. Such a bog existed at Dunquin in the Dingle Peninsula until the Office of Public Works covered it with an Interpretive Centre.

As I rounded the Peninsula, the clouds decided to do their job, the rain pelted down and it was time for the waterproofs. Cows grunted at me as I climbed over what seemed to be the remains of old settlements, walled field systems and enclosures, and what looked like hut circles and shell middens. I had read that many of the prehistoric remains on this headland were uncovered by great storms in 1990 and I was very conscious as I walked that what I was looking at may have lain largely untouched by human hand for two thousand years. A hare started and leaped away, bounding into the distance. Irish hares are bigger than English hares: according to some know-alls, this is because the Irish hare is a different strain but I put it down to Guinness, bacon and cabbage. A pair of oyster catchers close by rose into the swirling air to drive off a gull that was threatening their nest, and on the shoreline sandpipers peeped and flicked and fluttered.

All around me was decay and renewal, that smell of the sea that means the beginning and ending of things. It is easy to see why the Celts had such a great belief in the importance of edges. The only things that didn't seem to be in a state of decay or renewal were the man-made jetsam, the plastic dayglo fishing floats and the nylon ropes and crates that the sea had spewed out onto the shore.

I followed the hook of land round to Dog's Bay but the rain was so bad that my glasses misted up on the inside and were covered with rain on the outside. I got a bit lost after I'd crossed the connecting spit of land and, half blind with spray and steamed-up glasses, I ended up having to climb over the churchyard cemetery wall to get back to the road, ripping a hole in the seat of my trousers in the process.

Later that year, in early autumn, I came back to Roundstone and spent a joyous late afternoon climbing Errisbeg from the south-west. I was on my way from Galway to Clifden along the coast road and, although the weather had been dull and glum as I left the city, the sky lightened as I headed west. As I came into Maam Cross the clouds were breaking, and by the time I reached Recess the sky had cleared completely and it looked as though the day was going out in a burst of brass.

It was almost four o'clock when I reached the old quarry on the road west of Roundstone, but I had a flask and a few hours of daylight to spend with every prospect of good light on the tops. I went through the old gate and, following my nose, climbed steadily towards the rocky hump of Errisbeg. My route brought me shortly to what looks like a natural mountain lake but is, in fact, a man-made reservoir whose waters were once used for some long-ceased mining operation. Not a breath stirred and I was alone except for the odd crow and sheep. It is at times like this that I realise how much noise and clamour we all have to put up with in our lives and how lucky I was to be alone on an Irish hillside on a golden autumn afternoon – no telephones, no traffic fumes, just the birds and sheep and a soft warm breeze blowing in off the sea.

Errisbeg has not always been a place of such peace and quiet contemplation. Letterdyfe House, north of Roundstone, was at one time the home of the Robinsons (nothing to do with Tim), agents for various Connemara landlords responsible for many grievous evictions. During the Land Wars of the 1880s, after years of bullying and 'ethnic cleansing' by the agents, local people drove the Robinson cattle over the cliffs of Errisbeg in retribution.

The land rose ahead of me and I scrambled through a series of gullies and over several false summits until I came to the old trig point that marks the summit of Errisbeg. From there I cut across

The summit cairn of Errisbeg backlit in the evening sun

to another peak that was topped with a conical cairn. A haze softened the light and smoothed out the features of the land below, although I could see Tin Whistle Bay clear enough, and the smudge of Slyne Head far to the west. There are several rocky summits on the top of Errisbeg and from the most northerly one there is the best view you will ever get of the whole of Roundstone bog, while further off to the north east are the Twelve Bens. West towards Clifden lies the Derrigimlagh bogland where Marconi opened his telegraph station in 1907. It was from here that he broadcast the first wireless telegraph messages accross the Atlantic to Nova Scotia. Not far away, a huge, carved limestone wing planted on the bog commemorates the crash-

landing place of Alcock and Brown who, in 1919, became the first men to fly across the Atlantic.

I wandered around for a while looking at the pools of peaty water that dot the summit of Errisbeg. It is said that if you wash your hair in this cold mountain-top water, it will go white instantaneously. Since I have been going grey at the temples recently (which my mother insists looks 'extinguished'), I decided to give it a miss and began my journey down. As the Robinson cattle found out, there are a few cliffs on Errisbeg and, though in good weather the hill is perfectly safe, in poor weather you would need to take care because some of the faces are well hidden.

As I scrambled down an easy gully between the cliffs, I could see Roundstone far below and away to my left. I had reasoned, before setting out, that rather than retracing my steps or cutting over to the north, I would be able to drop towards Roundstone and follow a *bohareen*, that I could see now just below me, to the road, and from there I could hitch back to the car. But the best laid plans of this mouse and man ganged very much aglé. I sat for half an hour at the stone bridge at the end of the *bohareen* trying to hitch a lift, but, for the first time in Ireland, I had no luck. Either I had become invisible or people were just in too much of a hurry to get home. But what matter, I had a fairly long but pleasant road walk back to the car as the west-bound sun washed the flanks of Errisbeg with a soft crimson light. Later, as I made my way over to Clifden by the old coast road, where the air is so bracing they call it the 'Brandy and Soda Road', I stopped to watch the sun sink into the Atlantic, a dusty brass ball laying long reflections across the salt pools and low bars of Ballyconneely Bay.

A Connemara pony on the flanks of Errisbeg, evening coming in

20 Derryclare by the Devil's Staircase

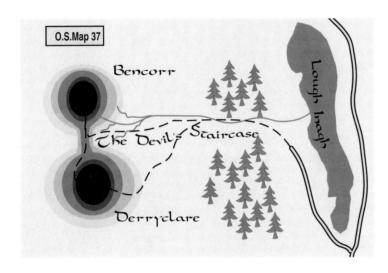

O.S.Map 37

Bencorr

Lough Inagh

The Devil's Staircase

Derryclare

It's not often I disbelieve someone, particularly a mountain man like Joss Lynam, general editor of the *Irish Walks* guides, but when he pointed towards the Devil's Staircase and said that we were going to climb that way out of *Log an Choire Mhóir* (the Lake of the Big Corrie) and on to Derryclare, I remember muttering something about 'bloody mountain goats' and wondering about my walking partner's sense of judgement. In the event of course Joss was right, the gully, though it looks formidable, is a safe and easy scramble on to the Twelve Bens (*Na Beanna Beola*).

I had met Joss a few years before at a mountaineering conference across the water in Buxton and had asked him what his favourite walking country was in Ireland. 'The Twelve Bens of Connemara', he answered without hesitation, so one summer, when I found myself in Ireland for a few days' unexpected holiday, I phoned Joss and arranged to meet him at Ballynahinch to spend a day walking in what so many maps mistakenly call 'The Twelve Pins'. Ballynahinch, by the way, is the wettest place in Ireland. In 1923 it rained on 309 days.

Once described as 'the father of Irish mountaineering', Joss probably knows more about the hills of Ireland than anybody else, though his climbing isn't limited to his own country. He has climbed extensively in Britain, the Alps and the Himalaya, and anything he writes about the mountains is well worth reading. He is a civil engineer by profession, and when we walked together that summer he had just returned from the island of Skellig Michael off the coast of Kerry; there he had been supervising conservation work on the ancient beehive huts and the sheer paths and stone stairs of that monkish and mystical barren rock out in the Atlantic. I had spent a day there filming a few years before and had been greatly moved by that bare rock stack with its vertical cliffs and dizzying paths. I had wondered, at the time, how the monastic settlement with its beehive huts had managed to survive there at all, yet they lived and worshipped on that bare rock from the sixth to the ninth century when the Vikings 'cut the foundation to the bone'. When I asked Joss about it, he told me that the soil was brought across eight miles of turbulent sea from the mainland in the monks' own *curraghs*, and the fields in which they grew their crops and on which they fed their goats were all made from that soil which they tilled with seaweed, sand and manure. They lived on a diet of fish and goats' milk and spent their lives on the wildest edge of Europe in prayer and meditation, much as Buddhist monks do in the rocky fastnesses of the Himalaya to this day.

It was a wild day when we set out for the hill from Bally-nahinch. Weeks of gale-force winds and summer rain had left the whole of the West sodden and glistening. But today the cloud had climbed clear of the mountain tops, and it looked as though it was set fair to stay that way for a while.

We parked the car by Lough Inagh and set off through the forestry towards the combe. The way through the woods is a forest ride and, as we rambled on, I grumbled about Sitka spruce and blanket afforestation and how I wished people would plant more deciduous hardwoods like oak and beech. Joss told me I was an old romantic with no business sense and I agreed. We left the forest behind and climbed into the mountain combe, the stiff breeze keeping the temperature down and cooling us off as we gained height. As we travelled further into the combe I saw ahead of me what seemed like a sheer and impassable wall of grey quartzite.

'Which way now?' I asked, and Joss pointed at the Devil's Staircase. Old Nick gets blamed for a lot of things in Ireland: the Devil's Mother looms above Killary Harbour, he has a Punch-bowl under Mangerton and his Ladder is a good way of getting up and on to Carrauntuohil. All in all, he's been a busy boyo in the Irish mountains.

I see the Devil simply as a folklore figure now, a corruption (in the horns and pointed-tail sense) of older pagan gods like Cer-nunnos, but there was a time when he was a very real person to me. My Irish grandmother had a major mission in life, which was to put the fear of God into me – as though I were some kind of empty vessel into which she would pour 'fear of God' from a big jug. Part of this mission meant filling my growing mind with stories about banshees and curses and Old Nick. In her rock-solid faith, she saw the Devil as a real and powerful spirit, the father of Lies. I used to lie awake on stormy nights, terrified by all the sounds in the house, hearing, in every rattle and creak, the claw scrapings and footprints of Satan himself coming for me. She further terrified me by telling me that the Devil was a mas-ter of disguises and often appeared as a mortal with his horns hidden under a bowler hat, his hoofs in a pair of shoes and his tail tucked away in his trousers. One dark November night a col-lector that I had never seen before from the Prudential Insurance Company called at our house. I opened the door to his knock-ing and saw a sinister-looking man in a bowler hat caught in the light from the hall. I suppose until the day he died he never understood why a seven-year-old boy started screaming and then ran back into the house, only to come out again holding a crucifix and to drench him with a bottle of holy water. 'He's an imaginative child', was all my grandmother said by way of explanation when she came out to give him the money.

I looked at the Devil's Staircase, hitched up my rucksack and plodded on behind Joss, still wondering whether there was

The spatter of the lakes and tarns of Connemara seen from the summit of Derryclare

something I should know about him that nobody in the Irish climbing world had told me yet – stuff to do with full moons and hairs on the face. But, as I said at the beginning, it was a tough but safe scramble to the top. In fact, I was quite proud of myself because I reached the saddle well ahead of Joss who was somewhat out of breath, puffing and wheezing like a steam engine by the time he reached me. From the top of the Staircase we headed up Bencorr (*Binn Chorr*) just to say we'd done it, and then doubled back to the saddle where we found some shelter and ate our lunch. A fierce wind was threatening to tear our skin off, hurtling thick clouds in from the west, through which sudden slender shafts of sunlight swept over the darkened land like searchlights. Across the valley, the Maumturks were coming and going from view under a belt of rain: we could see a constant rainbow over *Binn Chaonaigh*, for the cloud was fragmenting regularly in one spot now to let through a single slab of light. It was one of those beautiful and wild Connemara summer days when you feel as though you are on the very edge of things.

It was too blustery to linger long, so we set off for the summit of Derryclare, an easy ramble along a broad arête, though the high wind meant we had to lean forward into the wind and push hard until we were almost clawing our way through solid air. At the summit cairn we met another mountaineer with a coil of rope, and a young boy whom he had brought out onto the mountains for his first climb. What an introduction to the hills – Derryclare on a day like this! Below us, Connemara stretched out towards the Atlantic, an endless spatter of lakes and tarns in a sea of bogland and black clouds, with slashes of light coming in off the sea.

Rather than retrace our footsteps, we decided to descend the

Joss Lynam on the summit of Derryclare

mountain by a broad shoulder that led south to easier ground from where we could cut back eastwards to our starting point. So we dropped below the summit and began a gradual and graceless descent back to the Inagh valley. The quartzite rocks of the Bens are covered with a thin layer of slime that makes them more treacherous than ice when wet. I lost count of the number of times I ended up on my backside. Every couple of minutes or so, my legs would shoot out from under me and a very creative string of curses would sail out into the wind, while Joss bent over double behind me, trying to laugh and get his breath back at the same time. Then, as sure as eggs come from hens, a couple of minutes later Joss himself would go flying – all of which made the descent interesting if slow and painful.

Back at the car Joss was concerned that he was so winded and tired and couldn't understand why he felt out of sorts; he normally runs up and down mountains like Derryclare without any problem. A few weeks later, he dropped me a line to say he'd found out why he had been so puffed. He'd gone for a check up and the doctor had whipped him into hospital and performed a heart by-pass operation. A few months later he was better than new, and out in the Himalaya, climbing with a team of Irish climbers, all over fifty. It must be the bacon and cabbage that makes Irish mountaineers such hard men.

21 A Walk in the Maumturks

The Maumturk Mountains (*Sléibht MhámTuirc* – Pass of the Wild Pig) lie in a line running south-east to north-west, across the Inagh valley from their bigger brothers, the Twelve Bens. Made from the same quartzite rock that gives the summits of the Bens their shimmering silvery appearance, they are every bit as wild and tough; classic high hill-walking country. There is a walk that covers the whole length of the Maumturks but it is a serious day's undertaking and requires transport at each end. It's a serious day, not just because of the length (twenty miles from Maum Cross to Leenaun) but because the terrain is difficult and the walk involves a fair amount of ascent and descent, including several steep and sheer faces. Added to this, there are few escape routes in poor weather. There are a number of shorter, circular walks you can take in the Maumturks, however, my favourite being the walk from Maumeen (*Mám Éan* – Pass of the Birds) north-west to *Loch Mhám Ochóige* (no easy translation). It takes in the highest of the Maumturk peaks and in good weather gives you a glorious day out.

One hazy summer's morning, Pat and I left the car at the side of the road near Illion, and followed the Western Way along the valley to Maumeen. Across Lehanagh Lough, Derryclare and Bencorr shone in the early morning sun, and beyond ourselves there was not a soul about. There was that great sense of space you get on clear days in Connemara, a breadth of sky and ahead of us silvery hills rising from the valley floor.

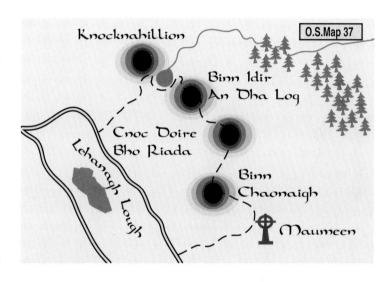

From Maumeen, we followed the old pilgrims' path to the pass and St Patrick's Well (*Tobar Paidraig*). Here there is an interesting modern statue of the saint and a Stations of the Cross that follows a round on the saddle of the pass. St Patrick slept here in a small cave (*Leabh Paidraig*) but, though he looked across the valley at the Twelve Bens, he vowed he would never set foot on them. Therefore, so legend has it, this is the furthest west that Patrick came in Connemara. There are various saints' beds throughout Ireland and for years I puzzled over why they should

Pat looking down into Glean Fada from the frost-shattered rocks of Binn Chaonaigh

be so important. Then I read that one of the main functions of the Celtic shaman (and, later, priest) was that by his dreaming he would foresee and prophesy events of great importance to the tribe. Thus, his *Leabh* was imbued with mystical powers. The chapel and well used to be the site of a special 'pattern' or pilgrimage (*pátrún* – patron saint) and each year people would gather to say the rosary and make the Stations of the Cross on the pass. It became associated with a great deal of *potheen* drinking, dancing, fiddle playing and faction fighting (though no one seems to have been much hurt and Steve MacDonogh suggests that it was perhaps more ritual fighting than real enmity) and the clergy banned it. It was revived a few years ago and now, much more soberly and decorously, it takes place every year.

The holy well on the pass at Maumeen was, in all probability, a sacred Celtic (and possibly pre-Celtic) site that was taken over by Patrick and his followers in their crusading drive across Ireland. Cleverly, the new religion took on the most important aspects of the old, assimilating and absorbing them, so that the sacred wells and mistletoe of the druids became the holy water font and the Christmas kissing decoration of the Christians. I do have one argument with the sculptors of the statues of St Patrick that you see all over Ireland. The majority of the older statues of the saint were destroyed during the Reformation, and it was not until the nineteenth century that the churches were able to replace them. When they did so, they got Italian statue-makers to churn out the St Patrick Mark One statue, showing the saint, hand raised in blessing, crozier in the other, and a full beard flowing over his robes. St Patrick, as a true product of the Roman Empire, would have been as clean shaven as Brutus, Nero or

The statue of St Patrick at the holy well

Julius Caesar. An end, I say, to all beards; let the statues be shaved clean and the record set straight.

The well holds the coldest, sweetest water you'll taste and, since it's the last you'll get on the Maumturks for a good while, you should fill up your bottle or your flask here. We left the pilgrim's path at Maumeen, where it begins its descent towards the Failmore River and the *Gleann Fhada* (the Long Glen) and struck up the hillside towards the first of the peaks we would be crossing that day, *Binn Chaonaigh* (Mossy Peak). We climbed slowly by quartzite slabs and outcrops in a sea of heather and rough sedge grass. The Atlantic winds make sure that only the hardy and tough can survive up here, although you might find the occasional wood violet, as we did. I thought it strange that a woodland flower could survive in these rough conditions, but I was told that the violet is a relic of the old forests that used to grow on these mountains. In fact, the hump we had climbed over just before St Patrick's Well is called *Cnoc Doire Bhéal an Mháma* (the Hill of the Wood at the Mouth of the Pass). Derryclare, across the valley, is an anglicisation of *Binn Dhoire Chláir* – the Mountain of the Oakwood of the Plain – so in years long gone there must have been a sizeable forest here. It was probably cleared by the landlords, like most of the great Irish forests.

The summit of *Binn Chaonaigh* is a broad and featureless jumble of fractured quartzite, capped by a cluster of cairns that is set in an ocean of white stone. From here you can see over to Lough Corrib, the whole of Connemara, the Twelve Bens and the Atlantic beyond. From the summit, a shoulder leads to a smaller peak, Binn Mhairg, and the views from there down into *Gleann Fhada* are wonderful. We sat there for a while in the lee of the wind. Bars of sunlight swept over the summit which, like *Binn*

Chaonaigh, is covered in chips of quartzite, frost-shattered and as blinding as a snowfield in the strong sunlight. Route-finding amongst that wasteland of fractured rock, is quite difficult, and we had a few false starts finding our way to the next peak, *Cnoc Doire Bhó Riada* (Peak of the Wood of the Tame Cow). The ridge below the summit, in particular, takes some finding: you have to walk west, looking for an easy gully that leads you down to the ridge, otherwise you are faced with a scramble over rough and tumbling scree with the prospect of an interesting roll into a steep-sided corrie to the east. With the new map (which I didn't have at the time), route-finding is much easier; all we had that day was the picturesque blue and yellow thing, which would have looked nice framed and hung on the wall, but was not much use in the high winds and confusing white wilderness of *Binn Chaonaigh*.

We had our lunch on the summit of the tame cow's little hill and then dropped steeply down to another saddle, before climbing just as steeply up to *Binn Idir an dá Log* (the Hill between two Hollows). This is the highest point in the Maumturks (2,307 ft) and from here you can see over to Killary Harbour and the Mweelrea Horseshoe. There was a strong wind so we didn't linger. All the ways off the summit looked bad. We chose the least of several evils, which meant traversing a quartzite ridge eastward, and then scrabbling down a great deal of bad scree that slid away before us continuously to the corrie lake of *Lough Mhám Ochóige*. I heard occasional mutterings of something that sounded like 'grounds for divorce', a phrase I seemed to remember from somewhere else, coming after me down the wind, but they were too indistinct to make out fully.

The lough is in a wild and beautiful place on the high mountain pass between the summits of Knocknahillion and *Binn Idir na dá Log*, and we stopped there for a while to fill our water bottles before beginning the long descent from there to the road. Be warned, we wasted some time by trying to go west round the lake to pick a way off the saddle but there is no way off in this direction unless you have a hang glider in your rucksack. The best way seems to be to circle the edge of the lake in an anticlockwise direction, and then look for a steep but grassy slope which leads down to the infant river that falls below Knocknahillion. We took that route and followed the stream all the way down back to the road. The sun was bursting through the cloud and the wind dying now.

On our way, we stumbled across a massive lump of bog oak, half hidden in the black peat, a relic of the once mighty oak woods of the Inagh valley. Earlier that week I had bought a beater for my bodhran carved from a piece of bog oak. Heavy and black, the notice in the craft shop described it as 'at least five thousand years old', although I had to wonder how the carver could be so exact. In the soft ground around the peat bog were the stars of butterwort and clumps of long-leaved sundew. While I was kneeling to look at the sundew, a bird screeched overhead and, looking up, I saw what I'm sure was a peregrine falcon. It is certainly the right kind of country for that lovely bird.

An old man was footing turf into cocks to dry, and we stopped for a bit of a chat. He told us that the emigrants from these parts would often take three things to the new world with them, a lump of turf from the family bog, a bottle of water from the family well and a chip of stone from the family hearth. I noticed his bicycle leaning against a stack of turf at the roadside, a picture in itself that will be gone in a few years' time. The death of the Irish bicycle: someone surely will write a book on it. They could do no better than to quote the words of Flann O' Brien. In his marvellous book, *The Third Policeman*, he explores the symbiotic relationship between the Irish and the bicycle in a way which will never be bettered. Claiming that, since all things are made of molecules, and since one thing hitting another causes an exchange of molecules between the two things, he goes on to argue that there are some people in Ireland who are more than two-thirds bicycle and some bicycles that are more than two-thirds people. 'Did you never notice,' he argues, 'the way a bicycle will insinuate itself into the house and lean against the wall near the fire?' I never tire of Flann O' Brien, one of Ireland's great comic writers.

That night we went for a drink in the Field Tavern just down the road from our B and B in Leenaun. It was here that some of John B. Keane's play, *The Field* was filmed. I was having a drink with John B. a few years ago in his bar in Listowel when he told me how some of the critics had described his story of one man killing another over a small field as 'far fetched and unrealistic'. Later that week, the Irish press was full of a story of a County Mayo man who was hacked to death with a turf spade by a neighbour, simply because of a dispute over a field border. Nothing is of more moment in Ireland than land.

22 Killary Harbour

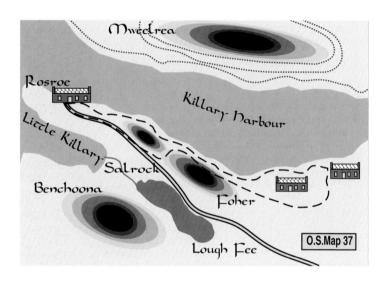

Killary Harbour (from *Caol* – a narrow sea passage and *rua* – red) is a great sea lough that cuts nine miles into the heart of some of the wildest hills in Connaught. The country's only sea fjord brings the Atlantic to Leenaun and close under the skirts of the Devil's Mother. The steep flanks of Mweelrea Mountain and Ben Gorm slope down to the lough on its northern side, while to the south lie the hills of Letterettrin and Foher and the smaller lough of Little Killary. The fjord is so safe for shipping that the British Navy sheltered here in the First World War, and, during the Second World War, German submarines came in to weather out storms.

A beautiful green lane follows the lie of Killary from the quay at Rosroe to Leenaun – the 'Famine Road' an old lady called it when I told her where I'd been walking. 'That's the way the people went when they walked from the West to Doo Lough House to try and get relief during the time of the Potato Famine, and many of them died along the way.'

The Famine Road can hardly have had much traffic on it in the last hundred years yet it is still broad enough along most of its length for a horse and cart. In many places it is kerbed and in parts has been cut through solid rock, so it was certainly an important route in the past, leading on beyond Leenaun, under the Devil's Mother and the Maumturks and on to Lough Corrib and Galway City. A good low-level walk, perfect for a poor day or families with small children, follows the green way along the side of Killary Harbour from Rosroe almost to Leenaun and brings you back over a narrow pass through the last of Foher hill to find your way back to the harbour.

One summer's afternoon I left Leenaun and took the wild and lovely motor road to Salrock and the little harbour at Rosroe to walk the green way by Killary. I have travelled by Lough Fee under the glowering Benchoona many times and it never ceases to thrill me. The peaty waters lap at the edge of the road while, across the lake, the hill stands massive and powerful. I parked

The old green lane beside Killary Harbour

my car carefully close by the An Oige Hostel and packed my rucksack with cameras, sandwiches and the usual flask of stewed tea. The hostel used to be a house and it was here that Ludwig Wittgenstein, the logical positivist philosopher, spent several summers in the late 1940s writing the second volume of his great treatise *Philosophical Investigations*. I must warn you that I have read the book and have come to the conclusion that he stole most of his ideas from Myles Na Gopaleen who used to come to Rosroe, dapping for basking shark with legs of lamb. One of Wittgenstein's arguments, 'If we weren't here we'd be somewhere else', is a direct lift from Na Gopaleen.

Wittgenstein must have been fairly unhappy in the place, though, because he seems to have done little but whine. He complained about the vast numbers of earwigs that lived in the area and moaned to the lady at the post office about the lack of any suitable detective fiction in her shop. I suppose that's just what you need when you are a Logical Positivist – a bit of Mickey Spillane.

Musing on this and other matters, I left the harbour and took the main road east for a few yards (I did put it back) before cutting up a lane (I did sew it together again) by a white-washed cottage that led me on to the old green track. There was a low grey sky and a cool wind coming off the Atlantic, but the clouds didn't look too threatening and the forecast was fair. I followed the lane until the stone walls gave way to more open country. Beneath me the lough, whipped up by the wind, was choppy and rough, with blown foam rolling up the shore. Far below, two men were clambering aboard a mussel raft from a motorboat. The rafts look ugly, strung out along the lough, but they provide local jobs and seem to be less damaging to the ecology than

salmon farming which leaves the sea bed beneath poisoned and sterile. The mussel beds have ropes hanging from them to which the mussels cling. After two years they can be harvested and the eco system has been left undamaged. The salmon cages, on the other hand, keep a non-shoaling fish static for a long time. The sea-floor beneath such salmon cages is often foul and lifeless because, for the salmon to fatten and prosper, they must be kept away from the kind of tides that are needed to scour the sea-bottom free of the deposits. The salmon also have to be fed an artificial, high-protein feed and pesticides to kill off the parasites that normally affect these unnatural systems. It's hard to see how this kind of development can ultimately do the environment anything but harm.

It was an easy and pleasant walk along the side of the fjord, with Mweelrea coming and going under the low cloud on the far side, and a little over an hour after leaving Wittgenstein's *Caladh na Gailseacha* (the Quay of the Earwigs) I came to some empty cottages. A man was looking around one of the cottages with his small children and I stopped for a chat. He was a Mayo man, now living in London, and the house belonged to his family. He told me that people had been living there fifty years ago, but now they were flown like the wild geese and their children were spread all over the world.

The man walked off towards Leenaun and I cut up behind the cottages, following a track that he had pointed out to me as a way back to my starting point. It was another green lane, heading towards a cleft in the mountain to the west. 'There's a pass there called the Salroc Pass,' he had told me, 'and it leads over to Little Killary. There's the remains of a chapel and holy well in the woods where St Roc used to pray. That's how Salroc got its name. Local people used to carry the dead over the pass to be buried. If you look closely you can see a rock with a big hole in it. The people used to place a stone in the hole for good luck as they went by. It was a smugglers' route too. They used to bring rum and tobacco out of Little Killary and carry it over the Salroc Pass and onto this lane. Then they'd take it through to Leenaun and over to the east.

Behind the deserted cottages, sloping down the hillside were the remains of 'lazy beds'. The poorer Irish were driven by the landlords onto the most marginal land where there was nothing but peat bog and bare rock. The women dragged seaweed and sand up from the shore in baskets on their backs, and the men, after they had cleared the slopes of as many rocks and stones as possible, mixed this poor mixture with whatever soil and manure they could find. So they made their fields and grew their only crop, the potato, on these impossible slopes. All over the West you can find these lazy beds and never did a name carry more desperate irony. Across the lough, the afternoon light, shining low from the west, brought out the contours of more lazy beds running up the flanks of Mweelrea like corduroy, and I could make out the ruined walls of long-deserted cottages. This place is named on the map as Derreennawinshin. There is not a road or a track to be seen, just the bare ruined cottage walls, the overgrown lazy beds and a terrible sense of the desperate state of the poor people forced there by the land hunger of the 1830s and 1840s.

According to the man from London there was a holy well somewhere on the hillside above the smugglers' path but I couldn't find it. Perhaps it has become overgrown and lost, as often happens in the least populated areas. The path itself was less easy to find than the green lane, but by sticking just under Foher's shoulder, I found my way to the rocky path that climbed to the Salroc Pass. The promised break in the weather that the radio had spoken of that morning failed to arrive, and the grey hood that had lurked over Mweelrea dropped to just above the lough as a thin drizzle began to fall. 'A soft day' they call this in the West. I pulled on my waterproofs, had a drink from the flask and then climbed up into the narrow defile of the pass.

Below me was Little Killary, and above it in the trees the roof and chimneys of Salrock House. The Thomsons, an English family, once owned the house and planted many of the trees that now grow so thickly above the lough shore. The father of the household, Alexander Thomson, was a blackguard. He had married into the Millar family, who owned the house originally, and one of his first actions on taking over the ancestral home was to evict as many tenants from the estate as he could, following the Scottish method of replacing them with more profitable sheep. It was largely because of his efforts that the area around Killary is so sparsely populated today. His daughter, albeit more of a human being than her father, was somewhat eccentric and, although she looked after her tenants quite well and made great efforts to relieve their distress during times of famine, was still a big chip off the old block. She zealously defended the family's fishing rights in Little Killary and thought nothing of swimming the river to catch poachers on the other side.

By the time I had rambled back to the quayside, the rain had stopped and a fitful light spattered across the sea and the mountains, one shaft shining on Gap Island: the Gaelic poet Seán Mac Conmara lived here during the years of the Famine. As I drove

The lazy beds on the hillside above Killary Harbour

south to Renvyle House (once the home of Oliver St John Gogarty, the model for James Joyce's Buck Mulligan and author of *As I Walked Down Sackville Street*, a wonderful account of Edwardian Dublin) and my bed for the night, the sinking sun turned the sea to brass and I stopped the car to walk along the fragmented and stony coast for a few miles. It was still and warm at the dimming of the day. An oyster catcher called in alarm close by while, out in the surf, people in sea-canoes paddled westward towards the setting sun.

County Mayo

All the counties in Ireland have mottos or slogans (call them what you will) after their names: Kerry's is 'Up the Rebels', Donegal's is 'Pride of All' but Mayo's is simply 'God Help Us', for Mayo is, if not the poorest, then certainly one of the poorest counties in Ireland. Much of Mayo is bogland, classic bogland. You can stand in the north of the county and see nothing about you but bog reaching for miles. As if the poverty of its soil was not hard enough to bear, Mayo suffered terribly during the Famine and had more than its fair share of rapacious landlords. The famous Captain Boycott who gave the world a new word was agent to such a one.

One of the most notorious absentee landlords of all time is Lord Lucan, whose family still owns the town of Castlebar. Where the famous Lucky Lucan is now is a matter for barside conjecture, though it's my belief that he is taking it in turns to ride Shergar with Salman Rushdie and the crew of the *Marie Celeste*. Whatever, the sensible tenant farmers of the Castlebar region are refusing to pay rent until the bold Lucan shows himself. The managers of the estate are hopping mad, of course, but, as the farmers explain, they owe rent to Lord Lucan and are perfectly willing to pay it just as soon as he comes and collects it in person.

The plight of the Irish people was so terrible during the Potato Famine that news of the disaster quickly spread to America. In 1849, the chief of the Chocktaw Indians was in Washington

A lone figure walking towards Doo Lough and the Devil's Mother

signing a peace treaty with the American president and heard of the dreaful famine in Ireland. He went back to his tribe and collected 700 dollars (more than a million pounds in today's values) which was sent to help the starving Irish. In 1995 the chief of the Chocktaw Indians, Gary White Deer, flew to Manchester to take part in a Famine Awareness week organised by Manchester's Irish Community, many of whom are Mayo people.

The Great Hunger was a blow from which Mayo never recovered and when emigration followed on the heels of famine and eviction, the county was bled of its best; 20,000 people left the western seaboard in the first years of the 1830s, almost all from Mayo. In 1841 the population of the county was 388,887, by 1851 it was 257,716, a decline of almost a third in ten years. When I worked on the building sites in Manchester in the early seventies, most of my fellow navvies came from a handful of villages and towns in Mayo. Bill Sloyan who taught me my very first tunes on the tin whistle was from the village of Killshemock. Working on a drama-documentary on the Irish navvy recently, I went out to the building sites and new road sites to take pictures of the navvies at work. I was not surprised to find that most of them were Mayo men.

I was talking to a farmer once in Dentdale, high in the north of the Yorkshire Dales. 'There used to be a lot of Irishmen came to t'Dales for the hay-timing. Every year they used to come for the hay. We had the same two men came every year. Most of them were from Mayo. They called themselves the July Barbers, so called because they came in the summer-time to shave the fields.'

A few days later I made this poem which I too called July Barbers.

JULY BARBERS

From Mayo, God help us, each summer they came
And stood to be hired in Salt Kettle Lane
And the farmers would pass with a swagger and a nod,
A hand slap, a wink, the chink of a few bob
    To drink 'your man's health' and the bargain was struck -
Binding them to the land.
The truck
Picked them up when the pubs had all shut
And tipped them, drunk and staggering,
Into the lamplit yard, their beery breath
Wreathing round the moth-danced flame.
Then it was weeks of
Scything, raking, turning, loading,
Sun-up to the edge of light
When blood filled the sky
And men grew field-long shadows.
Sleeping an hour they rose, swilling the night
Out of their eyes at the trough, washing
The gall of loneliness from their mouths,
The smell of bacon fingering the air
As mist smudged a heron on the river and a curlew
Bubbled at the orange ball that rimmed the fell.

Some nights they sang in Irish beneath a shaking moon,
Moving through the watery light
Over a land fecund with seed and fruit.
They combed the hayfield mowing to the lilt
Of an old song and called God's blessing on
The fields pan-scrub chin, well razored.

'Tis a shave will last all year, mister!'
Later, from the barn the farmer heard
The soft murmur of Gaelic chanting,
'Like bloody Ju Ju it sounded, Methody ranting.'
Peering through a crack he saw them kneel
Circled in the lamplight as horny fingers
And Pen y Ghent became Croagh Patrick.

Mayo has Ireland's most holy mountain, Croagh Patrick, upon which St Patrick fought with the old gods of Ireland. It has the last great wilderness in Ireland, Nephin Beg, with its vast boglands and wild hills. It is great walking country with some of the toughest walking in the whole island. The hills of Cork and Kerry are wild and the Derryveagh mountains of Donegal are bare and desolate, but there is nowhere wilder or more remote than the Sheeffry Hills and no mountain as savage as Mweelrea.

I suppose our understanding of a place is coloured by both the way it looks to the eye and by the inscape of stories and legends, music and people that we meet along the way. I have had some of the wildest and most joyous of times in Mayo in places like Westport and Achill, when the music and dancing has gone on well past the witching hour, and I have had some of my finest days on the hill there, too, yet at all times I sense an underlying air of sadness as though, in the middle of a sunny day, a cloud has suddenly passed over the land, bringing a moment of reflection. Drive from Louisburgh south to Leenaun on an autumn evening across the great boglands that stretch out to the Sheeffry Hills and on by Doo Lough and I think you will understand what I mean. There has been a terrible hurt here that will take a long time to heal.

23 A Ramble Round Cong

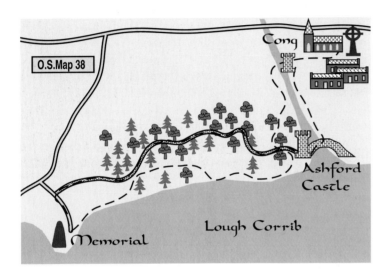

One of my grandfather's favourite films was *The Quiet Man*. He watched it over and over again, partly because he thought he looked a bit like John Wayne (he didn't, he looked more like Alastair Sim) but mostly because the landscape reminded him of home. The film was shot around Cong in west Mayo in 1951 and many of the houses and bars in the village still claim their fame as Quiet Man this or Quiet Man that. Close by the village is the House of the Quiet Man where Maureen O'Hara lived in the movie. As the years have gone by

and Big John has ridden to his last shoot-out in the sky, the world outside has largely forgotten the flickering black and white images that showed the imagined Ireland of Maurice Walsh's short story, but the film and the men and women who made it are still very much a part of the folk memory of the village.

But like many other places in Ireland where films have been made, Cong is worth knowing for much more than a brief fling with Hollywood. People often drive in to the area, have a quick look at Ashford Castle and the Abbey, drive on again and miss so much, for Cong lies in borderland where Connemara and Mayo meet. The name Cong is a corruption of *Cunga Feichin* – the isthmus of St Féichín who founded a monastery here at this most holy spot in AD 627. His first church had the lovely name *Cillín Breác* – the Little Speckled Church. After Féichín's church had fallen to dust, the Augustinians built the twelfth-century Cong Abbey, known as one of the 'Royal' Abbeys of Ireland because it was founded by a High King.

It is easy to see why this place should have been chosen as an especially holy site, given the very special significance the Celts gave to the borders between land and water, for the narrow limestone isthmus at Cong separates two of Ireland's largest and most beautiful lakes, Lough Corrib and Lough Mask. Only three miles wide, the isthmus is threaded by a series of underground channels and the waters roar their way across the barrier far below, with not one overground stream or river to join the two lakes together.

To describe Cong as beautiful would be like saying that Mount Everest is big. A small but very interesting booklet published locally by J. Fahey in 1986 is entitled *The Glory of Cong* and I think that *glory* really is the right word. The waters that resurface close by the village run past one of Ireland's greatest abbeys and through old and untamed woodlands coursing by Ashford Castle, one of Ireland's great houses, to Lough Corrib, Galway and the sea. It is a place of peace and stillness now and must have been so when the abbey was founded, but there have been battles here too. The first recorded battle in Ireland took place at Southern Moytura, close by Cong, when the dark people of the Fir Bolg were defeated by the Túatha Dé Danaan and, from those unrecorded days of myth, until Brian Boru finally crushed the Vikings at the Battle of Clontarf in 1014, it must have seen many a raid and massacre.

I stood in the ruins of Cong one bitter winter's day, when the wind thundered in off the lough and bare trees tossed and swung as though alive, and I remembered how on days like this, according to an old Irish poem, the monks would be thankful that the gales would keep away the Norse raiders:

> Bitter the wind tonight
> Combing the sea's hair white:
> From the North no need to fear
> The proud, sea-coursing warrior.

The twelfth-century abbey must have been one of the most powerful in all Ireland judging by the treasures which were kept here.

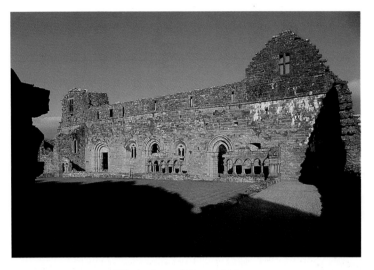

The ruins of Cong Abbey

The *Bacall Bui* (the great Cross of Cong), the *Fiachal Padraig* (Patrick's Tooth) and the *Cathach* (the Battle Book of the O'Donnells) were all in the keeping of the Abbot of Cong and, after the Dissolution in the sixteenth century, were kept hidden in a trunk by a succession of parish priests. They are all now in the National Museum in Dublin. The Cross of Cong is one of Ireland's great treasures and has at its heart a crystal cabochon enshrining a relic of the cross of Calvary, sent to the then High King, Turloch Mór O'Conor, from the Pope in Rome.

The reliquary holding St Patrick's Tooth is an extremely fine example of high Irish art and the *Cathach* covered in jewels, silver and gold, held the very book that brought about St Columba's exile on Iona, the copy of the Vulgate Psalms over which so

The Caves of Cong

much blood was spilt on the battlefield of Drumcliff in Co. Sligo.

There is an easy, gentle walk around the woods of Cong that takes you to no high-level adventure but on another kind of journey – woods and water, the edges of land and lake, a different kind of beauty and a different kind of exposure. Go alone or with a close friend and go as much as possible in silence. On a dull day in August, with dense elephant-grey cloud down to a leprechaun's kneecaps and no prospect at all of a walk in the hills, I left my bed and breakfast in Leenaun and drove behind the Devil's Mother heading for Cong. A walk in the woods, out to Lough Corrib and back by one of the old green lanes seemed a good way to spend the day.

I left my car in the Abbey car park (never leave your car in the car park of an Irish church on a Saturday afternoon – the reason why will be made clear) – and crossed the river by the bridge that leads to the woods under a fine stone arch. At its apex was the carved head of the last of the High Kings of Ireland, Ruari O'Conaire. (A passing thought that this was the real King Cong

flitted across what the previous night's *sesiún* had left of my brain, but I let it go.) Children were fishing from the stone platform of the Monks' Fishing House that stands over the river, prattling happily as they scoured the water with a little net on a bamboo stick. When Cong Abbey was founded, the fishing house was built on a stone platform over the river. There is a hole in the floor of the house and through the hole the monks would lower a salmon net. A line ran from the net to the monastery kitchen where it was tied to a big brass bell and, each time a salmon was netted, the bell would ring and the monks would know that it was salmon again for dinner. Lough Corrib salmon are fairly plentiful now, but I suppose they were more plentiful still in the unpolluted Middle Ages. I can't help wondering whether the novelty of the little stone house didn't pale after a while. You can imagine the monks hearing the tinkling of that bell as they bent at their labours in the field and each one saying silently in his heart, as he crossed himself for his uncharitable thoughts, 'Oh, no! Not pigging salmon again!'

I walked on into the heart of the great woods, following an easy path through the green shade to the loughside and here the weather suddenly turned from grey to blue and gold, the clouds all indigo, ragged and torn with blue slats of sky and slashes of sun. I had a flask and some sandwiches with me, so I sat on a driftwood log on the pebbly beach and watched three children throwing stones for a dog that turned and jumped and twisted and barked as it leapt up at the pebbles. The game went on for ages, neither children nor dog tiring of it. The children's mother sat close by on the grassy bank, feeding a new baby. We got to talking, as happens all the time in Ireland, and it turned out that she was born in England of Irish descent and had moved here from London when she married an Irishman. So often I have come across this movement across the Irish Sea, people coming home back to their roots, even though they may have been born a sea away.

I stood up to go and nodded towards the dog. 'That's a nice dog you have there.'

'I thought it was your dog', she said.

'Well, whoever's dog it is, it's having a great time.'

I followed the woodland path again until the trees opened out at a high point above grassy slopes and rhododendrons where there is a chalet and a massive obelisk. Local tradition insists that the chalet was built in a day by the man who then had Ashford Castle, Lord Ardilaun. He built it as a present for his wife Olive on her birthday. The couple seem to have been very much in love throughout their life together and on her husband's death Olive had the great obelisk built at her husband's favourite spot. Summer sunsets from this point are music for the eyes and it is said that standing here looking out towards High Island (*Árd-Oileán*) one evening inspired the lord to take 'Ardilaun' for his title.

The sun was losing itself in a tangle of clouds that were rolling in over far-off Galway Bay and, since I had no title to take, I took the way back into the woods, following a back lane to Ashford Castle.

The castle, built in the early eighteenth century by the Browne family, came, after Lord Ardilaun had owned and enlarged it, into the possession of the Guinness family in 1852; they greatly enlarged it again before selling it to the Irish State in 1938. The castle was then sold on into private hands and converted into an hotel in 1939. In general, it is not open to the public (unless you're rich enough to be staying there) but I worked out that my grandfathers, uncles and I must have contributed so much to the Guinness family fortunes over the last hundred and fifty years that in moral justice we own at least half a wing of this stately pile, and I had a good wander round. It was full of Americans in Aran sweaters ordering afternoon tea from little Irish girls with black hair and blue eyes, scuttling around in pinafores. My boots were muddy and my T-shirt sweaty, so, in spite of my being a shareholder, I left, feeling out of place.

From the castle I followed an old green lane back to the village. There I discovered that my car was jammed in by the Saturday evening Mass-goers. In my day, Mass was on a Sunday and missing it without a very good reason was a mortal sin. Nowadays, the Sabbath apparently begins on a Saturday evening, which means that modern-day Catholics (the softies) can get their Mass-going over on a Saturday after tea and have all Sunday to go fishing or play football or lie in bed and read the papers. But I was only stuck for half an hour. Mass is a very

Children and the unattached dog playing on the edge of Lough Corrib

short affair nowadays and the emerging crowd sprinting to their cars and zooming off was like a Le Mans start. You've more chance of being knocked down and injured by racing Catholics on the roads around Cong on a Saturday after Mass than you have of falling off Croagh Patrick.

I spent some time wandering round the Abbey ruins cursing its destroyers. I often try to imagine old ruins like these as they must have been before the Dissolution. They must have been like small cities with their gardeners and scribes, their bookbinders, cooks and fishermen. And the great chapels with the statues and the woodcarvings and relics, the libraries with their priceless books, all of them destroyed, all of them laid low. Of the glory that was Cong Abbey now nothing but the shell of the old building remains.

The modern church next to the ruined abbey is worth a visit for its Harry Clarke window alone. Clarke was born in Dublin on St Patrick's Day, 1889, to a Yorkshire father and an Irish mother, a fearsome mixture. He became a book illustrator (his illustrations to Faust are truly amazing examples of 'decadent' art in the Beardsley style) but is better known perhaps as a stained-glass worker. His lovely windows can be found all over Ireland, from Bewley's Café in Dublin to the rebuilt church at Cong.

I had a quick look at the dry canal before I left. The canal, often cited as the ultimate Irish joke, was in fact built by an English engineer, Mr Nimmo, using local labour as part of the Famine relief in this area. It was intended to link Lough Corrib and Lough Mask, thus making steamer transport possible from Galway Bay to the head of the northern lough. The four-mile canal with its sluices, lock gates and fine stonework still remains where the hundreds of navvies dug it out over five years for a wage of fourpence a day. But it had one serious flaw: being based on limestone bedrock (which, as every schoolperson knows, is porous) the canal could not hold water. Even in winter the water only reaches half-way to Cong.

There are many other things to see around Cong – cairns, standing stones, and more limestone caves than you can shake a stick at, including the Pigeon Hole, Kelly's Cave and, most notorious of them all, Captain Webb's Cave. Webb was a local Bluebeard who seduced the young maidens of Cong at an astonishing rate, despatching them, once he'd tired of them, down the deep pothole that carries his name. He did away with a round dozen of them in this manner but came unstuck with the thirteenth who grabbed him instead and threw him down his own hole. All of this was more than two hundred years ago and Cong's local maidens today are probably on their way to university to read Law and Astrophysics and are much too smart to be outwitted by blackguards like Captain Webb. He is said, by the way, to have earned his name 'through a physical deformity' – one wonders if it was his feet?

Close by Cong is Moytura House, the childhood home of Oscar Wilde, and Lough Mask House, where the foul Captain Boycott was land-agent to Lord Erne. When the Lord's thirty tenant-farmers asked for a twenty-five per cent reduction in their rents, Boycott, on the orders of his dotty County Fermanagh employer, offered them ten. The tenants decided *en masse* to send him and his family into isolation ('to Coventry' as Parnell described it). The servants were warned to leave the estate, which, knowing what was good for them, they did. There was no corn cut, no horses shod or watered, and Boycott and his family were avoided and ignored by all the locals. Not a shop would serve them, not a man or woman would work for them. Captain Boycott had to rise at four each morning to keep the estate going, and his poor wife, for the first time in her life, had to learn to cook, clean and do for herself. Lord Erne, incensed at seeing his agent so treated, brought in more than forty Ulster Protestants by train to harvest the corn. They were met at Clare-morris station by a detachment of the 15th Hussars and marched under escort to the big house, fifteen miles away. It rained constantly all the time they were there, so much of the harvest was ruined. At one time, there were as many as fifteen hundred British Government men in the area – all to protect less than fifty labourers. It eventually cost Lord Erne almost four hundred pounds to harvest a crop worth less than a tenth of that. Captain Boycott was sickened by the affair and left with his family for Dublin, where his hotel was 'boycotted'. He departed immediately for England, never to return, and thus the Captain attained his place in history and in the dictionary, if not in the hearts of the Irish.

But there are so many stories, and so little time. Did I tell you about the ruins close by Cong Abbey, of the home of McNama-ra, the Irish Robin Hood, who burgled the rich to help the poor and whose horse Venus once carried him over a thirty-foot gorge? Did I tell you about the holy island of Inchagoill with its fifth-century church? They will have to wait for some other time.

I was due back in Leenaun for supper so I drove westwards by the road above Lough Corrib, looking down on Hen Castle standing out in the lough on its small tree-fringed island. Fur-ther north, sun-burnished clouds rolled over the Maumturks before me as I headed towards the Devil's Mother.

24 The Devil's Mother

The Devil's Mother (*Magairlí an Deamhain*) lies at the eastern end of Killary Harbour, an outrider of the Partry Mountains. From the Leenaun–Louisburgh road, it doesn't look much of anything, a great hump of a hill with steeply sloping flanks. In truth, it's a stiff climb but a rewarding one because the views from the summit are superb and you are almost certain to have it all to yourself because, like many of the hills of Mayo (Croagh Patrick excepted), the Devil's Mother gets few visitors. The day I climbed it had a glum and grey beginning. Killary Harbour was funnelling all the foul weather from the Atlantic along the fjord, and once the weather hit the Devil's Mother, it just rolled up it and squatted there. The mountains all around were no better, Ben Gorm and Mweelrea had vanished in the thick mist and drizzle that was driving in out of the west.

However, when a sliver of blue showed just after breakfast, I decided to hang around Leenaun to see if it would clear long enough for me to get on the hills at all that day. I sat on the car park wall by the Leenaun Cultural Centre, looking down the lough and listening to the morning news from Radio Eireann on my car radio. The IRA had called a ceasefire and, as the news was coming through from Dublin, Belfast and London, the sky began to break and the first sun of the day came streaming down the fjord, almost as though the weather was in sympathy with the awakening of hope.

I parked in a fisherman's lay-by two miles out of Leenaun on

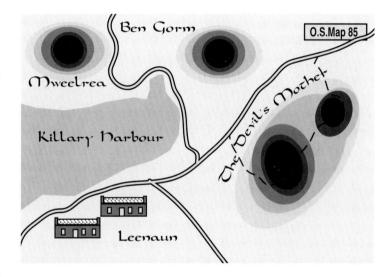

the Louisburgh road and filled the rucksack with waterproofs, food and cameras. I was going to follow a straightforward route up the flanks of the mountain onto the ridge which would take me directly to the summit. From there I planned to travel southeast then north following a long spur back down to the road.

The climb to the ridge was long, hard and dirty; it was slippy underfoot and the flanks of the hill turned into a severe boggy slope with lots of nothing at the bottom. Had I slipped badly and rolled, I would have gone a long way. The clouds

Pat on the ridge leading to the summit of the Devil's Mother

drove in again and the wind got up to gale force by the time I made the shoulder below the first of the mountain's summits. You could have sat on the wind. I carried on climbing the near-vertical bog to the first unnamed summit which, when I checked the map, is only 1815ft high. At first I wondered why I had found it so tough, but then realised that I had started off at sea level, so I didn't feel too bad about puffing and gasping up the last hundred or so feet.

From the summit I followed a wonderful, though fairly boggy ridge to the Devil's Mother proper. I stood there holding myself stiffly against the wild winds; black clouds raced overhead with sudden slashes of sun; below me was a sullen and dark land, Lough Nafooey to the east in rolling shadows, and Killary in the

west all mirky and forbidding. Then, just as suddenly, the sun broke through and the land was transformed again. Aross the valley, the corrie of Ben Gorm and, beyond that, the confused mass of Mweelrea were burnished by the wild light. I got in the lee of a small crag to have lunch and then began the descent. I described it in my journal for that day as 'a hard but not impossible descent. In mist, it would be easy to take the wrong spur and end up back in Leenaun, which would mean a three-mile road walk back to the car.' Going down was a bit of a knee-shaker but I dropped down fairly quickly. The weather closed in yet again and as gusty showers swept down the fjord I found a fairly easy way off the last of the ridge, though, as ever, there was a bog, a ditch and a barbed-wire fence just before the road.

When I got back to Leenaun, I sat in the Cultural Centre having a cup of tea with Michael O' Neil, the local historian, writer and fluent Irish speaker who built the centre.

'*Taimid ag súil ar an Sliebhe*. (I've been walking on the mountain),' I trotted out in my beginner's Irish.

'*Cad Sliebhe?*' (Which mountain?)

'*Magairllí an Deamhain*,' I replied. 'The Devil's Mother.'

Michael took a sip of tea, looked at me over his glasses and checked to see if any nun or Japanese lady tourist might be in earshot:

'You see, that isn't the real name of the mountain at all. When the sappers came round here making the maps of the country, they asked the local people what the names were of the various hills and rivers and loughs. "That's the Devil's Mother," said the old man they asked, because he was too embarrassed to say the proper word. Not that the old Irish were embarrassed among themselves, only when there were strangers amongst them. You

View of the fjord-like Killary Harbour from the shoulder of the Devil's Mother

see, the real translation is The Devil's Bollocks – but that would not look very nice on a map now, would it?'

I told him I thought it was a shame that the robustness and the bawdiness of much of Irish literature and art, such as is found in Merriman's poem 'The Midnight Court', had all become part of a secret sub-culture. Then I remembered something John B. Keane had said to me once when we were talking about the works of one of Ireland's great folk poets, a man whose work has hardly ever appeared in the anthologies of Irish poetry, Sigerson Clifford. Clifford was a schoolteacher from Kerry and his work, though it owes much to the folk ballad, is fine poetry, some of it glorious. Although he was loved in his native Kerry, he was ignored by the critics and scholars of the Dublin literary scene. 'Those middle-class intellectuals in Dublin,' said J.B., 'have done more to destroy Irish culture than the British ever did.'

That night in my hotel bedroom I took out my Irish-English *foclóir*. I was almost sure the colloquialism wouldn't be found there so I looked up 'testicle'. There it was, as true as Michael had said: 'testicle – *magairle*' and the plural would be *magairlí* and *Magairlí an Deamhain* is nothing to do with the Devil's Mother at all. I had spent the day climbing the Devil's Bollocks and felt a great deal better both for knowing it and having done it.

25 Mweelrea

Mweelrea (*maol ribhach* – bald grey hill) is the highest mountain in Connaught, a hard unforgiving massif standing between the dark and ghost-riddled waters of Doo Lough and the great fjord of Killary Harbour. The horseshoe walk that takes in Mweelrea and Ben Lugmore and Ben Bury has some fierce cliffs and crags that make it, in my opinion, one of the toughest hills in Ireland. In poor weather it could be a killer. I wondered at the names of Ben Lugmore and Ben Bury. Ben Bury, known also as Oughty Caraggy could perhaps be *Binn Búr* (Peak of the Boar) but Ben Lugmore is harder to translate. Being a romantic old fool I would like it to mean Great Mountain of Lugh – the god of light who gave his name to Lughnasa, London and Lyons, but Paddy Dillon reckons it is really *Binn Log Mhór* -The Peak of the Big Hollow, which I think may be correct but much more boring.

Climbing the Mweelrea horseshoe one autumn, I had one of the hardest days out in the hills I have ever had. I had been staying in Clifden and was making my way northwards to Louisburgh and Westport, hoping for some climbing on the way. Mweelrea had eluded me all summer, seven days out of ten it had been hidden under a cap of thick cloud when the rest of the country was under clear blue skies. That morning, coming north towards Leenaun, it was obvious that, although the valleys were clear and in full sun, there was still a great deal of cloud hanging around the mountains. Strange, inverted cloud was rolling over

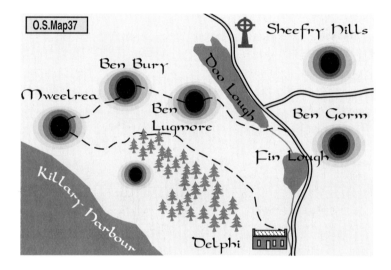

the Maumturks like a waterfall, pouring down the flanks of the hills into the Inagh Valley. The sun, burning through the mist, gave a sharp, almost unreal edge to the morning. I looked over at Mweelrea. For the first time all summer it was almost clear of cloud, just a fine, white, thin veil hanging over the last few hundred feet. It looked as though I might be in with a chance.

At Leenaun I filled the rucksack with cartons of drinks. Mweelrea was going to take five hours at least and I wanted to make sure that I had plenty of liquid. I drove to Delphi just south

Ben Gorm in sunshine, inspiring over-optimism

of Doo Lough, parked the car and looked up at the horsehoe. Mweelrea was clear, although there was a constant thin cloud swirling around on the ridge between Ben Lugmore and Ben Bury. But it looked as though it was set to clear out completely and had all the signs of turning into a lovely day, so I set off walking towards Doo Lough and the footbridge that crosses the stream at its southern end. On the east side of the lough the Sheeffry Hills were wearing a hood of cloud, but everywhere else seemed clear.

I crossed the footbridge and began climbing. It was a tough slog up the shoulder of Ben Lugmore with the occasional hands-on pull over slabs that were steep but not too exposed. I stopped every so often to look back at the glen falling away below me; a school bus purred along the valley road beneath my eyrie like a tiny white maggot. Above me I could see that the cloud I had seen rolling over the ridge had dropped slightly lower but it still looked passable. The summits had been just above the clouds when I left, so I assumed that the mist would still just be clinging to the ridge. I climbed on, soaked with sweat, through air that was alternately still and chill, an indication of why the cloud inversion was taking place. Still air rising up the south side of the ridge was meeting cold air on the knife edge itself. I climbed through the cloud into warm sunshine and sat below the summit to take a break, laying my shirt out to dry on a boulder, sitting there bare-chested in the warm sun.

I scrambled on through craggy outcrops, following a set of bootprints I had noticed lower down on the mountain, and a couple of stiff pulls brought me onto the summit of Ben Lugmore just as the mist closed in again. The summit was a fairly featureless waste of rock outcrops and peaty pools but the

Looking across the glen to Ben Craggan; note the school bus

stranger's footprints led on in the right direction so I followed them through the mist. As the mist suddenly cleared for a moment I saw that I was on a very impressive knife edge, leading between Ben Lugmore and Ben Bury. The arête is safe enough if you keep slightly below it to the south but to the north there are some horrific cliffs.

I took a bearing and went on, the going underfoot much better now. Then the mist thickened and visibility dropped down to a handful of yards. I had a good map and a compass so I checked my position carefully. One thing I had to avoid was going too far north and making a descent on to the north-east ridge where rope work is needed. The mist ebbed and flowed and at times I walked above a milky sea with the black fang of Ben Bury rising through it like an island. I made the summit just as the mist closed in again and then a very strange and unsettling thing happened.

A raven suddenly flew at me through the cloud, skimming my head. I flinched as its wings beat above me then turned to watch it settle on a rock close by, where it screeched out a harsh rattle-like cry. It may well have been my imagination but I could have sworn that the bird was directing its calls at me, whether warning or mockery I don't know, but in the rolling mist on that sharp peak with all the crags about me, I felt more than a little inclined to believe the bird knew something. In the Buddhist Himalaya, ravens are birds of good luck and are often kept as pampered pets, fed on tid-bits and wear little brass bells round their necks – but I wasn't in Nepal or Zanskar, I was in Mayo in the west of Ireland and in Celtic mythology the raven is always a bird of ill omen. Every raven in Ireland is said to have three drops of the Devil's blood in it, and there I was, mist-bound on a savage summit with lots of nothing on either side of me, being heckled by a black thing with three drops of Old Nick inside it. My membership of the Catholic Church has lapsed but I now tried to remember the Perfect Act of Contrition as I saw my obituary passing before me – 'Kind to most animals and a good climber for his size. Perished while trying to strangle a raven on an Irish mountain in thick mist.' Then, with one last strange gargling call, the black messenger flapped away into the cloud.

I knew that I couldn't sit there all day waiting for the mist to clear so I took a careful bearing and scrambled down from the peak towards the saddle between Ben Bury and Mweelrea. As I set off the cloud piled in again, turning from a light mist into dense fog, and the world about me became a grey ghost. There was nothing but nothing all around me, and some of that noth-ing had big holes in it. I walked on the bearing for a few hundred yards and found myself on the edge of a very nasty looking crag with more nothing beneath. I sat down. The new 1:50,000 Irish maps are good but they don't show crags, just lots of contour lines close together and, since a good deal of the horseshoe is like that, I hadn't a clue where the hell I was; even with map and compass, it was impossible to decode the landscape around me in this mirk. I was alone, the weather was foul, I was on a mountain I didn't know and nightfall was at the most three hours away. Then I remembered the two most important words in any mountaineer's lexicon – 'Don't Panic'. I looked at the map again. Then I panicked. I was in dense clinging fog on a high mountain summit with no visible way off and the land falling away from me on three sides. I could hear running water to my right which could, I reckoned, have been the Bananakee River that runs down from the saddle to Killary. Following that down would take me miles out of my way to Uggool or the road end at Dadreen where, if I was very lucky, I might be able to get a thir-ty-pound taxi ride back to Delphi.

I knew I needed to head more to the east but sensed nothing but empty space in that direction. The friendly bootprints had vanished in a jumble of scree and boulders. Whoever it was had either sprouted wings or had had better weather than me and had found his way off. All I could see before me was a steep shale slope leading to nothing. I cast around looking for clues and came to a crag edge that was a serious scramble leading to who knows what. I checked the map again, setting it against the compass. It told me I was in a fix. I had been making a mental note of escape routes and knew that, if I had to, I could climb back up a little and make my way off by a steep flank that looked as though it might be hard work but at least seemed free of crags and cliffs. I decided to sit it out for half an hour. The day was wearing on and, even if I got lucky, I would be getting back to the car as the sun was falling. But I reckoned I could spare thirty minutes.

It felt like a terribly long wait, but after quarter of an hour the cloud lifted and I could just see my way down on to the saddle between Ben Bury and Mweelrea. I scrambled down and belted along the col, losing more height than I liked, and then climbed through thickening mist along the ridge to the summit of the Bald Grey Hill. Here again I could have gone wrong for there are three peaks to choose from, but the compass and map guided me through porridge to the highest mountain in Connaught. Below me (2688ft below) was Killary Harbour. It could have been ten feet below for all I knew. I took another bearing and found my way off down the ridge towards the valley, eventually dropping below the cloud into early evening sunshine.

It was five o'clock and I still wasn't off the mountain. It was here I made another bad decision. One of the guide books shows a route that drops down to a saddle and climbs another un-named hill before leading down to the road. I decided to walk out by the glen to avoid another climb. It would have been easi-er climbing the hill. The walk out was a nightmare, boggy and slutchy. Every few hundred yards there were gullies and ditches full to the brim with the run-off from forestry plantations. I wasted time trying to go round these drains and in the end gave in and either leaped them or sploshed through. It took a long, long time and I was very, very, very miserable. I didn't get back to the car until almost seven o'clock, and there was peaty water and slutch up to my magairlí. I had had what you might call an

interesting day out, one that underlined the fact that you should never ever take Irish hills lightly – they are serious places.

The mood I was in was not lightened by the drive northwards. Doo Lough was dark and oppressive but I stopped at the side of the road above the lough as I always do, to stand in silence by the memorial there, for the story is one that demands silence. It is a testimonial to a terrible tragedy.

At the height of the Famine, six hundred starving people came into the town of Louisburgh looking for food or admission to the workhouse. They were turned away and told to see the two paid Poor Law guardians who would be holding a board meet-ing at Delphi Lodge the next day. The following morning four hundred of them set off, some in rags, some half naked, all of them barefoot, through a bitter cold spring day to cross ten miles of the wildest and bleakest country in the west of Ireland. At Glenkeen they were forced to ford a river swollen by recent rains and between there and Doo Lough they followed a high goat track, fording more streams and rivers along the way. When they reached Delphi Lodge, the guardians, Colonel Hograve and Mr Lecky, were at lunch and would not be disturbed, so the soaked and starving people were left to wait amongst the pine trees. When the two gentlemen finally came out they refused the people relief and told them to make their way back to Louis-burgh. There were no roads through that grim pass between the Sheeffry Hills and the Mweelrea Mountains, just narrow high goat tracks above the lough. Night was closing in and a savage wind brought a hail storm in from the north-west and, as they passed above a cliff known as the Stoppabue, sudden gusts of wind drove many of them off the cliff and down into the lough. The rest carried on northwards through worsening weather.

The ridge of Ben Bury with the ominous mist rearing up below

Those who did not die along the way died at the second crossing of the Glenkeen River. Not one of the four hundred survived.

I turned away from the memorial and drove northwards, the autumn night gathering around me as I left the great glen behind and crossed the rolling boglands to Louisburgh under a sky as dark and dour as the waters of Doo Lough.

26 Croagh Patrick

Croagh Patrick, or 'the Reek', as many know it, is more than just a mountain, more than just a hump of shattered rock rising up above Westport. Like Mount Sinai and Mount Olympus, Croagh Patrick (*Cruach Phádraig*) is the home of gods and saints. The gods were pre-Christian and the saint is Patrick himself, the Briton who was captured and taken into slavery by the Irish and who then escaped to Rome where he became a Christian. After his conversion and ordination, at the beginning of the fifth century, Patrick asked to be allowed to return to Ireland to convert his erstwhile captors from their worship of the old pagan gods. It was upon Croagh Patrick that he stood to banish from Ireland all the snakes and demons, all the old gods and spirits. The Tripartite Life of St Patrick, written in Irish around the tenth century, tells us that Patrick fasted and prayed on the mountain for forty days, and goes on:

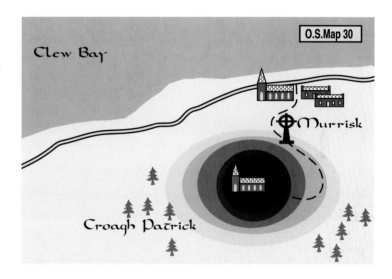

> Now at the end of those forty days and forty nights the mountain was filled with black birds, so that he knew not heaven or earth. He struck his bell at them, so that the men of Ireland heard its voice and he flung it at them so that its gap broke out of it, and that bell is Brigit's Gapling ... no demon came to the land of Ireland after that.

On the east face of the mountain is a cliff called Lugnademon (*Log na nDamhan* – Hollow of the Demons) down which the demons (in the guise of snakes) are said to have been banished. St Patrick's Bell and the beautiful reliquary that held it are in the National Museum in Dublin. Thus Croagh Patrick is Ireland's holiest mountain.

Time and again in Ireland you are conscious of the unwritten history of the land, of the book of the earth unfolding under your feet as you walk. There are stories under every field and every stone, every stream and ruin has its narrative and almost every hill is the scene of some murder or haunting, battle, eviction or ambush. It is no surprise that, for its size, Ireland has spawned more books than any other country. The land is almost as full of stories as stones.

Some miles to the east of Croagh Patrick, lies Ballintober, starting point for one of the hardest routes up the Reek. The abbey there has withstood all the trials of both the Reformation and the Cromwellian pogrom and Mass has been said there continuously since 1260. In the graveyard of the abbey, his grave marked by a great tree, lies Seán an t'Saggart (John of the Priest). At first you might be forgiven for thinking that the name was something to do with a priest called John or a holy man of that name. But it is nothing of the kind, Seán an t'Saggart was a priest-*taker*, a man who, during penal times, informed to the authorities the whereabouts of any priest. When he died, the local people took his despised body and dismembered it, scattering it all about the countryside in vengeance for the priests he had caused to be tortured and killed. The local priest, however, told them that judgement was not theirs and commanded them to gather up the bits of the corpse and bury it under the tree that is now known as Seán an t'Saggart.

On the last Sunday in July (around the time of what used to be *Domhnach Chrom Dubh* – Black Crom's Sunday, the feastday of the most powerful of the old gods that Patrick overthrew), the mountain swarms with people following the old pilgrims' route from Murrisk on the coast to the summit, many walking with sticks, some of them barefoot, and a few on their knees, to hear Mass and to say the rosary on Ireland's Holy Mountain. Such devotion is unknown elsewhere in the Isles of Britain and it was this kind of devoutness and faith that drove another lot of snakes off the mountain, the *gombeens* who wanted to mine for gold.

An exploration company discovered gold under Croagh Patrick in the late nineteen-eighties and estimated that the richness of the ore would yield half an ounce of gold per ton in at least twelve quartz veins. They wanted to remove 700,000 tons of gold-bearing ore. There was an outcry at the suggestion that the Holy Mountain should be mined, not simply from an ecological point of view (the cyanide used in gold extraction would have poisoned the waters and the spoil from the operation would have been enormous) but because, as the Revd. Dr. Joseph Cassidy, one of the strongest and most vocal opponents of the scheme, said: 'Croagh Patrick does not merely occupy space. It straddles history. For Irish Christians it is our foundation mountain, the mountain where our father in faith fasted and prayed. It symbolises the religious aspirations of our people and their upward journey to God. Digging into the Reek is not just digging into a mountain. It is digging deep into history and into the religious sensibilities of our people.'

In 1990 the Minister for Energy decided not to renew the exploration licence but it was a battle that could well have gone the other way and it says something for the mentality and morality of some developers that such an idea was ever considered.

One grey morning I was sitting with Pat in a tea-room in Westport having a quick bite when I overheard an English voice at the next table. There are a few English living in the Westport area and not all of them are nice. Some, like this lady, still have the colonist's mentality. 'The Irish are lovely,' she said loudly, 'but they can be so infuriating. I've been waiting almost three weeks for the builder to come and finish the guttering on the extension. "Mr Sloyan," I said, "when will you come?" "Oh," he said, "I'll be round soon." "When's soon?" I asked him. "Well, its closer than later and not as far as never." I was furious but what can you do? They're nice people, and one doesn't want to fall out with them, but I do wish they had more sense of time.'

I almost suggested that she go back to Dorking, or wherever it was she came from, and where I'm sure they've plenty of sense of time, but instead I just looked at Pat and said, 'Come on, let's go and climb the Reek.'

We left the car in the car park at Murrisk and stood under the statue of St Patrick with his false beard and looked up at the mountain. It was clear as far as the saddle and cloudy beyond but the forecast wasn't bad and the path is so well defined that it is surely impossible to lose, so, with an optimism that years of walking in Ireland should have laid to rest but hasn't, we set off up the old pilgrims' path. There are other ways onto the mountain, but this is the easiest and, I think, most interesting. The other popular route from Ballintober involves twenty-odd miles of linear walking and means a taxi ride or a lift back to your starting point. On a grey misty day the easy way up will always do.

I'm convinced that this holy mountain has a powerful magnet of some kind at its core because it felt as though I was wearing lead boots, the kind deep-sea divers wear. It seemed twice as hard as it should, despite the route being on fair paths. Two little boys with their father skipped past us (well, their father wasn't skipping, but you know what I mean). Then an American girl and her boyfriend zoomed by, but we were later to see them burnt out on the saddle so we didn't mind that too much. We plodded on towards the cap of mist; I've only ever seen this mountain in sunlight a handful of times in thirty years.

Just before we reached the cloud ceiling, we were overtaken by a rangy farmer in green wellies with his jacket under his arm, who was going up the mountain track as though he were going for a stroll after a heavy breakfast. He quickly left us behind, melting into the cloud. We followed, climbing steadily. Beneath us, the coastal plain and Clew Bay opened out but not enough for us to see more than a few of the islands that are scattered about it. One for every day of the year they reckon. The bay was once a drumlin field and when the sea flooded it millennia ago the drumlins were left like a school of whales facing west from the bay to the Atlantic. The day was very humid and warm under the thick grey duvet of cloud so that, by the time we reached the saddle, I was lathered with sweat and feeling fairly penitential. Then the cloud dropped further and thickened, and the pearl-grey day took on some of the aspects of Purgatory. In fact, it is said by some scholars that Dante took his idea for The Mountain of Purification in the *Purgatorio* from stories he had heard of Croagh Patrick and today I could believe it. From the saddle, there is a steep climb over rough, unstable stones that slide away with every step you take and that strange magnetic force seemed still to be tugging at my feet. I kept having to pause for breath, but, by taking it slowly and carefully, we made it to the cloud-covered summit where we could just make out the Chapel of St Patrick and *An Leabha Phádraig* (St Patrick's Bed) through the mist.

The chapel was built on the site of St Patrick's original chapel at the turn of this century, with all the materials being brought up on the backs of donkeys. As at Maumeen in the Maumturks, the Bed of Patrick is of special importance because it would be there that the saint would have had his dreams and visions.

Pat, the penitential pilgrim, plodding up the bouldery path; hard enough in good boots, in bare feet it must be torment

Something struck me as I sat by *Leabha Phádraig* drinking tea. The pilgrims who climb the mountain circle many of the sites on the pilgrimage in a clockwise direction, just as Buddhist pilgrims do in Ladakh and Zanskar. St Brigid's Cross turns clockwise too and is a sunwheel not very different from the swastika, which is often found as a symbol in Buddhist monasteries as well as carved on rocks across Europe. There seems to be so much common ground between Buddhism and the Celtic pagan/Christian religions of Western Europe that either they have a common Indo-European source, or Man responds in a similar way to his environment no matter where he is. The notion of the pilgrimage as a journey that echoes the journey the soul makes between Life and Death is common to many religions and a few years ago, while travelling in America, I came across a Hopi Indian text that proclaimed 'Our journey is our religion.'

We sat on the summit in the cloud for a while before retracing our steps down the scree slope. As we dropped below the cloud, it began to rain and the rain kept us company all the way off the mountain. Yet it was still strangely warm and humid, and by running off the hill I overheated and became dehydrated so that, just above the statue of St Patrick, I ducked my head in the stream that follows the path and drank deep. It was a toss up which tasted sweeter – the mountain water or the Liffey Water we had in The Shebeen on the way back to the digs. With a head

Musicians and dancers in Matt Molloy's bar

of foam you could walk on and a black body the colour of a nun's habit, it didn't touch the sides and sizzled when it hit the bottom.

That night in Matt Molloy's bar in Westport there was great music and dancing and the local police inspector insisted on my helping him to ensure that the Bushmills workers' jobs were secure. As a result of this I slept all the way to the Dublin boat in the car the next day while Pat drove. Missing my share of the driving means I now have to climb the Reek again as a penance.

27 Croaghaun

There is sorrow in it, as there is in all sharp beauty. Standing there with the gulls crying and the larks shivering in the sky and the wind going through the heather, a man gets cold with the beauty of it and is glad to be alone.

H.V. Morton, *In Search of Ireland*

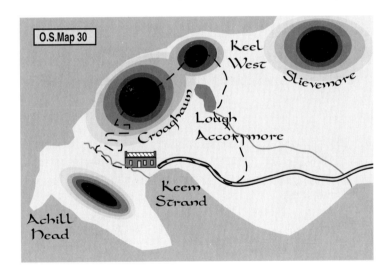

When I was a child I used to look at the map of England and Ireland and think that England looked like a witch on a broomstick while Ireland looked like an owl flying towards her, its beak the hook of land east of Strangford Lough, and its wings the counties of Galway, Mayo and Sligo. Achill Island is one of the feathers in the wings. It is a very special place, and very different in a way that I can't quite put my finger on. It may be something to do with the light, or the sense that, as on the Dingle Peninsula, you are on the very edge of things here and that, beyond Achill Sound, things become very different. There is a self-taught painter called Alex McKenna living on Achill who has captured the light and colour of that island better than any pen or camera. His work is hard to find but worth searching out.

Achill only just qualifies as an island, because a very short bridge joins it to the mainland and if someone dumped a couple of thousand tons of quarry bottom down there, it would be isthmused to the rest of Mayo and not be an island at all. But island it is and a wild and woolly place in winter too. I heard a story when I was there last of a Dublin engineer who was sent out to the island for a year to work on some government project. He thought it was paradise during the summer but by the time he'd sat out half the winter with day on day of thick dark cloud, the wind ripping the tiles off the roof and rain blowing straight through the windows he was a jibbering wreck and had to be helped off the island by kind men in white coats. One of the furthest points west of west, where the weather can change in seconds and where life has always been lived on the edge, it isn't surprising that the natives of Achill – like island people everywhere – have a self-reliance and a tough sense of humour that marks them out as 'different'.

The first time I went to Achill, in the late seventies, there was sea mist down to a hundred feet above sea level and a thin soupy drizzle was blowing in off the sea like something out of the first few pages of *Great Expectations*. I half expected prison hulks riding beyond the bar and a Magwitch behind every gravestone – and this was June. But bad weather never lasts long in the West and within hours the cloud had lifted and the world had opened up again.

Achill has two wonderful mountains, Slievemore (*An Sliabh Mór* – Big Hill), a great beached whale of a hill with a deserted village at its foot, and Croaghaun (*Cruachán* – steep-sided mountain), which has some of the highest sea cliffs in Europe, dropping almost two thousand feet straight to the sea as though a giant blade has sliced through a humped mountain and left it falling sheer to the waves beneath. Eric Newby, one of my heroes, climbed Croaghaun and described it thus: 'It was difficult to believe that I was now on the edge of the highest sea-cliffs in the British Isles, because beyond twenty feet in any direction, up, down, or sideways, it was impossible to see anything at all. All I could hear was the sea sighing far below and the dismal crying of the gulls.'

I've been lucky, I know, that each time I've come out to the far west of Achill the weather has been superb. One summer's

morning on a sunny cloudless day I left the car at Keem Strand and walked back along the road towards Dooagh. Clare Island, Croagh Patrick and the mountains of the mainland south of me were blue and hazy in the early morning light. After a mile of road walking, I left the tarmac and contoured round across rough ground to the uneven track that leads to the *cwm* lake of Lough Acorrymore. The lough has been damned to provide water for Dooagh and has a concrete wall and the usual waterworks architecture, and the end result is quite brutal in such a beautiful spot.

I crossed the concrete dam and made my way over to Lough Corryntawy and started climbing. It was a long slog over poor ground, grazed to the rock by sheep and drenched by months of rain but, taking it slowly, I gradually made it onto high ground. A farmer in wellies with his sheepdog raced past me driving a flock of sheep towards Slievemore. He'd probably been up since dawn and had run up and down this mountain several times already. I climbed on, consoling myself with the thought that he was probably carrying nothing other than a sandwich and a packet of fags while I was lugging a bag of cameras and a tripod.

As I gained the shoulder marked on the map as Keel West, I could see the seaward side of Slievemore sweeping down to Blacksod Bay and the whole of Achill opened out below. Further out to the north, the fragmented and gnawed Peninsula that runs south from Belmullet, forming the western wall of the bay, shimmered in the haze.

Under the southern flanks of Slievemore is a deserted village with a cluster of roofless houses and a lonely and overgrown graveyard. In that graveyard lies a group of sad graves. Young men and women used to go from Achill to Britain, as they went

Slievemore seen from the ridge leading up to Croaghaun

Achill Sound from the flanks of Croaghaun

traditionally from all over Mayo, looking for seasonal work hay-making, berry-picking or lifting potatoes. From Achill they went mainly to Scotland where they were called Tattie Howkers. They started work at dawn and finished only with the coming of night. They slept, ate and lived in stone bothies, all for five old pence an hour. In 1937 the last train to run to Achill carried the bodies of ten of those migrant workers: the oldest was twenty-three and the youngest only thirteen. They had all been killed

when their bothy at Kirkintillock burnt down, and now they lie under Slievemore, returned to their island home.

I climbed higher through the heat of the early afternoon until I gained the ridge. From there I could see over to north Mayo and Sligo, though Benbulbin was hidden in the heat haze. The summit ridge is rather airy, with rifts that shoot straight down to the sea, so I trod a very careful path to the summit and then followed a narrow arête to a second, slightly lower, summit. To my right, a gash in the rock fell sheer to the sea and, thankful that there was no wind, I leaned over and looked down at the waves slamming into the rocks 2,192ft below. On a windy day or when low cloud and drizzle are washing in off the sea, this would be a hairy spot to be indeed, the edge is crumbling considerably in places and there is evidence of a number of rockfalls and the raw scars of new gashes opening up. I dropped down to slightly below the summit and sat in a sun trap to have my lunch and dry out my sweaty shirt. From my eyrie I could see the beach at Keem Strand quite clearly and I could hear the shouts and calls of playing children mingled with the slow fall of the surf. I sat for ages in the hot sun, so long in fact that I ran out of time and, instead of dropping from the summit down to Achill Head and following the southern cliffs back to Keem, I took the shorter route back, following the river that runs south-east between Benmore and Croaghaun. It's a knee-cracking descent to the river, steep and slippery, and you need to thread your way through numerous outcrops of rock, but I took it slowly and,

once down at the river, followed it back to the road. Some ruins stand on the river's banks; these are the ruined buildings of the famous Captain Boycott who managed his own estates here before moving out to Lough Mask where he became land agent for the aforementioned Lord Erne. His substantial buildings stand empty and tumbling now, something he could hardly have foreseen all those years ago.

I left the ruins behind and crossed the stream to cut up by some old coastguards' cottages to the road and the strand. Parents were packing up deck chairs and towelling down children who were complaining that it wasn't time to go home yet and couldn't they have one last swim? Long shadows crept across the sand. I thought of my own childhood memories of summer seaside days, that eternal swell and sound of the sea and the sun-sizzled skin and salty swimming costumes on the beaches of long ago. As I drove towards the mainland by quiet winding roads, I passed by families out in the small fields turning hay by hand in the dying sunlight, the last of the summer's hay gathered in.

County Sligo

I've thought long and hard about Sligo and what it is that makes it such a special place and I still haven't come up with any sensible answers. It may be that so much of it is linked with the poetry of its great son, W.B. Yeats; it may be that, like Clare and Donegal, it is a great county for traditional music; it may be that there are a lot of great pubs; it may be that there is so much myth and magic in County Sligo that every bush and stone tells a story; or it may be the landscape which varies from the gentle seascape of Rosses Point to the wildness of Benbulbin and the Ox Mountains. It may be all of these rolled together or it may be nothing at all but the essence of the place itself; I don't know. It beggars my powers. What I do know is that it's a hard heart that wouldn't fall in love with Sligo and its people.

It is a land of gentle rivers and deep still lakes, of mountains and music and poetry, of soft wooded valleys and sheer dark cliffs on wild and murderous sea coasts, and it is a land where mystery and legend are never far below the surface. In an old street in Sligo town, for example, is a butcher's shop where the butcher, Michael Quirke, suddenly hung up his apron a few years ago, exchanged his mincer for a hammer and chisel and became a woodcarver. The butcher's block is still there but the window now displays carvings from Irish mythology instead of pork chops and links of sausages. And the carvings are not comfortable, touristy leprechauns and Colleen Bawns, but hard and powerful images drawn from the pagan sagas and hacked out of

the timber looking as though they have just been found in a bog. In Catholic Ireland, Michael Quirke is a consummate pagan who sees the life force and the power that lies below all the old legends and, if you sit with him for half an hour as he hacks and carves away in his workshop, you will learn more from him about Irish mythology than you will from any book. I have sat with him and watched him turn a lump of lumber into Balor of the Evil Eye while he has recounted the story of the *Fir Bolg's* battle with the *Túatha Dé Danaan*. Now, in the last decade of the twentieth century, he retells stories that predated Christianity as though they had happened in Sligo the week before.

It is no small wonder that Yeats saw Sligo as the land of his heart's desire and that this Protestant son of the Ascendancy returned here as often as he could. He wasn't, in fact, born in Sligo but in Dublin. He lived there until he was three when his father, the painter John B. Yeats, shipped them all over to London, where W.B. spent most of his childhood, only returning to Ireland when he was fifteen. His grandparents, the Pollixfens, had an old and interesting house called Merville in Sligo and the young William Butler and his brother Jack (who later became one of Ireland's greatest painters), used to spend the long summer holidays there. These visits coloured the young poet's life, for he would move each summer from the grey realism of London's Regent's Park into a land where people still believed in the banshee and the fairy people, in ghosts and hauntings. Sligo

Sligo Town across the harbour in the evening light

The Sligo Maid

town now houses a Yeats' museum and has a fine statue of W.B. on the corner by the bank, his broad-shouldered jacket covered with a bee-like swarm of words.

In Sligo town too you will find McGlynn's Bar, a fine old singing pub where I have spent many, many happy hours, and Hargadans, one of the finest pubs in Ireland with its private booths and its marble and mahogany. Just across from the Yeats memorial and the phone box is Shoot the Crows, a great music pub, where the late Joe O' Dowd could often be heard playing

fiddle and where his son Séamus now carries on the family tradition.

South-west of Sligo town lies Tobercurry, the birthplace of Michael Coleman, the most legendary of all Irish fiddlers whose recordings, made in America in the early years of this century, had such a strong influence on the traditional styles of Irish fiddling. Sligo has mountains and music and poetry and sea, friendly people and great pubs and, if that isn't enough, then I don't know what to say.

28 Knocknarea

The host is riding from Knocknarea
And over the grave of Clooth-na-Bare;
Caoilte tossing his burning hair,
And Niamh calling 'Away, come away:
Empty your heart of its mortal dream.'
W.B. Yeats, *The Hosting of the Sidhe*

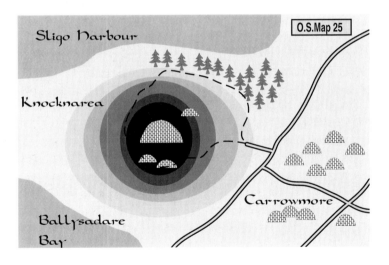

It's easy to dismiss tales of leprechauns, little people and banshees as blarney when you are sitting far away in England under an electric light and the BBC radio is wittering on about the Dow Jones Index. But in Sligo one time, standing at a holy well, I understood why the people around here believed in fairies so fervently.

The autumn day had turned suddenly from sunshine to black storm, a rush of air flew overhead for all the world like the beating of giant wings, then the still day turned into a wild lashing rainstorm. Common sense tells me the wings were just air currents rushing in to fill a void but common sense isn't the only way of looking at the world.

It was the Victorians who turned the fairies into wee creatures with gossamer wings. Many of the Irish fairies, the *Ban Sidhe*, for example, are of normal height. Leprechauns and other little people are often described as being the size of a small boy and there is a theory that the legends of the fairies and the little people grew out of sightings of the dark race of people that were here before the Celts, a short, swarthy race that lingered on long after the taller, fair-haired Celts had pushed them towards the west.

The summit of Knocknarea (*Cnoc na Riabh* – Hill of the King) stands 1,078 feet above sea level and on it lies the burial chamber of the most powerful Irish woman of all time, Queen Maeve – so powerful that she could send whole armies into battle merely to satisfy a whim, so powerful that she eventually became a Celtic goddess. She lies buried under a mound of stones, *Miosgan Meabh*, 40 feet high, 200 feet in diameter and 630 feet in circumference. The mound is said to contain 40,000 tons of stones and, whether or not you believe in the fairy nature of Queen Maeve, whoever is buried under that great mound must have been of supreme importance. I think we can trust local legend and assume that it was a great queen.

It was Maeve who was responsible for one of Ireland's fiercest battles, and the way the story is told, it seems that the battle was fought on the whim of a woman both powerful and strong but ultimately stupid. The story goes that Maeve and her husband, King Ailill, were indulging in some pillow talk one night when Maeve told him that she could never respect a man who was weaker than she, less courageous than she, or had less than she in worldly goods. (By Celtic law, a woman retained all her goods on marriage.) So the royal pair began totting up their bits and chattels, only to find that she was the lesser by a Great White Bull. Peeved at this, Queen Maeve set about finding a bull of her own, and soon heard of the Great Brown Bull of Cooley belonging to the King of Ulster.

Then followed what must be the most famous cattle raid of the western world, the *Tain Bo Cuilreadh* (The Cattle Raid of Cooley). Maeve despatched an army of her fiercest warriors north-east to Ulster to steal the bull and, in spite of the most valiant efforts of Cúchulainn, who seems to have been working

for the King of Ulster as a mercenary, Maeve's raiding party overpowered the northern forces and brought the Brown Bull back to Connaught. The story doesn't end there, though, for the White Bull and the Brown Bull took an instant dislike to each other and a fight took place in which the White Bull of Ailill was torn to pieces and tossed into the air by the horns of Maeve's Brown Bull. We can only conjecture at the dinner-table conversation in the house of Ailill and Maeve at the end of that hectic day.

It is interesting that a lot of people regard the old myths as nothing more than that, as though they appeared out of the air for no good reason. The land that lies about them seems too mundane to have been the battleground or love bed of a major epic. The Maeve who lies buried under that mound on Knocknarea was probably the wife of a tribal king, she walked through mud and slept on a low bed in a rough stone house yet, out of her story, the people wove a saga to be told by the fires through long winter nights. It is great myth that is made from the simple earth.

One summer afternoon I left the car in the little car park at the foot of the mountain and set off for the summit. It is a short but spectacular slog, and the country opened up about me wonderfully as I climbed. I was hot, and the camera pack I was toting felt like a small bungalow, but I had all afternoon, with nothing to drag me back off the mountain but the *sesiún* in Shoot the Crows that night. There was not another soul in sight and nothing to be heard but the songs of birds and the faint noise of a tractor fussing about in the fields somewhere far below.

With sweat stinging my eyes, I crossed the summit to the great

Walkers diminished by the mound of Queen Maeve's tomb

gombeen mind. Seán O' Faoiláin writes of Maeve's mountain: 'Myths suffuse the air like spray. One look at that flat-topped plateau of Knocknarea, one hint of its associations, is enough to subdue all disbelief.'

For this is where the hosts rode out from in *The Hosting of the Sidhe* and this is the land of *Red Hanrahan's Song About Ireland*. A great warrior called Eoghan Bel is said to be buried here on Knocknarea, standing upright, his blood-stained spear in his right hand and his face looking northwards towards his vanquished enemies. Below Maeve's great tumuli, on the north-facing shoulder of the mountain, is what is marked on some maps as the grave of an Iron Age chieftain. Smaller than the great queen's burial chamber, the tomb still commands a fine position looking northwards towards Sligo Bay '....on the side of the hill by which the northerns pass when flying before the army of Connacht.' Is this collapsed tomb perhaps the grave of Eoghan Bel?

On your first visit to Maeve's tomb, you get a special wish if you carry a stone up the mountain and deposit it on the cairn. On the other hand, it is supposed to be very unlucky to take a stone back down with you. The story is told of an American woman who made the fatal mistake of not only carrying a stone down off the mountain, but of taking it back to America with her. There somebody told her of the curse she had brought on herself. In a panic, she posted the stone back to Sligo, care of the postmaster, together with three dollar bills, which were to be given to some 'gosoon' (*garsún* – little boy) to take the stone back up the mountain. I've never been able to find out if the stone eventually made its way back there, but I do hope some little Sligo 'gosoon' got three dollarsworth of sweets and ice cream for his trouble.

white mound. The mountain summit really does feel magical, even to an old cynic like myself, and, on a day like this, with the mound of stones shining white against a blue sky, it was especially so. Alone on the summit, I sat in the sun, close by what seemed to be a group of smaller burial chambers. Below Knocknarea to the south-east is what was once one of the greatest collections of prehistoric burial chambers in Europe, a true Necropolis. In the area around Coloorey, something like three hundred and fifty stone chambers and standing stones were recorded. Over the years, all but fifty have been destroyed and carted away. Sligo council tried to turn what was left into a waste disposal site a few years back, but there was such an outcry that they backed off, the triumph of sense and sensitivity against the

View across Sligo Bay from the summit of Knocknarea; the bulk of Benbulbin is just visible on the other side

I wandered round the summit for half an hour or so, the whole of Sligo spread below me in the sun – Sligo Bay, Rosses Point and Coney Island with the causeway just showing, a spattering of tiny white farms on the green plain beneath me and the far off neb of Benbulbin smudged with heat haze. As I walked down off the mountain towards the plain it occured to me that I had spent more than three months of that year walking in Ireland like Yeats's Wandering Aengus.

Though I am old with wandering
Through hollow lands and hilly lands,
I will find out where she has gone,
And kiss her lips and take her hands;
And walk among long dappled grass,
And pluck till time and times are done
The silver apples of the moon,
The golden apples of the sun.

29 A Stroll By Lough Gill

When the weather is too poor to get up on to the tops there is still plenty of good walking to be had in Ireland. The back roads are usually quiet enough to be safe and there are woodland walks and coastal paths in plenty. One Sunday morning in spring, I took the Lough Gill road out of town with hardly a soul about, they were either all abed or at Mass. The weather was biting cold and grey, just the kind of day you wouldn't want to spend up on Benbulbin or over in the Ox Mountains. A few cars passed heading out for the lough, but generally I had the road to myself. The quiet back way to the lough passes close to a place called Cleaveragh (the place of the basket makers). It was here that salley (salix - willow) was grown for basketweaving and the Salley Gardens of Cleaveragh were the very gardens of Yeats's poem. He was inspired to write his piece by a few lines he had heard at a fair at Ballysadare. A ballad seller wandering through the crowd, with his sheaf of broadsides, singing 'Ye Rambling Boys of Pleasure' with the words

> She bid me take life easy as the leaves fall from the tree
> But I being young and foolish with her could not agree

inspired one of the loveliest poems (and songs) in the English language, 'Down by the Salley Gardens'.

At Tobernalt, under Carn Hill, there is a holy well, one of the many sacred springs of Ireland. According to Charles

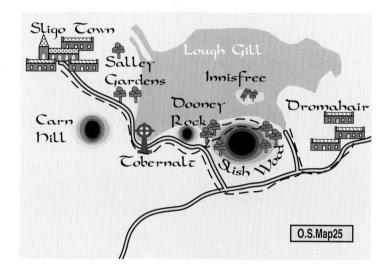

Plummer's *Lives of the Irish Saints*, there are almost 3,000 holy wells scattered about the country and perhaps many more unrecorded. The Celtic Christian church absorbed many of the practices of the early Irish pagans through a kind of symbiosis and the wells came to be associated with various saints and a variety of ailments. According to some, *Tober an Ailt* means the Well Under the Cliff, others say it means the Well of the Lunatics and that people came here to be cured of their madness. The well is still the site of a great pilgrimage in July when

Cross at the Holy Well at Tobernalt

hundreds come to pray and hear Mass and the water from the well is said to be renowned for its unusual powers, including that of increasing the prowess of football players. That such pilgrimages have survived is almost a miracle in itself since an Act of the Irish Parliament of 1704 decreeed that anybody found worshipping at a holy well would be soundly whipped and fined ten shillings.

The first time I came here, in the early seventies, there were rags and ribbons tied to the branches of the hazel trees that surround the well in a symbolic offering that goes back far into the past and that nobody seems to be able to explain. The worship of wells goes back to the early Celts and probably beyond, and since woods and groves were also thought of as holy places, you can be sure that a holy well in woodland like this one at Tobernalt is a very ancient, sacred site. Lady Wilde, mother of the more famous Oscar, tells in her book *Ancient Legends* of a blind man who came to Tobernalt and was cured. Turning to the people around him, he cried, 'I was blind from my birth and saw no light till I came to the blessed well; now I see the water and the speckled trout down at the bottom, with the white cross on his back.'

There is an altar above the well that incorporates an old Mass-rock, where priests would come to say Mass during the penal times when the Catholic religion was outlawed. Hundreds of people would gather in secret at night with look-outs posted, probably on Carn Hill and all the approaches. With the dawn, the outlawed priest would appear as though from nowhere, say Mass, give the sacraments and disappear again. There was a price on the head of any priest, and it is an indication of the strength of the people's faith that there were so few informers.

The Isle of Innisfree, the island of Yeats' poem

There are Mass-rocks all over Ireland and yet, as far as I know, they are unmarked on the map, only local tradition keeps the knowledge alive.

This spring morning I spent a quiet few moments at the well looking at the Mass-rock and the striking little stone crucifix that has been carved there in recent years. An old man saying the rosary at the well was the only other sign of life. I waited until he had finished his devotions and then drank from the waters, saying my own silent prayer. There is a wonderful aura at Tobernalt, it's one of my favourite places in Ireland,

Dooney Rock

with a great sense of peace and of something very old and very powerful.

Leaving the well, I took the road round the bay to Dooney Hill. Everywhere you go in this part of Sligo, the poetry of Yeats whistles through your mind like a wind. Dooney Rock is where the fiddler came from who, even though he has a brother and a cousin who are priests, will be invited first through the door of Heaven:

> For the good are always the merry,
> Save by an evil chance,
> And the merry love the fiddle,
> And the merry love to dance:
>
> And when the folk there spy me,
> They will all come up to me,
> With 'Here is the fiddler of Dooney!'
> And dance like a wave of the sea.

If you climb to the top of Dooney Hill and fight your way through the overgrown trees and bushes to the Rock, you can see across the lough to the far off hills of Benbulbin and Benwiskin, with Cottage Island beneath you with its ruined mediaeval chapel. Another such chapel lies on Church Island further across the lough, which, like St Finbarr's chapel in Goughane Barra, is one of the mystical places chosen by men of the early church for their lonely meditations. Local legend has it that there is an ancient city buried under Lough Gill, possibly a folk memory of a drowned lake-dwelling or *crannog*. A tourist fishing from a boat on the lough once asked his boatman if he had ever seen the fabled city. 'I have surely,' said the boatman. 'In fact, on a still summer's day you can see the turf smoke from the chimneys rising up out of the lake.'

Yeats once toyed with the idea of retreating to an island. His father had been reading *Walden* to him and the idea came to Yeats that he might build a hut like Thoreau's on an island in Lough Gill called Innisfree. He never did build the cottage, but his dream brought forth a poem, made, as he said, while he was in London and sick for the sight of home. Sligo, to Yeats, had always been the *Land of Heart's Desire* and, in those busy London streets, he was suddenly carried back to the country of his childhood, and one of the most glorious poems in the English language was born:

> I will arise and go now, and go to Innisfree,
> And a small cabin build there, of clay and wattles made:
> Nine bean-rows will I have there, a hive for the honey-bee,
> And live alone in the bee-loud glade.

The island lies much further on along the lake shore and was my ultimate goal for the day, but first I was heading for Slish Wood where Yeats slept out one night in order to call down upon himself some mystic experience. He was away all night and, when he got back home, ruffled and damp and obviously not having slept, the housekeeper thought he'd been out on the tiles with one of the local girls. She started laughing and snorting when Yeats protested that he had done no such thing, and the more he denied it, the more she laughed.

Coillté Teo, the Irish Forestry Department, for some reason have changed the name from Slish Wood to Lough Gill Forest, although, as a sensible afterthought, they have mapped out several walking routes around the area. There is one well-marked track through the forest, which wanders high above the lake and looked from the map as though it would be an interesting route. I followed the path and, as I climbed, the clouds that had been hanging over the land all morning began to thin and fade away so that, by the time I reached the high point of the forest path,

the land before me was awash with sunlight. I sat on a felled log in a clearing and looked down to the lough and over to its far shore. There was not a soul on the mountainside but myself. Looking at the map it would be quite possible for Coillté Teo to carry the path on to Trawane Bay facing Innisfree, which would be a lovely end to the walk. I hope they manage to organise this with the local landowners.

I thought for a brief moment that it might be a good idea to climb Killerry mountain. From where I had been sitting it looked quite close, but the ground between the forest track and the bottom of the hill is horrific, a mess of tangled briars and felled lumber, so instead I stayed where I was and ate my sandwiches. There's always another day and always another way up a mountain.

Since there was no way I could follow a route eastwards through the forest, I made my way back out of Slish Wood to the road and followed it all the way round the mountain to Trawane Bay and the Lake Isle. Free, from whom the island takes its name, was a young warrior who fell in love with a chief's daughter. To prove his love, she asked him to fetch her some fruit from the island. The fruit, however, was magical fruit, kept solely for the use of the local deities and guarded by a fierce dragon. Free swam across to the island and slew the monster, but he tasted the fruit himself and died. His sweetheart was so taken by grief at his death that she too ate the forbidden fruit and died by his side. They are buried together, so the story goes, in the heart of that magical place. Yeats's island of peace, by the way, also goes under the unpoetical name of Cat Island.

By the time I got to Dromahair it was opening time, and I was able to take a pint and a cheese sandwich from the landlord's

Yeats' grave at Drumcliff set against the flank of Benbulbin

daughter in Stanford's Bar, without having to swim across the lake. There was nobody but myself there, and a fine sandwich it was too, in one of the best old pubs in Ireland. It was at Drom-ahair that the man who dreamed of Faeryland heard the little silver fishes singing to him:

> He stood among a crowd at Dromahair;
> His heart hung all upon a silken dress,
> And he had known at last some tenderness,
> Before earth took him to her stony care;
> But when a man poured fish into a pile,
> It seemed they raised their little silver heads,
> And sang what gold morning or evening sheds
> Upon a woven world-forgotten isle.

I read somewhere that poetry is the closest we will ever get to magic and that a great poet will mine something deep and eternal and universal that goes beyond words. Call me a romantic fool if you like but I feel that the music of Yeats's poetry somehow touches on that deep magic and when you walk about Lough Gill your feet are treading on the very stuff that magic is made from and you must 'tread softly for you tread on my dreams'.

I didn't relish the thought of a long road walk back to Sligo, so I stuck my thumb out and the second or third car to come along stopped and gave me a lift all the way back to town. I had a quick bath and took myself and my banjo off to McGlynn's and, as my grandmother would have said, 'And why wouldn't you? Sure you're a long time dead.'

30 Benbulbin

No, not in boyhood when with rod and fly,
Or the humbler worm, I climbed Ben Bulben's back
And had the livelong summer day to spend.

W.B. Yeats, *The Tower*

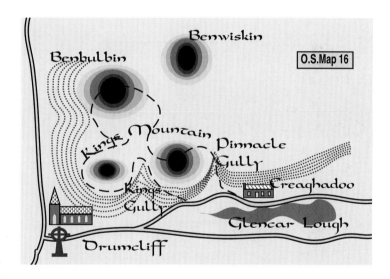

Yeats' grave lies in Drumcliff in the graveyard of the church where his grandfather was once rector. He lies beneath a simple grey stone slab, as he requested. On the slab are the words he asked to be cut into the stone:

> Cast a cold eye
> On life, on death,
> Horseman pass by!

These are the last lines of his poem *Under Ben Bulben*. (The Suirbhéireacht Ordonáis na hEireann now call the mountain Benbulbin.) I have been going to that graveyard for more than twenty years and, at the fall of light, particularly in winter when the rooks are settling in the skeletal sticks of the high trees, it is a powerful place. Away in the distance is the great stone prow of Benbulbin (*Binn Ghulbain*), while across the lane stands one of the most beautiful High Crosses of Ireland, St Columba's Cross.

It was at Drumcliff that the Battle of the Book was fought, a battle that took Columba out of Ireland for ever, away in exile to Iona where he founded one of the greatest holy communities of

the early Christian world. The book was a psalter, the *Cathach*, which Columba had secretly copied while staying with St Finian. When Finian discovered this, he demanded that the copy be given to him. Columba refused and the matter went before Dermod the High King, who made his famous decision, 'To every cow her calf, to every book its copy' and Columba was ordered to give the copy to Finian. Columba refused to accept this decision and called on his Ulster relatives for help. In AD561, three thousand of his men faced the army of Dermod under the flanks of Benbulbin. In the battle, thousands lost their lives and Columba, aided by an angel, won the book. It is said that Columba left his beloved Ireland in shame and repentance for exile on Iona where his self-given penance was to convert more to Christianity than had died in the battle.

The *Cathach*, though lost for a while, was later found and was carried into all their battles by the O'Donnells, the Ulster chieftains. The book is now in the Royal Irish Academy, while its case or shrine is in the National Museum in Dublin. I have stood many a time, my nose pressed on the glass of the case, looking at that jewelled shrine and thinking about it and about the power of the word and the book and how that power runs through the story of Ireland from the battle for the psalter to James Joyce's *Ulysses*, once banned in the country that now claims him as one of her greatest sons. When you realise that '*maru an filí ort*' (the curse of the poet on you) is an echo of the power of the Druid bards, you understand a little more about the power of the book and the word, and why the Catholic Church in Ireland had an Index of banned texts for so long.

Knocknarea, the High Cross, and Yeats' grave are all clustered together in this mystical corner of Sligo, and from the heights of Benbulbin you can see them all between the summit and the sea. The last time I climbed Benbulbin was on an early spring day, when the weather looked untrustworthy and I was in a pretty poor way. I'd been in Shoot the Crows the night before with Séa-

mus O' Dowd and a cluster of musicians, and the *craic* had been mighty. My theory that Arthur Guinness and Co. put something in their brew that makes you crave Vindaloo curry at fifteen minutes past midnight held up and I trudged around Sligo looking for a Taj Mahal or Light of India. The only place open was a fast-food joint. I should have known better. I ordered something dead on bread and a portion of fries. It was what I call a Yo-Yo supper, no sooner down than up, and I had a most entertaining night racing my intestines to the bathroom.

Next morning, thick-headed and feeling like I'd gone ten rounds with Cúchulainn and lost, I drove out of Sligo heading north to the back road to park close by Creaghadoo under King's Mountain. The clear night sky of the previous evening had brought a cool windy morning with blue skies and broken, but serious-looking, cloud. Charlie Roberts, the Uilean pipe-maker and piper, lives close under the mountain, so I called at his house on my way to Pinnacle Gully.

Uilean pipes, at one time known as Union Pipes, are Irish bagpipes, but instead of being blown like the Scots pipes, they have a bellows that is worked by the piper's elbow. There are several great Irish pipers, like Paddy Moloney, Liam Og O'Flynn and Davey Spillane, but I am afraid I will never be one of them. I once tried to play the Irish pipes. I spent a month trying to get a decent note out of them and failed. Imagine, if you can, wrestling with something that is a cross between the animate world and the handiwork of a bad plumber. It was like trying to get the pyjamas off a particularly recalcitrant and bad-tempered octopus with adenoid trouble that had somehow got itself attached to an antique stomach pump. I produced nothing but shrieks and screams from the belly and nose of this particular contraption and gave up before the neighbours reported me to the police as a serial killer. I shall not do it again.

Pinnacle Gully is one of the easiest ways up through the cliffs of Benbulbin onto the massif and I planned to climb up through the gully and make my way by King's Mountain to the trig point on the summit of the Ben. From there I would come back to the King's Gully in a sort of figure of eight, and make my way off the mountain down an old track. The cliffs of this great plateau run for miles and in poor weather getting on, off and across it can be a fairly hairy experience. I knew that the new 1:50.000 series map was available for the mountain, but none of the bookshops I had combed in Donegal and Sligo had a copy, so I would be using the pretty, but pretty useless, old series. Charlie pointed me towards a *bohareen* that would lead me towards the gully and told me to call in for a cup of tea when I came down off the mountain.

I followed the path, the cliffs dead ahead of me, and, climbing the ubiquitous wall, barbed-wire fence and ditch, struck off to my right to the scree slope under the gully. It was a bit of a slog, made doubly tedious by the fact that the numerous sheep on the mountain have gnawed it to the bone, and what grass there is left is like a thin green veneer covering the clay underneath. The previous year had been a particularly wet one even for Ireland and the mountain was sodden and slippy so that, to be blunt, it was like climbing near-vertical snot. The climb got quite hairy, too, because the flank of the mountain soon grew steeper, until it became a very dodgy slope with nothing for boots or hands to grip and I began to wonder if they made special clay-crampons for Irish mountains. I climbed, slithering and clutching at sprigs of chewed gorse, into the heart of the gully, where a natural stone staircase made the going better. 'This is going to be a piece

of cake,' I muttered to myself, but then the staircase met a featureless, slime-covered, blank stone wall and I had to contour out on more steep snot to climb above it. It was quite tricky and the sheep below me were giggling and talking about me in Irish. Back in the gully, I climbed on, coming after a few minutes to a scramble that was as near vertical as doesn't matter and, as I was dangling in space, again to the amusement of the sheep, the sky darkened and a sudden hail storm hit the mountain.

Visibility went down from twenty miles to twenty feet in as many seconds and I hung on with toes and fingers while I struggled to pull on my waterproof trousers and cagoule, without either falling off the cliff or dropping my rucksack. The sheep by now were rolling about, laughing hysterically. One of them laughed so much she was sick. I sat out the storm, drinking tea and trying to keep warm, staring out at a grey wall of mist and swirling hail. Then, as suddenly as it had come, the storm blew through and the land beneath opened up again. There were more sheep looking up now, one of them selling tickets, hoping for an encore. I climbed on through a tricky scramble, over a barbed-wire fence through more snot and up through a narrow stone defile onto the top; all in all, a hell of a climb. In dry, warm weather it would be a good scramble; in ice, snow and hail it was less than pleasant.

The plateau before me had no defining features or landmarks so I took a compass bearing and headed north-west. The hail returned but, compared to the previous storm, this was a half-hearted event, more a postscript to the other one. A fair bit of bog-hopping brought me to the head of King's Gully, and here I saw a small, white Celtic cross below me. I discovered later that it marked the spot where six anti-Treaty soldiers were ambushed

The approach to Pinnacle Gully

by Government troops while on their way over the mountain to the glen of Ardnaglass in September 1922, one month after the murder of Michael Collins. Irishmen killing Irishmen, there in that beautiful place, and more than seventy years later, not so many miles away across the border, a fragile peace had at last broken out. I walked on, across what felt like endless bogs, to the saddle of the Benwiskin-Benbulbin Horseshoe. From this point you get no sense of the knife edge that Benwiskin presents when seen from the north, but the views are still wonderful. The arms of the horseshoe stretch before you as the massive, green amphitheatre of Ardnaglass glen with its maze of turf cuttings and its bog road, falls away beneath. Had you a long summer's day, the walk from Glencar over the saddle and down into the glen would make a grand day out.

I carried on, following the compass, remembering from past experience that the summit is hard to find, but at last I came to the trig point. Beneath me stretched most of Sligo – Knocknarea, the Ox Mountains, Sligo Bay, Rosses Point and the bright Atlantic ocean shimmering under the bright spring sun. It was terribly blustery, though, and I soon got down behind the trig point for shelter. My hands, wrapped round the cup of tea, were still cold so I didn't hang around long. I stuck the monopod in the peat bog and took some photographs of myself on the summit to prove that I had been out in the hills and not in Hargadans, helping to reduce Ireland's Guinness mountain, then I headed south-east across the plateau to the south face of King's Mountain. I followed a route across the edge of a steep but not too dangerous slope and then cut back into the massif and into King's Gully, following it to its head before crossing the gully to take a fine, green path down what was obviously an old way over the saddle and down to Ardnaglass. It struck me as I walked that it might have been an old turf road.

The sun was full out now and I had a lovely walk back down to the intake wall and across sad, rushy fields to the road. At one point, as I walked on the road, heading for Charlie's house, two mad dogs attacked me outside a farm gate, but I went for them with my monopod and they backed off. Charlie's wife, Mary, made me tea and biscuits and we chatted until Allan, their son, came in from school and played the pipes for us. He's fifteen and wants to follow his dad into the craft. It was really pleasant to sit there after a long walk in cold winds, supping tea with someone like Charlie. A Geordie who has worked all over the world as a draughtsman and engineer, a mountain climber and musician, he married a Sligo girl and came to live here under the mountain and make some of the finest Uilean pipes in the world. He has orders from Italy and America; plenty of work and a lovely place to work in. Lying in bed that night, after another *sesiún* at McGlynn's, I read that Yeats' grave lies in the diocese of Elphin. Knowing his fascination with the world of *faery*, that must cheer him a lot.

31 Truskmore – the Big Cod

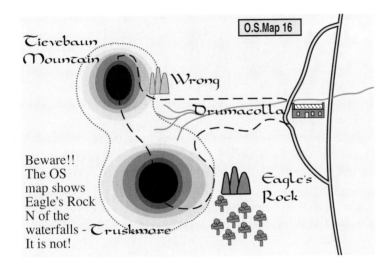

Tievebaun Mountain

Wrong

Drumacolla

O.S.Map 16

Beware!!
The OS
map shows
Eagle's Rock
N of the
waterfalls - Truskmore
It is not!

Eagle's
Rock

The mountains that edge the Sligo coast all echo the shape of Benbulbin, with steep grassy slopes leading to vertical cliffs. Benwiskin, Arroo and Truskmore shadow the outline of Yeats' mountain and they all present the same difficulties to the hill walker – in poor weather their slopes are greasy and the mist-shrouded cliffs are murderous. I did have good weather, though, when I walked Truskmore one hazy, still, autumn day with a gentle sun burning through light cloud and little prospect of a change. I'd decided to climb onto the mountain by Eagle's

Rock, a great fang that juts up as an outrider of the massif, like something more at home in Monument Valley, USA. *The Irish Walks Guide* for this area described a tough climb over rising ground and scree into the sanctuary of Eagle's Rock and from there it seemed an easy walk on to the plateau and over to the summit.

I left my car by an empty cottage and fought my way along a half-choked *bohareen* to open ground. Climbing a wire fence, I caught my trousers and ripped them. They were a very old pair and I was going to throw them away anyway so, with it being a sunny warm day, I decided to convert them to shorts. The cows watched with interest as I hacked away at the trouser legs with my Swiss army knife. 'Man turning himself into a scarecrow' must surely have crossed their bovine minds, sparking across the BSE holes like lightning across great ravines.

The sun threw Eagle's Rock into relief as I climbed, sweating and panting, towards the sanctuary. I took a point too far to the right into a gully that would have brought me under the cliff and had to make one of my least favourite moves, swinging out on a sheep track over lots of nothing until I made better ground. The scramble into the chasm over the jumble of a boulder choke was tough but didn't seem dangerous, until a rock the size of a tea chest went off below me and crunched and crashed down the gully. I didn't dwell too much on what might have happened if my leg had been under that. I was alone and nobody knew where

I was going. Although I had mentioned to the girl on the desk at the hotel that I was climbing Truskmore, I'm sure she hadn't taken it in.

Comforted by that small thought, I scrambled into the dark and dreary mountain hall. Extremely serious cliffs rose up sheer on each side and, at first viewing, my way out didn't look too nice either. It seemed like a sheer drop on to nothing, but by following a more stable boulder choke down out of the hole, I got to a sheep track that followed an easy line under the plateau edge. A misty autumn light washed over the Gleniff valley and I had a pleasant walk along a series of sheep tracks up on to the massif. The summit was still some way off, hidden behind rising heathery ground, so I took a compass bearing and began to climb. Not a soul, not a bird, nothing stirred, I could have been alone on the face of the earth at that time. Around me, the land stretched away, heathery and silent. Then, cresting a rise, I saw the summit still some way off but capped by a massive television transmitter aerial.

Truskmore is hardly a beautiful mountain, but it still doesn't deserve this. As I got closer, I saw that there was a smaller aerial close by and wondered idly if the big one had had a baby. At the mast I sat in the warm sun on one of the massive concrete blocks that hold the aerial up, eating some cheese and an apple, wondering if my bodily presence was causing interference on televisions all over Sligo and Donegal. 'Seán, there's a wee shadow on that corner of the tally. Looks like somebody eatin' cheese an' apple, so it does.' It also struck me that, at one time, the tops of great mountains were the dwelling places of the gods, and now the new god, the god of the haunted goldfish bowl, has taken over. Here, on the highest hill in Sligo, is the throne room of the gods of *Neighbours, Blind Date* and *Crinkly Bottom*. I decided that it was time for this pagan to be off.

From Truskmore (*Trosc Mór* – Big Cod) to *Tievebaun* (White Side) I followed the old county boundary ditch and wall that divides Leitrim from Sligo. To build this boundary must have taken thousands of man hours and yet I could see no reason for digging a physical line to mark the line on the map. Perhaps it was the same spirit that caused the construction of some of the great dykes of the British Isles, like Offa's Dyke between England and Wales, and the Devil's Dyke on Bleaklow in Derbyshire. The dykes stand proclaiming: 'This is my land, beyond here you are a stranger'.

The featureless summit of Tievebaun gives a wonderful panorama of Benwiskin in the south, the sea to the west and the Gleniff valley to the east, with the great massif of Arroo flanking it. It was too hazy for taking pictures, so I picked my way carefully along the rim of the plateau, looking for a way down. There is a broad and welcoming gully a short way along the edge but, looking at the map, I saw that it ended in something narrow that had 'Waterfall' written across it. (The word 'Waterfall' is missing from the new map so take care on this section.) Remembering that waterfalls are normally vertical, I walked on to where a steep slope took me down to a broad, sheep-spotted terrace.

I could see a scree run leading over the lip of the terrace with what looked like a cairn on its edge. I peered over. Steep, grassy slopes led down a long way towards an old green lane. I saw a series of sheep tracks that could be followed in a sort of zig-zag fashion and began scrambling down towards them. It was a steep and long but fairly safe descent, with wonderful views

Eagle Rock seen from the green lane

down into a landscape that was already tinted with the first colours of autumn, small white dots of farms, like foam on a russet sea. All day the pale but warm autumn sun had shone and, yet again, as happens on so many Irish mountains, I had not seen a soul.

I dropped down to a green lane that would take me back to the road and filled my water bottles from a mountain stream by some sheep folds at its head. Never has water tasted sweeter. In fact, I don't think there is anything better than pure mountain water from an Irish hill – particularly when it is helped along with a litle splash of Black Bush. That night in Shoot the Crows, Dervish, the young Sligo traditional band, were in great form and what better end to a day in the hills than the fire and sweet water of traditional music?

County Donegal

Oh I've just come round to see you all and sit with you a while
Because I love your voices and I love your own sweet smiles
I'll sit a while and talk with you until the cock doers call
For your hearts are like your mountains in the homes of Donegal.

Traditional Song

According to the information sheet in the Glenveagh National Park, it rains seven days out of ten in Donegal. I'm not sure that is true or, if it is, it must only be a bit of a spit and spatter for some of those days. Although I've had some of the wettest, coldest and windiest times in the mountains of Donegal, I've also had sunny, warm days, when not a breath was stirring and you could hear larks above you and the far off murmur of surf on some distant pebbly beach. It is impossible to describe Donegal in a handful of lines – it is the wildest place I have been to in Ireland and yet also the gentlest and, like the weather and the land, the people can be wild and gentle in turn. You can hear that in their fiddle music. It can be riotous, fast and swooping one moment, plaintive and tearful the next. Donegal is a land, you might say, of complementary contradictions and it is a land of dry wit, too, when the most outrageous things are said with only a slight twinkle just discernible in the corner of an eye.

I stopped on a lonely bog road one winter's afternoon to ask the way of a man who was stacking turf at the road's edge.

'Where will this road take me?' I asked.
'This road,' he said, 'will take you wherever you want to go.'

The cliff walk at Port

They've got a great sense of humour in Donegal: the English Tory party took its name from Tory Island off the coast of Donegal where the people are wild and tough and strong. What they didn't and probably still don't know is that Tory is the Irish for 'rogue'.

If you look at the pretty maps of Donegal, numbers 1 and 3 in the old 1:126,720 series, you will see that most of Donegal is golden and orange, which means that most of Donegal is over 1,000 feet above sea level: in fact, it has more than a hundred 1,000 ft peaks. Most of the low-lying ground is either in the long glens that run from the north-east to the south-west or is on the sea coast where it is fragmented by inlets like Rosses Bay and Gweebarra Bay. It is a beautiful county, in some places stunningly so, yet it is a poor county too, famine and emigration have left terrible scars here.

Donegal is the second biggest county in Ireland with more than a million acres of land. Yet only three-tenths of this is cultivable. There is a bridge in a lonely glen near Gweedore called the Bridge of Partings because, when the young people were setting out on their great journey of emigration, their relatives and friends would accompany them on a long day's walk as far as this bridge and there they would part, more often than not for the last time. The Wailing Wall in Jerusalem can hardly have seen more tears than this stone bridge.

Because it has some of the poorest land in Ireland and because, until recently, it was so inaccessible, Donegal was able to retain its music and its language in better health than in most other parts of the island. Irish is still the first language of many parts of west Donegal and a recent survey showed that this area had more than 50 per cent of the population as native Irish speakers. In the area round Gweedore and Glencolumbkille you will often hear Irish as the only language spoken. One reason for Donegal's special character may be that it has always eluded the grip of the English. In 1923, when partition took place, Carson, the Protestant leader, reasoned correctly that Donegal was better left out of the Six Counties because, being full of Catholics, it would only have voted itself back into the republic at the first opportunity, perhaps taking Fermanagh with it.

Another clue to the special nature of Donegal may be its close links with Scotland and the North. Many Donegal people travelled to Scotland for work and brought back with them hints of Scotland in the music and songs they picked up, and through the fiddlers of Donegal you will hear more than a tint of the thistle in the reels and schottisches. An expert (and I am not one) can readily distinguish between the fiddle styles of Sliabh Lucra (a great musical area on the Cork and Kerry border), Galway, Sligo and Donegal and they will always tell you that it's not just the bowing or the fingering or the tunes but something else not quite tangible. And as you stand and listen to the fiddlers in the Rusty Mackerel in Teelin or Teach Biddy's in Glencolumbkille, you will hear in those ringing Donegal strings the very soul of Donegal.

For the walker Donegal has everything – high mountains, sea cliffs, low coastal walks and glens; places where you can walk all day and not see a soul. I am not employed by the Donegal Tourist Board but I have to admit a certain bias and everybody I've ever sent Donegal way has, like myself, gone back time and again.

32 A Walk in the Blue Stacks

Paddy Campbell is a tidy wee man with red cheeks and a soft and lilting way of talking. His shoes were polished bright and he wore his best suit the morning I met him to ramble in the Bluestacks a long number of years ago when I was working on a BBC radio series in Donegal. I had imagined that we'd be off the road, climbing in some glen to a *cwm* or mountain corrie, where buzzards hung on skeins of wind, but, instead, we wandered the back lanes of his townland and met so many of his neighbours and friends and were invited in for so many pots of tea and plates of cakes that it took us all day to cover a handful of miles, at the end of which I had overdosed severely on tannin. Those miles, however, were amongst the best I've ever walked anywhere; nowhere have I met people more friendly and hospitable. We were beckoned into houses all along the lanes as we passed. The woman at one house had left Donegal as a young girl to spend all her working life as a clippie on the Glasgow trams and buses, returning when she retired to the quiet cottage under the hill in which she had been born.

Paddy, who wrote *Rambles in Donegal* and *From Quiet Glens to Noisy Streets*, is a gifted storyteller. Every house and crossroads and standing stone we came upon had a story attached to it, and Paddy knew the story and told it beautifully, in a soft musical voice as we wandered around the Bluestacks that day.

The *Cruacha Gorma*, or Bluestack Mountains, lie to the north of Donegal town, in the triangle made by the Barnesmore

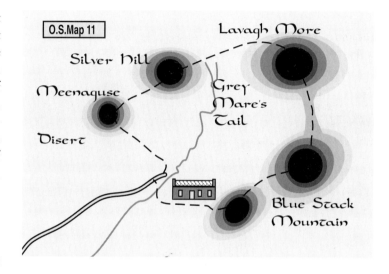

O.S. Map 11
Lavagh More
Silver Hill
Meenaguse
Grey Mare's Tail
Disert
Blue Stack Mountain

Gap and the Glenties to Ballybofey road. But they are, like the Burren, more a state of mind than a range of hills because, according to Paddy, the people of the Bluestacks are different from the people you might meet elsewhere. Like other Donegal mountain folk, they are gentler and shyer than lowland people, and although the number of native Irish speakers in the mountains is diminishing, as it is everywhere in Ireland, Paddy remembers a time when there were people around the *Cruacha Gorma* who would come to the fairs and markets and ask those who

Paddy Campbell and Jimmy McCrory by Jimmy's fireside

were more able in English to speak for them. And Paddy tells how the men of the Bluestacks are experts with sheep and sheep-dogs, their dogs only understanding commands in Irish.

We were walking one day along a quiet narrow lane above lovely Lough Eske, when Paddy suddenly dived through a gap in a hedge, shouting, 'There's an old friend of mine lives in here, Jimmy McCrory.'

I looked through the gap and saw a tiny, whitewashed cottage with a thatched roof. Paddy called out again and Jimmy's head came peeping round the door. With weathered features and eyes that you could only describe as 'merry', Jimmy was a softly spoken and gentle man, a bachelor farmer living quietly on his little patch of land. People knew him as a great Rambling Man in the

days before television and radio took over, when people would ramble from house to house of an evening, to sit and gossip, tell a tale or sing; what Johnny Crowley would call a *scairthing*. Jimmy doesn't ramble much now, but he has kept the old thatched cottage exactly as it was when his mother and father were alive, with its stone flagged floor and open fireplace.

When I went back to see him a few years ago, he was living in a prefabricated unit close to the old home, which has now been condemned. He has a bathroom and heating and is dry and warm, so I suppose in many ways it's a better life for him. But Jimmy has a great fondness for the old house and he still goes in and sits there quietly. It is full of ghosts now, singing and step dancing and having the *cráic*. Of those whose feet tramped the old earth floor of the cottage, some are in America, some are in England, many are dead, but Jimmy is still next door with his smile and his knitted cap. Following a bad fall from a tractor, rheumatics set in and he hasn't been able to look after his old house so well. Grass is growing all round the cobbles and it needs a bit of re-thatching, but Jimmy loves it, and when he gets stronger, he'll be in there weeding out the grass from the cobbles and tidying the place up for the ghosts and the memories that are in it.

The waters of the Grey Mare's Tail (*Rubal na Lárach Bainé*) fall 1,800 feet from the high cliffs of the Cock of Sruell to the floor of the lonely Sruell Glen and, on windy days, the gusts feather out the waters so that they look indeed as though a great horse is shaking its tail over the valley below. For years it has been a popular walking spot both for serious mountain men and women and for Sunday strollers. Above the waterfall stands Lavagh More (*Leamhách Mór* – Big Place of Elms) and facing it,

Pat walking on a track through Sruell Glen, with the Mare's Tail seen beyond

across the glen, the Blue Stack Mountain. There is a fine horse-shoe walk that takes in both hills and makes a grand day out. Paddy had led me as far as the road end that summer's day long gone, and had pointed me the way up by Meenaguse and the loughs under Silver Hill on to Lavagh More.

A few years later, I came back and walked the horseshoe on a lovely, soft June day. The lane to the Grey Mare's Tail leads to the head of the Sruell Glen, past the ruins of cottages that, until a few years ago, were still inhabited. There was a whole community living up here in the glen but, within a handful of years of their leaving, the weather has gnawed and clawed away at what was left of the family homes, and now weeds and trees grow through the cottage floors. Beyond the ruins, the lane melted into the bog and the peat, and I struck up to the left to scramble by a small beck through crags that would take me above Meena-guse and on to the rising ground between Silver Hill and Lavagh More. Under Meenaguse is the townland of Dysert. I once asked Paddy to define a townland and he found it very difficult. It is not a political area like a county, or a religious area like a parish. Some townlands straddle parish boundaries and parishes con-tain many townlands. It seems to be something like a mind-scape, the place you feel you belong to, and often its boundaries will be a river and a mountain. The townland of Dysert was famous once for its clay. It was said to have magical qualities and that rats could not live anywhere near where the clay was kept and, for that reason, the clay from Dysert was carried all over the world. I imagine that the Union of Pied Pipers and Affiliated Rodent Evictors was less than pleased about that.

I climbed on up the rugged slope, the valley with its ruined cottages falling away behind me. It was the kind of summer's day

hillwalkers dream of; the sky was clear and the sun was hot, though a strong wind racing in off the Atlantic drove any ideas I might have had about sunbathing on the summit back into the cupboard. The landscape was sodden, a giant green and brown sponge. Even the slopes were waterlogged, and every clod drib-bled water into my palm as I clutched at them to pull myself up. Flakes of stone slid away under my boot as I scrabbled for footholds on the rock. The outcrops were the safest place to stand; everything else was falling and sliding and melting as though the very mountains were dissolving. I dropped off the broad ridge of Silver Hill and worked my way round by a neck-lace of silvery loughs, until I was under the mountain. The Donegal sky was constantly changing, steel-blue with small ragged white clouds scooting in from the west. And the wind that was driving them in picked up strength and blew me along the rise between the peaks, helping to make the pull up to Lavagh More a little easier.

Around me on the wet and windy summit were clumps of quartzite boulders that looked for all the world like sheep, while below, sheltering from the mountain gale, were a lot of sheep that looked for all the world like clumps of quartzite boulders. I wondered if the sheep had any identity problems and would occasionally find themselves talking to rocks about nice patches of grass they had found. Then I decided that such thoughts had been brought on by the sunshine and the wind and the wonder-ful view over to Donegal Bay and that I ought to drop down off the summit and find some shelter in which to eat my lunch.

A steep descent brought me down to the saddle between Lavagh More and the Blue Stack Mountain. The whole glen was spread out before me, the Grey Mare's Tail plain to see, so I sat

Homes of Donegal

in a natural shelter between some boulders and opened my flask and unpacked the sandwiches. I suppose the saddle would have been a way over from the Sruell Glen to Ballybofey for the people of the glen, but it must have been a long hard walk. Full of tea and soda bread, I left the col and slowly slogged my way up to the summit of Bluestack. From the top, the panorama took in Lough Eske and Benbulbin to the south, while westwards lay Slieve League and, faint and far off, the hills of northern Donegal.

I scrambled over massive boulders lined with quartzite veins and great glaciated slabs called boiler plates to sit in a sun trap for half an hour or so, looking out over the land below and won-

dering what was going on in the rest of the world. Clouds were rolling in from the sea as I followed the broad ridge off, through bogs and spongy land and down to the last farm in the glen. There used to be fourteen families farming here and now there is just one.

In this lovely glen at the end of a day of bright sun and glorious walking, a shadow passed over me and I felt the kind of sadness that can come upon you suddenly when you think about what has gone before. The old Irish bards used to say that there were three kinds of song, a song for laughing, a song for weeping and a song for sleeping. In Donegal you can hear all three in a single day.

33 The Cliffs of Slieve League

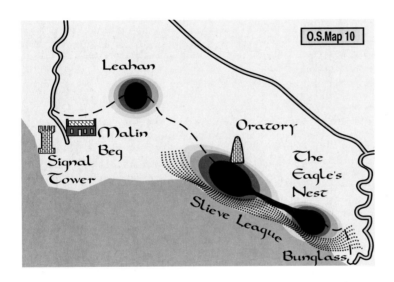

If you've no head for heights, then there's a part of the coast of Donegal that could well give you trouble. The One Man's Pass on the Slieve League cliffs is a narrow arête, with a huge gulf of air lying below it to the west, with nothing in it but 2,000 feet and a floor of sea. Water is soft, but not after 2,000 feet of foreplay. On the landward side, a slightly less serious crag opens up a drop of 700 feet and, between the 'rock and a hard place', the path is a yard wide and closing. On a sunny, still day it is safe, if a little exposed. On a windy day, if you were daft enough to do it, you'd need to cross it at a bum shuffle, holding on with everything you've got. A Dutchman walked the One Man's Pass a few years ago with a Walkman glued to his ears. Up there on the airy knife edge you can get sudden squalls coming from both seaward and landward sides and you need all your five and country wits about you. He didn't hear the gust of wind from the east that toppled him from the knife edge and he fell to his death. There is an easier and totally safe path, on the landward side, called the 'Old Man's Pass' and many people take that way, avoiding the arête.

The Slieve League cliff walk is one of the great walks of western Europe, marred solely by the fact that, unless you're staying in Carrick or fancy several miles of road walking, it is best done as a linear walk, for the hairy coastal road – and you can hardly call it a road – that runs by Carrigan Head is the only track that goes anywhere near the cliffs.

I first tried to walk the cliffs alone on a terrible day in early March, when Atlantic gales were dragging great sullen clouds over the sea and dropping them on the head of the cliffs. I gave up just below the One Man's Pass and went back to the car, wet, cold and miserable, but still alive. I may be daft but I'm not stupid.

I have walked the cliffs a number of times since then and they are wild. Once, on a darkening winter afternoon, I watched as the sea boiled with a strange, luminous light and the rest of the

Walkers on the skyline of Slieve League with the coast and mountains of Sligo in the distance

Slieve League

world around, sky and cliffs, grew grey, purple and savage. It's no place to be in foul weather.

A few years ago on a fine August day I was lucky enough to be offered a lift from Glencolumbkille to the cliffs by Tony Birtles, who was leading a group of hillwalkers from *Odeas Gael*, the Irish summer school that runs courses in hillwalking, Irish language and Irish dancing in that village throughout the summer. In Ireland, there is a generosity of spirit that includes the stranger in many things and, simply as a result of saying one night in Teach Biddy's in Glencolumbkille that I was hoping to walk Slieve League, I was invited along as one of the party. The summer school minibus would take us to Bunglass beyond Teelin where the road ends and collect us at Malin Beg at the end of the day.

The drive from Teelin to Bunglass and the place they call *Amharc Mór* (The Great View) is interesting in its own right. The track which the bus follows is only inches from the edge at times and, first thing in the morning, after a breakfast of kippers and porridge, with the taste of last night's Guinness still on you, the realisation that there is nothing outside the left-hand window of the bus but a rehearsal for eternity can be a sobering experience. The bus dropped us and set off back to Glencolumbkille.

There was bright sunlight all about us with just a handful of clouds rolling in from the west. It looked set to stay fair all day. We shouldered our packs and struck off along the path. The narrow but safe track on to the cliffs is well defined and follows the edge all the way. From Bunglass (which means The End of the Green) the trail curves into a cleft and climbs steeply under a massive overhang to The Eagle's Nest. There (if it's not too windy) you can lie on your belly right on the edge, and look down at Atlantic rollers smashing into the great seastacks they call the Giant's Desk and Chair. At the Eagle's Nest you are on the first leg of the ridge walk that takes you to the One Man's Pass and, as you climb towards the arête, the world opens out below you. To the east are Teelin Bay and Tawny Bay while, inland, the hills stretch away to the north to Slievetooey and Crockuna and further north-east lie the hills of the Glengesh Horseshoe. On that lovely summer's day, we could see the white cap of Errigal to the north, and south to Croagh Patrick, seventy-five miles away.

But ahead of us stood the last climb to the knife-edge of the pass. There were ten of us on the walk and, though the day was clear and bright, the wind, as we climbed, grew stronger. By the time we reached the arête it was gusting strong enough to make a crossing of the One Man's Pass dangerous for a large group without ropes. So we took the Old Man's Pass just below the ridge and, once beyond the arête, climbed up the far side to look back at it. A yard wide at its narrowest point and about forty feet long, I would like suckers on my feet before I crossed it on anything other than the stillest day.

Once beyond the pass, the going gets much easier and we climbed the last few feet to the summit of Slieve League, a flat moonscape of frost-shattered stones. Just below the trig point to the east is the oratory and holy wells of St Assicus, goldsmith to St Patrick. Ireland has more than fourteen hundred saints, but only five of them are recognised by the Vatican. This is probably a hangover from the days when the Celtic Church, with its married clergy and women priests, was a definite threat to the gathering might of Rome. If you were to ask people today which place has a greater feeling of spirituality, Rome or the hills of Donegal, I think I know what the answer would be. Having said that, some of the saints do seem faintly dubious: St Comgall of

Bangor was said to possess miraculous spit which could shatter rocks, St Dympna is the patron saint of sleepwalkers, while St Fiacre is the patron saint of gardeners, taxi drivers and haemorrhoid sufferers. But in case you think I mock, let me tell you that King Henry V let his troops ransack the shrine of St Fiacre and the king died not long after of septic haemorrhoids on the very feast day of St Fiacre. So be warned!

Leaving the summit we headed for Leahan, crossing the boggy saddle between, to climb that almost conical hill in bright sunshine. But, though the weather had seemed settled when we set out, it was changing now and, as we stood on the peak looking west to Malin Beg and the ocean, we could see the rain clouds that the weather forecast had talked of that morning crowding in towards the land. We moved quickly down the hill towards Trabane and the coastal track and, as we gained level ground, the rain began to fall and the signal tower on the headland stood out stark against a thunderous orange light as the afternoon sun was lost in the hurrying storm. We put on waterproofs and headed on through lashing, chilling rain, an indication of just how quickly the weather can change in the west of Ireland.

We took shelter in one of the holiday cottages used by *Odeas Gael*; there was nothing to drink but whisky and strong tea to warm us up, and nothing to do until the storm wore itself out but sit before a turf fire, eating soda bread and biscuits and yarning away. I was quite sad when the bus came to take us all back to Glencolumbkille.

One of the twelve crosses of St Columba's 'round'

34 A Ramble Above the Glen

It is not nostalgia to say that we have lost something: we must face up to the fact that the evolution of our 'civilisation' cannot be assumed to mean progress. We have lost something when we cease to interact; when we cease to come together in groups to enrich each other's lives; to stimulate; to rely upon our wit and our spirit; to inspire and support each other.

Fr. McDyer of Glencolumbkille, *An Autobiography*

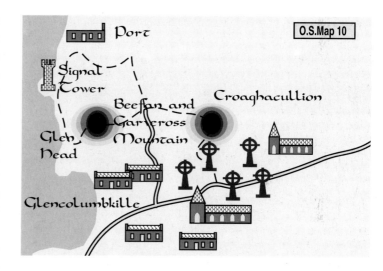

There is a magic about Glencolumbkille that is hard to define. Somebody once called it Ireland's best-kept secret and they may be right. James Byrne, the Donegal fiddler, lives in 'the Glen', as locals call it. He is a stocky farmer with broad, workman's hands that you would hardly think could hold a fiddle, let alone coax magic from it, but James comes from a long tradition of Donegal fiddlers like Con Cassidy and John Doherty and those tough, hard hands play some of the best music you will ever hear; musicians from all over the world come to play with James and learn tunes from him, and if by chance you get to hear him in Teach Biddy's one night, when the *cráic* is mighty, then you must count yourself extraordinarily lucky indeed.

St Columba has a strong association with the glen which bears his name. He built himself a retreat house in the Glen and came to meditate, pray and preach here. The circular path he trod while meditating was remembered by the people and is commemorated with twelve crosses, many of them cut with Celtic designs, others carrying key patterns. It is probable that many of the crosses were pagan originally and that lines and circles were added to pagan designs to Christianize them. One cross, *Clon Aoineach* (the Stone of the Gatherings), has a hole in the centre of the cross head. Hole stones were of definite pagan origin and were used as binding or swearing stones. With hands or fingers joined through the hole, people would swear oaths and young couples would make their marriage vows. The crosses are visited each year on the saint's day, 9 June, and, during the *turas* (pilgrimage or journey), those who lean their backs against this cross and renounce the devil and all his works may, if they are in a state of grace, be allowed a glimpse of paradise through the hole in the stone.

St Columba was born not far from Glencolumbkille in Gartan in the north of Donegal in AD551 and a modern Celtic cross marks the site of his birth. He was educated by St Finian and was marked out as a child of great piety and devotion from the very first. Like many of the saints of the early Celtic church, he travelled hundreds of miles, studying at various monastic houses and seats of learning, a tradition that followed on from the wanderings of the bards and the *fili* – perhaps going back to druidic times. Columba in his wanderings founded abbeys at Durrow, Derry, Swords and Kells. He is said to have written three hundred books and to have founded at least as many holy houses before his self-imposed exile, after the Battle of the Book, to Iona where he died aged seventy. Columba may also have suffered from the first recorded case of vachophobia, or whatever it is that you call fear of cows, for he would not allow one anywhere near his religious houses. He is quoted as saying: 'Where there is a cow, there is a woman, and where there is a woman, there is mischief.'

Glencolumbkille has attracted many people over the years, some of them quite famous. The composer Arnold Bax stayed here many times and became infused with a deep love of the Glen and its people that informed and underpinned much of his music. He was first inspired to go to Donegal by reading the poetry of W.B. Yeats as a very young man in the early years of this century, and once said, in a talk on BBC Radio, 'Yeats's poetry means more to me than all the music of the centuries.' Many of Bax's compositions were inspired by the untamed scenery and the changing weather conditions of the Donegal coast. He wrote in a letter from the Glen: 'This place gets all the wind there is ... life is much the same here as it was a hundred years ago and there is no civilisation worth speaking of . . . all this progress of humanity has not counted for very much.' The poet Dylan Thomas rented a cottage at nearby Port for a few weeks one summer but all they remember him for in the Glen is that he then left without paying.

When first I came to Glencolumbkille a fair number of years ago, it was on a dreary, cold winter's day and the village was in a depressed state. Emigration and despair gripped it and there was a sadness that was almost breathable. Now it is a brighter and more cheerful place, thanks very largely to the inspiration of one man, the parish priest of the Glen, the late Fr McDyer. Distressed by the unemployment and decline that was causing the emigration from his parish of its finest young people, he set about creating local industries that would revitalise the community. He badgered Dublin until the government put up the money for a fish-processing plant, then a holiday village with thatched cottages, and finally a folk village where you can see traditional Donegal cabins, house tools and furniture that were in use until well into this century. You can also buy Irish books and music there because the area is part of the *Gaeltacht*. The cultural centre close by the folk village is a vital part of the community and

Odeas Gael, the Irish summer school, runs its courses there from Easter until the autumn.

One Easter I went over to Glencolumbkille, taking the ferry from Stranraer, and driving across Ireland with snow and sleet and rain following me all the way. Easter was early and the winter was having its last laugh at us. Calling in at the Glenveagh National Park on my way across country, I was welcomed as the first visitor that year. There was no red carpet, though, not even a free cup of coffee in spite of my heavy and unsubtle hints. (I shall not first-foot it next year.) After towing a car out of the ditch at the side of the snow-covered road under Errigal, I sat under the mountain half the afternoon, hoping it would clear enough for me to climb the hill and claim my first Irish mountain of the year, but it didn't and I went on my way. I was travelling to the Glen to take a week's course in Irish at *Odeas Gael* and hard work it was, too. Living in Manchester, I don't get much chance to speak Irish, but here I was made to speak it all the time, so that it is now the fifth language in which I can confuse people.

After three days, my head was so full of Irish, Guinness and music, that I ducked out on a set-dancing class to go for a walk on the hills instead and had a great walk up Croaghacullion, the hill that forms the north-east arm of the Glen. I had just enough time, I reckoned, to make it to the old signal tower on Glen Head and then along the cliff path to Port. It was a lovely evening and, with narry a soul about, I left the last of the village behind and took a narrow road north towards the mountain. I followed a *bohareen* for a while on to open country and then climbed steadily up the rocky slopes of the hill. The glen opened out below me as I climbed, the Protestant church standing out alone, and the small white specks and clusters of cottages bright in the evening light. Slieve League rose up beyond the village, dark and snow-streaked, and the far off braes were washed with sunlight and bars of shadow. From the shoulder of the hill I could see, far below, a perfect rath and hill fort in the field in front of a farm house. In some parts of Sligo and Donegal these raths were still lived in late in the eighteenth century.

The map shows half a dozen fair-sized loughs on the summit of Croaghacullion, but I was either on the wrong mountain or the map is wrong because I could only see a couple of peaty pools below me to the west and a bog or two further north. Perhaps one man's bog is another man's lough. From the summit I dropped down to an old bog road where half-submerged plastic bags in the bog and small eroded stacks of turf were evidence of last year's turf cutting, and climbed up again westwards towards the falling sun, to the summit of Beefan and Garveross Mountain, a grand name for a featureless hump. The land fell away before me westward to the sea and on the cliff top above Glen Head was the old signal tower, another in the chain of early-warning posts that are dotted all along the coast, and twin sister to the one at Mizen Head. A few sheep watched me curiously (if sheep can have that emotion) as I dropped down towards the tower, perhaps wondering if I had any goodies for them. When they saw I hadn't, they ignored me and carried on munching at the scant grass.

Beyond the signal tower, the wind battered the cliffs, lashing the waves on to the rocks below me. I went close to the edge but, noticing that a few slabs of soil had crumbled off recently, I took care not to go the same way. I had that wonderful feeling that comes to me so often in Ireland of being alone in the midst of great beauty. The light had that warm tint to it that washes

Evening light over hayfields and cottages

everything with a faint copper flush, and it was easy to understand, standing on the high cliffs above the sea, how saints and mystics came here to the West to find peace and calm. I rambled on along the cliffs past the great nose of Sturrall and dropped down a few hundred feet until I saw ahead of me the bay at Port and the smudge of Toralaydan Island. The village is deserted now and it is hard to believe that in 1940 there was a thriving fishing community there. With more time I might have gone right down to Port and walked back by lanes and roads under Crockuna to the Glen, but the day was dimming and I had my banjo to tune and a shower to take before the *sesiún* that night. So I contoured round until I hit the old bog road that took me back by a stiff climb to the saddle between Croaghacullion and Beefan and Garveross Mountain. I aimed for the transmitter mast as light started to fall and beyond that the track took me down the easy way by Cloghan to the village, just as lights were coming on in the houses and families were sitting down to their evening meal.

35 Errigal

Here in the hollow of the mountains
it is more peaceful than a country chapel.
I walk, cap in pocket, silently
down the mossy carpet of the aisle,
down between the grass-clump-pews,
and at the altar-height stand a moment,
while a faint breeze - the altar boy -
dispenses heather incense everywhere.
Cathal Ó Searcaigh, *Tearmann*

Like a volcanic ash cone, Errigal Mountain (*An Earagail*) stands high above Dunlewy, its quartzite peak shining silver on bright days, dull and leaden on those days when the Atlantic winds drive cloud and the mist inland towards Glenveagh. An outlier of the Derryveagh Mountains, the mountain stands sentinel above some of the wildest and most remote country I have ever been in. As far as the eye can see, moor and bogland stretch east and northwards, featureless and bare, great mountains thrusting up above the glens like sleeping dragons, and, beneath, a tiny ribbon of a road threading its way through.

There are few houses to be found once you leave Dunlewy, for the people were driven out of this area by the terrible evictions of the last century, when great areas of the West were cleared of the peasantry. The general excuse given was that they had not paid their rents and the landlord could not afford them on his land. In

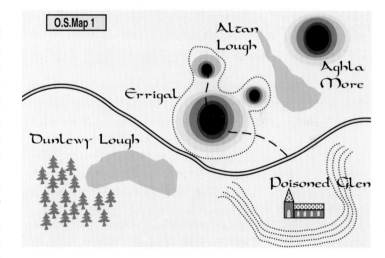

O.S.Map 1

Altan Lough

Aghla More

Errigal

Dunlewy Lough

Poisoned Glen

reality, it was an act of clearance as evil as the ethnic cleansings in Bosnia. Stories, the stuff of nightmares, are told of families thrown out into the bitter cold and snows of midwinter, their cabin walls broken down with battering rams so that they couldn't return. At least John Adair of Glenveagh Castle, who owned the ninety square miles north of Errigal, was honest; he cleared the tenants off his land simply because they were a bother to him. Heartbreak Valley was the name by which Glenveagh was known then. On 1 April 1861, the valley was sealed off from the outside world by a squad of military police and Adair's eviction gangs moved in. The screams of women and the thud of the battering rams could be heard all across the glen. Two hundred and fifty-four people were turned into wandering beggars that day. Some were taken in by relations, some went to the workhouse, and 150 of the young and fit went to Australia. But John Adair had cleared his land and now had his untrammelled view.

A later owner of Glenveagh Castle, Henry MacIlhenny, an American millionaire, renovated it as a holiday home. His wife created the gardens, while MacIlhenny, solicitous for the comfort of his guests, had steam pipes run out under the lough to raise the temperatures of the lake's waters, thus creating the world's largest outdoor heated swimming pool. Glenveagh is now a National Park, and the castle with its fine furniture and hangings is open to the public. A herd of six hundred red deer roam these uplands and, in winter, when the snows lie thick, they come down from the high ground close to the buildings of the park headquarters.

It is a wild but beautiful land with some of the finest mountains in the West – Muckish, Aghla Beg, Aghla More, Errigal and the Derryveagh and Glendowan Mountains. Errigal is an easy mountain to climb, although it does have a narrow arête between its twin peaks that should be given a wide berth in icy or windy conditions. The easiest way up follows a line of posts that cross the bog from the road that leads east of Dunlewy towards Glenveagh, and one autumn day, at the end of a long week spent in the West, I found myself at the foot of Errigal in the early afternoon, with about four hours of daylight left and eight hours to spare before the boat I was to sail home on left Larne. I had a few bottles of water and a packet of biscuits, so I threw the cameras and the rest of the gear into the rucksack and set off up the hill.

A hazy, soft, warm light smudged the shapes of all the surrounding hills like an artist's thumb as I climbed higher, the Derryveaghs sliding away into the haze and Dunlewy Lough a bronze mirror behind me. At the end of the line of posts, the trail becomes a steep scree slope similar to that on Croagh Patrick and, after a fair pull up its slithery length, you arrive on a narrow shoulder. Below and behind you, lovely Altan Lough lies curving round the base of Aghla More.

There is a fair amount of summit furniture on this rocky shoulder, the most recent a stone memorial to Joey Glover, an Irish mountaineer, killed by the IRA in 1976 'by mistake'. I said my own kind of prayer for Joey and moved on across the shoulder to a handful of unstable cairns that stand beside a modern 'hut circle' built by climbers as a wind-shelter. I left my rucksack in the shelter and raced on to the first of Errigal's two summits and then, with a great deal of care, followed the narrow ridge of the One Man's Pass (sister to that on Slieve League) to the northern peak. There was nothing but a light breeze and the path was dry and clear, but the fact that it was only two-foot wide and was

Errigal Braes

surrounded by a lot of nothing helped to concentrate the mind greatly. I didn't linger long there but turned and made my way back to the shoulder and the wind-shelter, where I had a drink out of the way of the breeze and looked at the hazy land about me.

Earagail means 'oratory', so presumably at some time there must have been a hermitage up here, where an unknown monk spent his days in fasting and wrestling with demons. I have searched the books and asked those who might know but have found no mention of the monk or his cell. One book I read said nothing at all about the oratory, but told me that every five years the World Domino Championships are held on Errigal. I looked down into the haze to see if there were any domino players making their way up the hill and do you know there were - domino players by the hundreds were making their way up Errigal that

day, and each was carrying a box of dominoes under one arm and a flying pig under the other.

Down below, a shimmer was all that could be seen of Dunlewy Lough, with the vague shape of the Poisoned Glen leading away from it to the south-east. The glen gets its name from a spurge that grows in its wet hollows, a plant that is poisonous to sheep. It is a dark and drear-looking place in certain lights; no road goes in to its heart and the ruined church that stands at the mouth of the glen helps to make it look even more empty and deserted. Dunlewy is home to Cathal Ó Searcaigh whose poem stands at the head of this chapter. He is a great poet who writes exclusively in Irish and I was lucky enough to hear him read his own poetry at a gathering in Glencolumbkille a few years back. It is powerful and beautiful stuff and if, like me, you have little or no Irish, it is available in translation and worth seeking out.

The ruined church in the Poisoned Glen; even on a bright day there is a sense of gloom about the place

The descent from the mountain was steep but easy. The light was falling and my car just a dot in the far distance across the bog below. It was my last day of walking in the hills in Ireland that year and, as I made my way to the car in the gathering dusk, I felt the land close in around me and I had a great feeling that this was the end of something and yet the beginning too, as though I would be leaving Ireland for another year and yet leaving part of myself behind, a part that will bring me back over and again.

The old name for Donegal is *Tirconail* (the Land of Conall) and as I drove under Muckish at the edge of light, with torn purple clouds coursing across the crests of the hills and the autumn day turning to night, I remembered a fragment of a poem called 'Tirconail' by Patrick MacGill, 'The Navvy Poet', the common labourer and 'knight of the shovel', who went from Donegal to work on the 'diggings' in England and who produced a wealth of truly great writing. I knew the first two lines by heart and spoke them quietly as I left the mountain behind. The next evening I read the rest of the poem back in my house in England under the crags of Combe Scar with a Donegal light in the sky:

Errigal has listened to the light feet
On the dancing floors of Gweedore!
Curving and curtseying,
The white bones of the time-forgotten dancers
Are one with the waters
That thresh your shores,
Tirconail.

For they were and are not,
They are and will not be!
And thus, I, too,
The onlooker of a moment will go. My moment as nothing,
The strain of a fiddle in the twilight,
A low wind on the hills.
Tirconail!

Late sunlight behind the cross on the summit of Errigal

The Parting Glass

The Parting Glass

Of all the money that ever I had
I spent it in good company,
And all the harm that ever I done,
Alas it was to none but me.
And all I've done for want of wit
To memory now I can't recall,
So fill to me the parting glass,
Goodnight and joy be with you all.

If I had money enough to spend
And leisure time to sit awhile,
There is a fair maid in Sligo town
That sorely has my heart beguiled.
Her rosy cheeks and ruby lips

I own she has my heart in thrall,
Then fill to me the parting glass
Goodnight and joy be with you all.

Oh, all the comrades ever I had,
They're sorry for me going away,
And all the sweethearts ever I had
They wish me one more day to stay.
But since it falls unto my lot
That I should rise and you should not,
Then I gently rise and softly call,
'Goodnight and joy be with you all.'

The Parting Glass - Traditional

Index